Family
Relations

CURRENT ISSUES IN THE FAMILY SERIES

Series Editor
Timothy H. Brubaker, *Miami University*

The pace of change in contemporary society has had an enormous impact on the workings of its most important institution, the family. This series of volumes explores the various dimensions of societal change and how the family is changing with them. Each edited volume contains the latest theory and research from leading scholars in the family field on a topic of contemporary concern. Special attention is paid to the impact of this research on the work being done by family therapists, family life educators, and family policymakers.

Volumes in this Series

1. Timothy H. Brubaker (ed.)
   FAMILY RELATIONS: Challenges for the Future

Other series volumes are in preparation.

Family Relations

Challenges for the Future

EDITED BY

Timothy H. Brubaker

1 Current
Issues
in
the
volume Family

SAGE Publications
International Educational and Professional Publisher
Newbury Park   London   New Delhi

For information address:

 SAGE Publications, Inc.
2455 Teller Road
Newbury Park, California 91320

SAGE Publications Ltd.
6 Bonhill Street
London EC2A 4PU
United Kingdom

SAGE Publications India Pvt. Ltd.
M-32 Market
Greater Kailash I
New Delhi 110 048 India

Printed in the United States of America

Library of Congress Cataloging-in-Publication Data

Main entry under title:

Family relations: challenges for the future / edited by Timothy H.
Brubaker.
p. cm.—(Current issues in the family: V. 1)
Includes bibliographical references and index.
ISBN 0-8039-3945-0.—ISBN 0-8039-3946-9 (pbk.)
1. Family—United States. 2. Marriage—United States. 2. Sex
role—United States. 4. Parenthood. 5. Work and Family—United
States. 6. Family violence—United States. 7. Family social work—
United States. I. Brubaker, Timothy H. II. Series.
HQ535.F346 1993
306.85'0973—dc20   92-31802
                                                                CIP

94 95 96 10 9 8 7 6 5 4 3 2

Sage Production Editor: Judith L. Hunter

*This volume is dedicated to the contributors to the
Family and Child Studies Center Lecture Series,
Miami University, Oxford, Ohio.*

Contents

Acknowledgments

While the development of any edited volume is the result of numerous individuals working in a cooperative way, this one is unique because it is the first volume supported in part by contributors to the Miami University Family and Child Studies Lecture Series. Nearly one half of the chapters presented here were originally presented as lectures at Miami University and then revised for inclusion here. The contributors to the Family and Child Studies Lecture Series are recognized for their support of the initial presentations.

Numerous individuals within the Family and Child Studies Center participated in the completion of this project. Foremost is Mary Tharp, who professionally prepared correspondence in organizing the contributions and devoted numerous hours to typing the combined reference list. Without her, this book would not have been completed. Judy A. Kimberly spent many hours on a variety of mundane tasks associated with the project. Her willingness to assist in any way, as well as the cheerfulness with which she performed her assignments, are greatly appreciated. In addition, Maureen Callahan, Paula Dolloff, Connie Ferger, Joni Schweier, and Katherine Stoops provided assistance in immeasurable ways. Appreciation is expressed to all of these individuals who persevered through the turbulence of change and the doldrums of procrastination.

Mitch Allen of Sage is a person whose encouragement, patience, and wisdom have influenced this volume. Not only has Mitch's support been unwavering, but his commitment to scholarship is commendable. Without him, the information within this the book could not have been completed. His high level of professionalism and his friendship are appreciated.

The support of the Family and Child Studies Center of Miami University is recognized. In addition to providing support for the lecture series, the center provides an environment in which to pursue intriguing ideas.

To all, a hearty thanks for completing a voyage that took much longer than expected but its completion is celebrated. Thanks for the support.

Series Editor's Preface

The pace of change in contemporary society has had an enormous impact on the workings of its most important institution, the family. This series of volumes explores the various dimensions of societal change and how the family is changing with them. Each edited volume contains the latest theory and research from leading scholars in the family field on a topic of contemporary concern. Special attention is paid to the impact of this research on the work being done by family therapists, family life educators and family policymakers.

—Timothy H. Brubaker,
Miami University

PART 1

Changing Family Perspectives

1

Challenges to the American Family

TIMOTHY H. BRUBAKER
JUDY A. KIMBERLY

During the past several decades change has characterized American families. As American society changes, the structure and functions of American families have been altered. For example, most families have changed to accommodate two earners; many children live with one parent; and remarriage has resulted in a vast array of stepfamily relationships. Within both the popular press and scholarly literature, questions about the survival of the American family have been voiced. The increased diversity of family forms has led to predictions of the demise of the American family. While contemporary American families are characterized by more heterogeneity than in the past, they continue to be important to individuals. The fact that there is no single type of American family in the 1990s should not suggest that the family is evolving out of existence: rather, it is changing to meet the demands of the changing 1990s.

As the diversity among American families increases, a greater range of problems arise. Berardo (1990, p. 809) noted that "the expanding range of alternative marriage and family forms brings with it not only new freedoms and responsibilities but also associated problems." Traditional beliefs and values are challenged and institutional structures of the broader society are modified. For example, the increased number of dual-worker parents has had an effect on the American educational system. Similarly, churches and religious groups (traditional supports

for family life) have had to address the issue of family stability as the
divorce rate has increased.

Demographic Trends

Demographic changes within the American family vividly describe
the wide range of family forms. According to Jaynes and Williams
(1989, p. 571), demographic trends for all American families occurring
over the past three decades include "declining rates of marriage, later
ages at first marriage, higher divorce rates, an increase in female-
headed households, a higher proportion of births to unmarried mothers,
larger percentages of children living in female-headed families, and a
higher percentage of children living in poverty." These demographic
trends suggest the genesis of some stresses associated with these divergent family forms.

Marriage

According to the United States Bureau of the Census (U.S. Bureau of
the Census [USBC], 1989c), marriages averaged 1.5 million annually
from the 1950s through the 1960s. The 1970s showed a decline in the
number of first marriages for women, while the rate of first marriages
for women in the 1980s remained relatively constant at a rate of 2.4
million annually (Norton & Moorman, 1987; USBC, 1989c). Norton
and Moorman (1987) suggest the stabilization of these rates may be
attributed to "a period-based hiatus, a reflection of differential cohort
behavior, or the acceptance of and adjustment to a new set of societal
norms or standards" (p. 4). Regardless of whether one of these possibilities or a combination of them is responsible for explaining the period
of stabilization, the decrease in rates of first marriage has begun again
in the 1990s. Presently, the rate of first marriage per 100 single women
aged 14 to 44 is 8.2 (USBC, 1989b), a rate matched only by the all-time
low of the Depression years.

Despite this decline in first marriage rates, marriages continue to be
the primary source of family formation (USBC, 1989c). However, this
family type, after fluctuating considerably, has also declined steadily
over the past 20 years. Married-couple families dropped from 87% of
family households in 1970 to 82% in 1980 and 79% in 1990 (O'Connell
& Bachu, 1990). One suggestion is that the permanence of marriage has

weakened enough to cause persons to make more tentative and limited commitments to marriage (Glenn, 1987, 1991; T. Martin & Bumpass, 1989). In spite of this alarming trend, the weakening is not so devastating that it will eliminate marriage, as estimates show that approximately 90% of the population will ultimately marry (Norton & Moorman, 1987; USBC, 1989c).

Age at Marriage

Since the 1950s the median age at first marriage has crept steadily upward, reaching highs of 23.6 years for women and almost 26 years for men in the late 1980s (USBC, 1989c). As would be expected with this postponement of marriage, the proportion of men and women of prime marrying age who have not yet married for the first time is also rising. Between 1960 and 1970 the proportion of men and women who never married showed little change, but from 1970 to 1988 sharp increases in this population occurred (USBC, 1989c).

Research devoted to the discussion of these trends usually falls under the category of mate selection and is then further divided into one of two categories: structural or nonstructural influences (Surra, 1990). Surra defines *structural influences* as those that are "concerned with the availability of marriageable partners" (1990, p. 847). Included in this category are variables such as size of the population with regard to one particular characteristic and the balance of men and women of marriageable age (also called the gender ratio or the marriage squeeze). The other set of influences "concerns social and personal preferences for certain mates, such as endogamy norms" (Surra, 1990, p. 847). Included in these norms are religious preferences, educational attainment, socioeconomic factors, and race (Surra, 1990). Age is also a factor in this category, as social norms and biases help dictate which mates are age appropriate.

Some of the ramifications of women delaying marriage are the increase in their educational attainment and their labor force participation out of economic necessity (L. K. White, 1990). Later age of marriage for women also affects fertility due to the increased risk associated with childbearing at later ages. Postponing marriage may also increase the number of premarital births due to the fact that women may spend a larger part of their childbearing years in an unmarried status. During the 1980s, out-of-wedlock childbearing was the second most common type of family formation (USBC, 1989c), with women as the primary head of the household. Combined with divorce in which women have received custody of their children, the number of single-mother heads of households has increased dramatically. However, there has been little change over the past several decades in the number of men who are single-parent heads of households and they remain relatively uncommon (USBC, 1989c).

Divorce

It should also be noted that while the marriage rate has been declining, the divorce rate has almost doubled the rates of the 1950s and 1960s and almost tripled since the 1920s and 1930s (USBC, 1989b). A stabilization of the divorce rate is expected in the 1990s, however, due to older ages at first marriage, which are associated with lower divorce rates (Norton & Moorman, 1987; Price & McKenry, 1988). Another factor attributed to the present stabilization of the divorce rate is the post-Vietnam War era of the early 1970s. Like other postwar eras, it was characterized as a period of unusually high divorce rates (Price & McKenry, 1988). The large baby boom cohort (those born between 1946 and 1960) passed through their twenties during 1965-1975, a period when they would be most likely to marry and/or divorce (Adams, 1986), so a stabilization of the rate was inevitable. "Thus, it is possible that a part of the rise from 1965-1975 was simply a function of the age of our population, and that the leveling off is in fact an indication of a high, but fairly constant, [divorce] rate in the future" (Adams, 1986, p. 332).

Remarriage

Remarriage after divorce was a relatively uncommon phenomenon until the 1970s (M. Coleman & Ganong, 1990). Prior to this time, remarriage usually took place after the death of a spouse. Currently, the majority of remarriages occur after divorce (USBC, 1989c), with almost 40% of marriages being remarriages for one or both partners (M. Coleman & Ganong, 1990). The time interval between divorce and remarriage has also diminished, to approximately three years (M. Coleman & Ganong, 1990; Pasley & Ihinger-Tallman, 1987), with almost two thirds of those remarriages being preceded by cohabitation (L. Bumpass, Sweet, & Martin, 1990). Thus new relationships are established relatively soon after divorce occurs.

With remarriage, as with divorce and marriage, demographic, economic, and social trends also serve as contributing factors in family formation decisions. Factors such as education and income have been found to influence the remarriage rate (M. Coleman & Ganong, 1990; Pasley & Ihinger-Tallman, 1987).

Regardless of the stresses and burdens the family unit seems to undergo, the family remains a ubiquitous institution in American society. With 90% of the population getting married at some point, the average family size consists of approximately 3.17 persons per family (USBC, 1989c), indicating the presence of children or elderly members. The majority of persons remarrying after divorce indicates membership in a family is an important element in most people's vision of a "quality" life. Family researchers feel the family is "here to stay" and the recent changes in the composition of the American family are adaptive alterations rather than signs of disintegration and decay (Berardo, 1990; Glenn, 1987).

Challenges to the Family

Future challenges facing the family are embedded in contemporary economic, political, and social structures. Changing economic opportunities have and will continue to influence family relationships. For example, as the economy expanded and more women sought employment outside the home, the number of two-earner families increased. With the increased income provided by two earners, families' standards of living increased and women were not as dependent on a spouse for economic survival. Thus families experienced change in several ways. First, some families were able to support life-styles that exceeded their expectations. Their material wants became material needs. Second, some women achieved independence beyond their marital and family relationships, thereby increasing their autonomy. At the same time, some women doubled their responsibilities by accepting the demands associated with employment in addition to their household burdens. Third, the financial independence generated by employment provided women with an alternative to marriage. Women could choose to leave a marriage or not enter a marriage because they could support themselves financially. Thus an expanding economy provided women as well as men with more life-style options.

The changing American economy (i.e., the move from a manufacturing to a service economy [Harrison & Bluestone, 1988; Howe & Parks, 1989], lower median income [Mishel & Simon, 1988], frequent restructuring and layoffs) suggests that men and women will become more vulnerable within the workplace. As the economy experiences contraction, American families will be more likely to experience economic distress and possible dislocation and change. As Voydanoff (1991, p. 432) noted, "economic distress is a concept referring to aspects of economic life that are potential stressors for individuals and families. Major components include economic instability, employment uncertainty, economic deprivation, and economic strain." Changing national and global economics have an influence on American families and may be one of the major challenges for the American family in the future.

Changes in the national economy can expand or limit opportunities for families. As individuals anticipate or actually experience economic changes within their family situations, spouses, children, and others will probably feel strain associated with the new situation. Adaptability will be a crucial skill as the contemporary family addresses the challenges associated with economic change.

Politically, the changing status of women has had, and will continue to have, an influence on family life. While there may not be pay equity on the job, there have been attempts to legislate equity between men and women. Thus women who are abused by their husbands can seek assistance from the legal system as well as social service programs. Gender parity in divorce settlements has become an important ingredient within domestic courts. The increased emphasis on the status of women has challenged the way in which families interact on a daily basis and how roles are defined. For example, both men and women are economic providers in many families but men continue to be recognized as the breadwinner (L. Thompson & Walker, 1991). As the parity in the status of men and women increases, will husbands and wives share recognition as breadwinners? If both are recognized as breadwinners, will both be responsible for household activities?

Within the family studies field, the emerging feminist orientation to the family provides a theoretical perspective that challenges traditional views. As Ferree (1991, p. 117) states, "the feminist perspective redefines families as arenas of gender and generational struggles, crucibles of caring and conflict, where claims for an identity are rooted, and separateness and solidarity are continually created and contested." The traditional divisions of power within the family are being challenged; consequently, spouses are encouraged to examine who is responsible for making decisions within the family. This examination and possible change can foster strain within the family.

For the feminist, the historical and political contexts of the family are crucial elements in understanding the way men and women perform their family roles (Allen, 1987; Ferree, 1991). Contemporary families embody present interpretations of the historical definitions of family responsibilities and roles. Husbands and wives define their own situations within the context of the current political climate. The feminist perspective of the family is based on the following premises (Walker, Martin, & Thompson, 1987): (1) Women are oppressed because they are not taken seriously and are denied equal access to the valued things of society; (2) individuals cannot be separated from the social structure and the personal is political within everyday life; and (3) feminists are a part of the system and, at the same time, they are outside of the system trying to change the prevailing view of women. Thus feminists suggest that women are viewed as oppressed and are assigned lower status within the family as a result of the historical and current social structure. In addition to the personal aspects of the family, family relationships are also political, in which women do not have parity with men. Even though women are a part of the family, they can encourage changes in the traditional views of the family. This orientation has begun to influence the family studies field and challenges the way in which relationships are defined within families as well as within the family discipline.

The pervasiveness of marriage and the family is evidenced by the demographic description of the American family. There are, however, a number of challenges faced by the contemporary family in the United States as a result of changing social values. First, a variety of meanings are attached to the notion that today's family is characterized by a number of forms besides the traditional values of falling in love and marrying a lifelong partner as a young adult. Love and marriage for life may be the ideal, but realistically many individuals do not expect to be married to one individual for a lifetime. Second, while family life is important, the family has evolved into a voluntary association (Schwartz, 1987). That is, individuals marry, stay married, divorce and stay unmarried, or remarry, by choice. If marriage and family relationships are rewarding, the relationships continue. If rewards are considered low, the relationships may not continue. Thus one major challenge to the American family is the ability to deal with the potential change in marital relationships while at the same time assuring some continuity within the kinship network. Marriage has traditionally been valued as a relationship that provides continuity for individuals within a changing society. But, as Spanier (1989, p. 9) noted, "the health of the family in the future, I believe, hinges on our ability to marshall the forces of resiliency in the face of forces of discontinuity." Divorce may enable marital partners to move out of an unrewarding situation, but often children are involved and the effects of the marital change may be detrimental to them (A. Booth, 1987). It is this type of discontinuity in intimate relationships that challenges the family. Family members need to be concerned about the continuity between generations that is being developed within each family unit. For example, do children continue to value long-lasting relationships with both parents after divorce? If most mothers receive custody of children after divorce and children have infrequent contact with their noncustodial (father) parents, how is the father role defined by the children? What long-term impact does this have on the family relations of the children when they become parents? Research indicates that divorce can have both negative and positive consequences for children. Children of divorce are not uniformly impacted (Demo & Acock, 1988).

There is little doubt that the voluntary nature of family relationships may lead to discontinuous patterns within the family. Children are the most affected by the consequences of these disruptions, but there is little agreement on what to do about this situation. Beliefs in long-term marriages and continuous family relationships are being challenged and new definitions of intimate relationships are being created. Individual autonomy and the ability to be involved in rewarding intimate relationships are enmeshed within the social fabric of our society, but it may be important to minimize individual autonomy for the continuation of the voluntary association we have defined as *family*. The future of the American family is grounded in the changing family values that seem to reinforce a concept of family that is based on individual rather that familial fulfillment.

The changing definitions of gender roles have presented another challenge to the values of many American families. Although women have become employed outside the home, expectations that housework and decision making become more equally distributed between husbands and wives have not been fully realized. As noted above, employed wives and mothers are held more accountable than husbands and fathers for family responsibilities (L. Thompson & Walker, 1991). Concluding a review of research on gender and the family, L. Thompson and Walker provide the following summary of men's and women's responsibility within the family:

Everyday and ultimate responsibility for marriage, housework, and parenthood usually remains with women; and responsibility for breadwinning usually remains with men. Most women "help" men with provision, and many men "help" women with family work and parenting, although partners collude to sustain a belief that men are primary providers and parenting is shared. (1991, p. 95)

Changing perceptions of gender roles dramatically shifted the division of labor for married persons as well as patterns and policies within the workplace. As suggested by Ross, Mirowsky, and Huber (1983), contemporary marriages are shifting away from complimentary household divisions of labor where the husband and wife perform different but interdependent tasks, to a parallel pattern in which tasks are shared by partners. The challenge for husbands and wives is to negotiate mutually satisfying divisions of household tasks without overburdening one member of the marital partnership. In addition, corporate managers, policymakers, and co-workers are also being challenged to provide a supportive situation in which mothers and fathers can balance family and work responsibilities. The importance of these views can be seen in the form of recently proposed legislation amending existing parental leave laws to include both parents.

Despite moves toward a more egalitarian division of household tasks along with equality in the workplace, conflicting gender roles still present stressful situations for individuals within both the family and the workplace. While men may experience some discomfort with the changing responsibilities attached to new roles, research suggests that women are more likely to experience overload and feel stress as a result of increased responsibilities within the workplace, coupled with undiminished responsibilities at home.

The increased recognition of abuse within intimate relationships provides still another challenge to families and those individuals who work with families. Family relationships are often viewed as supportive relationships in which members are loving to one another. Research suggests, however, that a significant incidence of abuse exists in husband-wife, parent-child, sibling-sibling, and adult caregiver-older relative relationships (Gelles & Conte, 1991). Causes of this behavior within intimate relationships are complex and its existence may have long-term consequences. There is some evidence that abusive behavior in one generation is repeated in subsequent generations. As Gelles and Conte (1991, p. 329) observe, however, "the process by which violence is transferred from one generation to the next is more complex than simple modeling of behavior. When the cycle of violence occurs, it is likely the result of a complex set of social and psychological processes." The challenge is to identify the historical underpinnings of the abusive relationships to ferret out the causes of violence within the family.

With the potential for abuse in any intimate relationship (e.g., dating, marital, parental), the need for developing intervention strategies is crucial. Family life educators and social service workers need to help identify possible indicators of abuse. The challenge is to define, identify, and modify abusive behavior that occurs within the family, and when possible address the potential for violence before it occurs. By bringing the issue of abuse into the open, improvements can be made in the family balance of power and the quality of family relationships.

Recent economic, political, and social changes have challenged the ways families have traditionally functioned. Boundaries between family and work have become more complex and family roles have become more blurred. Differences between men's and women's roles have become more confused. Discontinuity between generations has become more frequent. Nonetheless, the family continues to meet these challenges and changes. To help families deal with the strains of change, family life educators, therapists, and policy specialists need information about the challenges facing today's American family. This book and other books within this series will provide the necessary information regarding the challenges confronting today's families.

Plan for This Book

This book addresses issues of continuity and resiliency of the family across the life cycle. Society's changing definitions of gender roles provide a backdrop for the discussions of transitions into marriage, parenthood, work, divorce, and abuse. The ability of the family to adapt to change and crisis is also explored. To assist the family in dealing with challenges, several intervention strategies are reviewed. Family life education, family therapy, and family policy provide three ways to reinforce continuity and assist in adjustment to discontinuity within family relationships. Educators, therapists, and family policy specialists are the professionals who can help the contemporary family deal with the challenges of the 1990s.

The first section of this book addresses changing family perspectives or the avenues by which families address the ways they balance continuity and change in their relationships. Beginning this section is David H. Olson's chapter discussing family continuity and change throughout the life course. Using the circumplex model as a foundation, he examines various challenges encountered by the family throughout the life course, such as marriage, family cohesion, and communication. Different types of family systems and the stressors and strains they impose on the level of well-being across the family life cycle are also discussed in this chapter. He concludes by providing a rationale for the use of multimethod assessment of family inventories. Olson's chapter helps to explain the family system's continuity and change across the life cycle within a developmental context and provides a sound model by which further family research can be conducted.

The next chapter of this section, by Joan Huber, outlines changing gender roles within the family. The effects of role changes on interpersonal behaviors, beliefs, and feelings in various social areas are discussed, highlighting gender role issues such as caring for elderly family members, the division of household labor, the effects of remarriage, and the effects of single-parenthood on children. Huber suggests that technological and economic developments in the past century are largely responsible for the present challenges of contemporary family gender roles.

The second section—Challenges to the Family—encompasses many of the areas of family life that are in flux. Judith L. Fischer and Donna L. Sollie focus on the transition from single life to marriage to open this section, looking specifically at the network supports and coping strategies of young adults. The stresses of remaining single for longer periods of time lead to challenges both within the family unit as well as to the individual and the community. A longitudinal comparison of persons who remained single, persons who were single initially but who became married, and persons who remained married during the period, was made. Even though the transition to marriage was hypothesized to be stressful, singles appeared to be more vulnerable to the buffering effects of social support (i.e., availability of friends and embeddedness in the friendship network) than their recently married counterparts. What this implies for singles moving into marriage, is that the newlywed stage becomes a critical time for balancing time with friends and with one's partner. It is also noteworthy that if the transition to marriage is not perceived as stressful by the single person, the support of friends may not be as integral to that individual's social network as it is to those singles who see the transition to marriage as a stressful event.

In the next chapter, Douglas R. Powell reflects on the escalating interest and efforts to support parents during the early years of child rearing. As new configurations of family demographics continue to emerge, with increases in the number of single-parent households, in women in the labor force, in divorce, and in mobility, the challenge to find ways of fostering the parent-child relationship become more difficult. Striking a balance between child, family, and institutional needs requires a great deal of flexibility and adaptability on the part of the parent. Consequently, Powell addresses ways to facilitate this adaptation and methods for institutions/programs to help relieve some of the burden.

Patricia Voydanoff untangles the complex issues involved with the shift in economic and family structures. As other authors, she also applies the multiple role perspective; as a balance between the interdependent roles of worker, parent, and spouse is sought, conflict can ensue. The challenges to the family that arise from this interdependence are that the provider role, typically assumed by men, will now be, and already is, shared with women. As more women participate in the labor force, work/family issues are no longer viewed as strictly women's issues, rather they become relevant to both men and women. Attempts to accommodate the changing nature of work and family responsibilities and the internal dynamic processes of how men and women combine and coordinate their roles are major issues that will continue to face the American family in the future. Voydanoff illustrates the need for equity between men and women in work loads, both at home and on the job, as well as discussing the demands these new roles and relationships will make on the family.

As stated above, trends in marital disruption are well documented in the literature. Divorce, remarriage, redivorce, stepfamilies, half-siblings, cohabitation, and death are all factors in marital disruption experienced by families. In "Families and Marital Disruption," Marilyn Coleman and Lawrence H. Ganong explain the determinants that have become a standard part of the American family experience. Challenges to the children of divorce, both as young children and adult children, are examined, along with the challenges faced by other family members (i.e., parents, grandparents, siblings) when a family member divorces.

In addition, the changes from nuclear families to blended and extended families are discussed as they confront the relationships between family members in a variety of ways and settings.

Sally A. Lloyd and Beth C. Emery scrutinize abuse in the family by examining the effects of violence on children, the transmission of abuse in courtship and marriage, intergenerational violence within families, and the implications for intervention. Because the consequences of physical and sexual abuse of family members are so far-reaching, the challenges to those families at risk for violence and those currently experiencing abuse extend to all aspects of their interpersonal functioning.

In the following chapter, Hamilton I. McCubbin, Marilyn A. McCubbin, and Anne I. Thompson focus on the resiliency of families and what role family schema (the set of beliefs, values, goals, priorities, expectations) play in how families cope, endure, and survive crises. Family crises challenge families' established methods of functioning. Sometimes new patterns of adaptation and/or adjustment may be created, or present methods may be continued. Regardless, the interaction between family schema and family functioning is discussed and the efficacy of a wider scope of study is surveyed.

Intervention strategies designed to aid families in facing the challenges of family life in the United States are the focus of the third section of this book. First, family life education, whose purpose is to help strengthen and enrich family living and whose focus is on preventive rather than therapeutic measures, is examined across the life span by Charles B. Hennon and Margaret Arcus. They examine models currently employed in programming areas and call for grounding future education programs in theory and research, as well as tying family life education to counseling and therapy. Challenges to family life educators are enumerated in the current trends of the life-span approach to family life education.

Although marital therapy is a relatively young discipline, Anthony P. Jurich and Candyce S. Russell document the changes in the treatment response of current professionals in their chapter. Changes in the family are reflected in the challenges encountered by therapists in their sessions with individuals and couples. Again, family trends discussed above—such as divorce, increased women's participation in the labor force, and families experiencing addictions and violence—function as catalysts to develop new therapeutic models designed to assist families trying to cope with the changing complexities of American society.

Finally, Steven K. Wisensale focuses on family policy initiatives for the 1990s. Factors impeding the implementation of family policy in the

1980s, such as slow-moving policy initiatives and conflicts between generations for policy and financial support, are outlined. These factors will play an important role in the development of family policy in the 1990s. The challenges to the family rest with emphasizing the importance family issues are given by policymakers and the American public. If being well informed about family issues and taking an active part in the debate of these issues is a priority, the contention of this chapter is that the 1990s appear to be a dynamic era for family policy.

Changes within the patterns of U.S. families are evident as they adapt to social, economic, and demographic changes. These changes present challenges to individual family members as they reconsider their own values and expectations for one another. As members renegotiate their roles within the family and seek to mesh these demands with extrafamily demands (e.g., work), strain and crisis often develops. The challenge to family scholars and professionals is to develop educational and therapeutic programs, as well as policy, that undergirds family continuity during changes within the family structure. While families are resilient and adaptable, they continue to need support from family professionals. Therefore, understanding past and present family relationships is an important factor in recognizing and predicting the future challenges and directions of the American family.

2

Family Continuity and Change

A Family Life-Cycle Perspective

DAVID H. OLSON

Change and continuity are the most basic underlying concepts of both family development and life-span development theory. While life-span development focuses on the individual at multiple levels across time from childhood through adulthood (Baltes, Reese, & Lipsitt, 1980), family development emphasizes the family system as a unit. More specifically, while life-span development increasingly focuses on plasticity (Lerner, 1984, 1986), the same concept could be applied to family systems. Family system plasticity would focus on the extent to which the family system changes its structure and dynamics across the life cycle.

A definition of family development that integrates psychological development and the family system perspective was offered by Klaus Schneewind (1986): "Family development is a process of personality development within the family context taking its course in mutual relatedness" (p. 10). This definition emphasizes the importance of the family context for the development of an individual and also indicates the dynamic relationship between individuals and their family system over time. Based on general system theory, it follows that change in

AUTHOR'S NOTE: This chapter was originally presented as the Barbara T. Stegeman Lecture as part of the Family and Child Studies Lecture Series, Miami University, Oxford, OH.

either the individual or the family system would create some impact or change in the other system. This chapter presents a model that can illustrate various types of family systems. This model also assumes that these family systems would change across the family life cycle. In other words, the Circumplex Model of Family Systems is a dynamic model that assumes change, in contrast to individual personality types that are presumed to have higher levels of stability. The ideal method for capturing the process of family development would be the use of longitudinal studies. Unfortunately, most of the research in family development and theorizing has been based on cross-sectional studies that provide only a "snapshot" of families at various stages of the life cycle.

Circumplex Model of Marital and Family Systems

The Circumplex Model of Marital and Family Systems was developed in an attempt to bridge the gap that typically exists between research, theory, and practice. A variety of hypotheses have been developed and tested using the Circumplex Model. Some of the research has focused on types of family systems across the life cycle and how families cope effectively with normative stress (Olson, Russell, & Sprenkle, 1989).

Family cohesion, adaptability, and communication are the three dimensions in the Circumplex Model. These three dimensions emerged from a conceptual clustering of more than 50 concepts developed to describe marital and family dynamics. Although some of these concepts have been used for decades (power and roles, for instance), many of the concepts have been developed recently by individuals observing problem families from a general systems perspective (pseudomutuality, double-binds).

A variety of other theoretical models have focused independently on variables related to the cohesion, adaptability, and communication dimensions. Most of these models have been developed in the past 10 years by individuals having a systems perspective on the family. Evidence regarding the value and importance of these three dimensions is the fact that these theorists have quite independently concluded that these dimensions were critical for understanding and treating marital and family systems.

Table 2.1 Theoretical Models Using Cohesion, Adaptability, and Communication

	Cohesion	Adaptability	Communication
Beavers & Voeller (1983)	Centripetal Centrifugal	Adaptability	Affect
Benjamin (1977)	Affiliation	Interdependence	
Epstein, Baldwin, & Bishop (1983)	Affective Involvement	Behavior Control Problem-Solving Roles	Communication Affective Responsiveness
French & Guidera (1974)		Capacity to Change Power	
Gottman (1979)	Validation	Contrasting	
D. Kantor & Lehr (1975)	Affect	Power	
Leary (1957)	Affection Hostility	Dominance Submission	
Leff & Vaughn (1985)	Distance	Problem-Solving	
T. Parsons & Bales (1955)	Expressive Role	Instrumental Role	
Reiss (1981)	Coordination	Closure	

Table 2.1 summarizes the work of 11 theorists who have worked on describing marital and family systems. Most of the recent theorizing about family dynamics and intervention has been strongly influenced by general systems theory. Current work has focused on describing both clinical and nonclinical families or has been concerned with clinical intervention with families.

Marital and Family Cohesion (Togetherness)

Family cohesion is defined as the emotional bonding that family members have toward one another. Within the Circumplex Model, some of the specific concepts or variables that can be used to diagnose and measure the family cohesion dimensions are: emotional bonding, boundaries, coalitions, time, space, friends, decision making, and interests and recreation.

There are four levels of cohesion ranging from disengaged (very low) to separated (low to moderate) to connected (moderate to high) to enmeshed (very high) (see Figure 2.1). It is hypothesized that the central levels of cohesion (separated and connected) make for optimal family functioning. The extremes (disengaged or enmeshed) are generally seen as problematic.

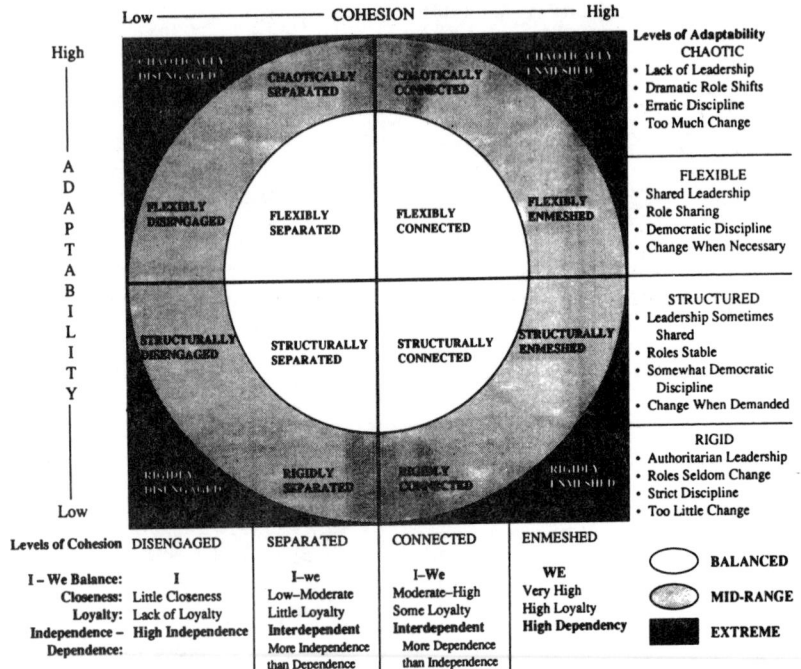

Figure 2.1. Circumplex Model: Couple and Family Map

In the model's "balanced" area (separated and connected), individuals are able to experience and balance the two extremes and are also able to be both independent from and connected to their families. Many couples and families who go to marital or family therapy often fall into one of the extremes. When cohesion levels are high (enmeshed systems), there is too much consensus within the family and too little independence. At the other extreme (disengaged systems), family members "do their own thing," with limited attachment or commitment to their family.

A disengaged relationship often has extreme emotional separateness. There is little involvement among family members and there is a lot of personal separateness and independence. Individuals often do their own thing and have separate interests. A separated relationship has some emotional separateness but it is not as extreme as the disengaged system. While time apart is more important, there is some time together and some joint decisions. Activities and interests are generally separate but a few are shared. A connected relationship has some emotional closeness and loyalty to the relationship. Time together is more important than time apart to be by oneself. There is an emphasis on togetherness. While there are separate friends, there are also friends shared by the couple. There are often shared interests. In the enmeshed relationship there is an extreme amount of emotional closeness and loyalty is demanded. Individuals are very dependent on each other and reactive to one another. There is a general lack of personal separateness and little private space is permitted. The energy of the individuals is mainly focused inside the marriage or family and there are few outside individual friends or interests.

Based on the Circumplex Model, very high levels of cohesion (enmeshed) and very low levels of cohesion (disengaged) might be problematic for individuals and relationship development in the long run. On the other hand, relationships having moderate scores (separated and connected) are able to balance being alone versus together in a more functional way. Although there is no absolute best level for any relationship, some may have problems if they always function at either extreme of the map (disengaged or enmeshed).

Marital and Family Adaptability

Family adaptability is defined as the ability of a marital or family system to change its power structure, role relationships, and relationship rules in response to situational and developmental stress. In order to describe, measure, and diagnose couples and families on this dimension, a variety of concepts have been taken from several social science disciplines, with heavy reliance on family sociology. These concepts include: family power (assertiveness, control, discipline), negotiation styles, role relationships, and relationship rules.

The four levels of adaptability range from rigid (very low) to structured (low to moderate) to flexible (moderate to high) to chaotic (very high) (see Figure 2.1). As with cohesion, it is hypothesized that central levels of adaptability (structured and flexible) are more conducive to marital and family functioning, with the extremes (rigid and chaotic) being the most problematic for families as they move through their life cycles.

Basically, adaptability focuses on the ability of the marital and family system to change. Much of the early application of systems theory to families emphasized the rigidity of the family and its tendency to maintain the status quo. Until the work of recent theorists, the importance of potential for change was minimized. Couples and families need both stability and change, and the ability to change when appropriate distinguishes functional couples and families from others. Marriages and families can range from having a rigid and authoritarian leader to being chaotic with erratic or limited leadership. A rigid relationship is one in which one individual is highly controlling. The roles are strictly defined and the rules do not change. A structured relationship is less rigid overall. Leadership is somewhat less authoritarian, less controlling, and is shared between the parents. Roles are stable but there is some sharing of roles. There are a few rule changes but not a lot of change. A flexible relationship is even less rigid. Leadership is more equally shared. Roles are sometimes shared and rules could change. A chaotic relationship has erratic or limited leadership. Decisions are impulsive and not well thought out. Roles are unclear and often shift from individual to individual.

Based on the Circumplex Model, very high levels of change (chaotic) and very low levels of change (rigid) might be problematic for individuals and relationship development in the long run. On the other hand, relationships having moderate scores (structured and flexible) are able to balance some change and some stability in a more functional way. Although there is no absolute best level for any relationship, many relationships may have problems if they always function at either extreme of the model (rigid or chaotic).

Circumplex Model: A Couple and Family Map

Another way to consider the model is as a descriptive map of 16 types of couple and family relationships; in other words, a Couple Map and a Family Map. The Couple Map is used to describe 16 types of marriages; the Family Map is used to describe 16 types of families.

The Family Map is important because people often use their own family-of-origin as a reference for the type of marriage and family they either want or do not want. People often either recreate the type of family system they had as a child or they may react by doing the opposite. Thus if a couple came from two quite different family systems or they prefer different types of family dynamics, it would be difficult for them to create a compatible relationship style that works for them.

The Type of Marriage, as illustrated in the Couple Map, is important for individual and relationship development. Couples need to balance their levels of separateness-togetherness on cohesion and their levels of stability-change on adaptability. These levels can be adjusted by a couple to achieve a level that is acceptable to each individual.

Balanced Versus Extreme Types of Marital and Family Systems

An important distinction in the Circumplex Model is between balanced and extreme types of couple and family relationships. There are four balanced types that are "separated" or "connected" levels on cohesion and "structured" or "connected" on adaptability. Figure 2.1 illustrates the four balanced relationships and the four extreme relationships: chaotically disengaged, chaotically enmeshed, rigidly disengaged, and rigidly enmeshed.

This typological system is conceptually compatible with other family system models like Constantine's (1986) family paradigm model, which contains four system types (open, closed, random, and synchronous) that can be either enabled or disabled. The four enabled types are conceptually similar to the balanced Circumplex types and the disabled types are similar to the extreme Circumplex types.

Three-Dimensional (3-D) Circumplex Model:
First- and Second-Order Change

In the three-dimensional Circumplex Model, the balanced types are elevated to the highest level followed by the mid-range types; and the lowest level are the four extreme types (see Figure 2.2).

Conceptually, this three-dimensional model enables one to incorporate second-order change into the Circumplex Model as proposed by Lee (1988). First-order change is that which occurs *within* a given family system type. Second-order change is the ability of a system type to change to another type. First-order change is curvilinear in that too much or too little change is problematic. First-order change refers to the amount of change on the dimensions of cohesion and adaptability.

In contrast, second-order change is linear and is illustrated by the three-dimensional Circumplex Model. Second-order change is also similar to Beavers's concept of competence as described by Beavers and Hampson (1990).

The three-dimensional model has the advantage of demonstrating more clearly the dynamic similarity of the types within the balanced, mid-range, and extreme types. The three-dimensional model more clearly illustrates that the four balanced types are more similar to each other dynamically than they are to any of the extreme types. Conversely, the four extreme

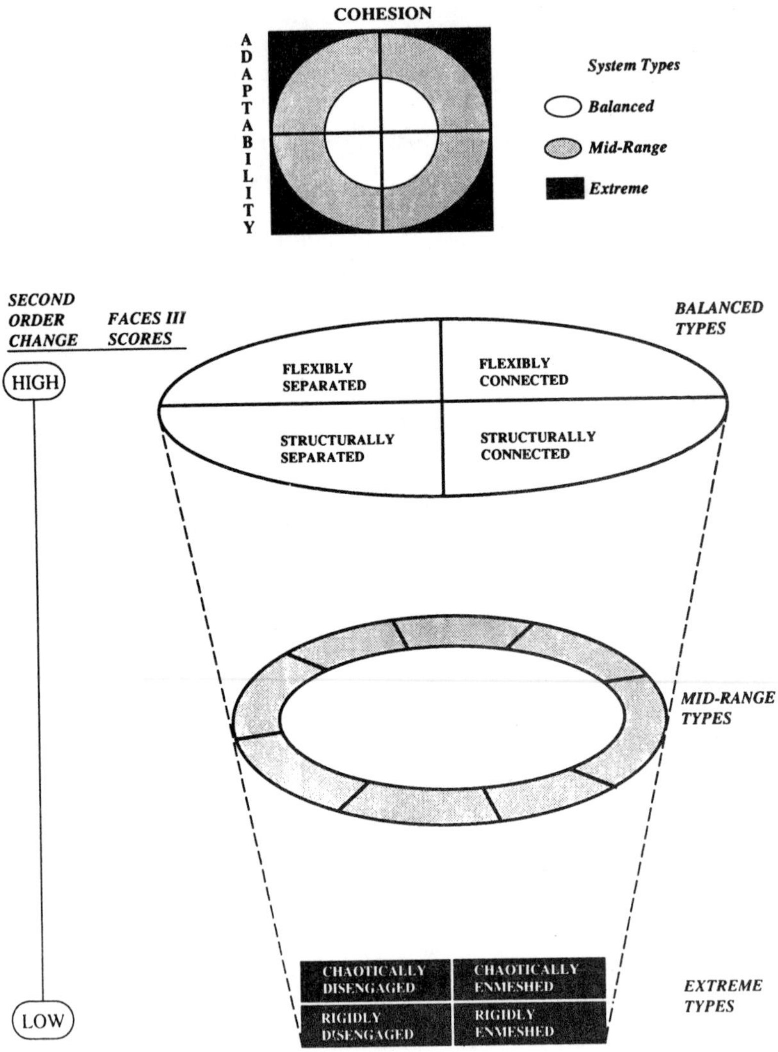

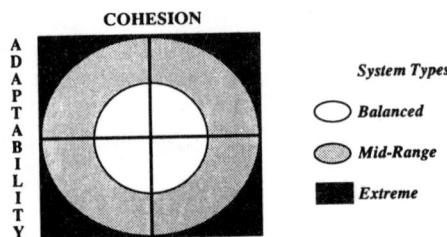

COHESION

A
D
A
P
T
A
B
I
L
I
T
Y

System Types

○ *Balanced*

◍ *Mid-Range*

■ *Extreme*

SECOND ORDER CHANGE   *FACES III SCORES*   *BALANCED TYPES*

(HIGH)

FLEXIBLY SEPARATED   FLEXIBLY CONNECTED

STRUCTURALLY SEPARATED   STRUCTURALLY CONNECTED

MID-RANGE TYPES

CHAOTICALLY DISENGAGED   CHAOTICALLY ENMESHED

RIGIDLY DISENGAGED   RIGIDLY ENMESHED

EXTREME TYPES

(LOW)

Figure 2.2. Three-Dimensional Family Circumplex Model

types are more similar to each other dynamically than they are to any of the balanced types. This clarifies the dynamic similarities within types that is often lost when looking at the Circumplex Model laid out two-dimensionally (4 levels × 4 levels).

Methodologically, FACES III, a self-report scale that answers family cohesion and adaptability, measures the three-dimensional model in a more effective way than it does the traditional four by four design. It is clear from the various methodological studies and from a review of the specific questions in FACES III that high scores actually measure balanced family types and low scores measure extreme family types. More specifically, high scores on cohesion are measuring "very connected" families (balanced) and high scores on adaptability are measuring "very flexible" families (balanced).

Studies with FACES III should assume it is a linear measure with high scores representing balanced types and low scores representing extreme types. This revised conceptual approach to FACES III also makes the three-dimensional model more similar to Beavers's System Model and McMaster's Family Model. It also helps clarify why FACES III statistically is correlated in a linear way to the Self-Report Family Inventory (SFI) by Beavers and Hampson (1990), the Family Assessment Measure (FAM III) by Skinner, Santa-Barbara, and Steinhauer (1983), and the McMaster Family Assessment Device (FAD) by Epstein, Baldwin, and Bishop (1983).

Marital and Family Communication

Family communication is the third dimension in the Circumplex Model and is considered a facilitating dimension. Communication is considered critical for facilitating couple and family movement on the other two dimensions. Because it is a facilitating dimension, communication is not graphically included in the model along with cohesion and adaptability.

Positive communication skills (i.e., empathy, reflective listening, supportive comments) enable couples and families to share with each other their changing needs and preferences. Conversely, double messages, double-binds, and criticisms minimize the ability of members of a couple or a family to share their feelings and, thereby, restrict their movement on these dimensions.

Hypotheses Derived From the Circumplex Model

One of the assets of a theoretical model is that hypotheses can be deduced and tested in order to evaluate and further develop the model. The following are hypotheses derived from the Circumplex Model:

1. *Couples and families with balanced (the two central levels) cohesion and adaptability will generally function more adequately across the family life cycle than those at the extremes of these dimensions.*
   An important issue in the Circumplex Model relates to the concept of balance. Individuals and family systems need to balance their separateness versus togetherness on cohesion and their level of stability versus change on adaptability. Even though a balanced family system is placed at the two central levels of the model, it should not be assumed that these families always operate in a "moderate" manner. Being balanced means that a family system can experience the extremes on the dimension when appropriate, but that they do not typically function at these extremes for long periods of time.
   Families in the balanced area of the cohesion dimension allow their members to experience being both independent from and connected to the family. On adaptability, balance means maintaining some level of stability in a system with the openness to some change when it is necessary. Extreme behaviors on these two dimensions might be appropriate for certain stages of the life cycle or when a family is under stress, but it can be problematic at all times.

2. *Positive communication skills will enable balanced couples/families to change their levels of cohesion and adaptability more easily than families at the extremes.*
   In general, positive communication skills are seen as helping marital and family systems facilitate and maintain a balance on the two dimensions. Conversely, negative communication skills impede movement into the central areas and thereby increase the probability that extreme systems will remain extreme.
   Positive communication skills include the following: sending clear and congruent messages, empathy, supportive statements, and effective problem-solving skills. Conversely, negative communication skills include sending incongruent and disqualifying messages, lack of empathy, nonsupportive (negative) statements, poor problem-solving skills, and paradoxical and double-binding messages. Although many studies have investigated communication and problem-solving skills in couples and families, these studies have not specifically tested the relationships of these skills to the hypotheses derived from the Circumplex Model.

3. *To deal with situational stress and developmental changes across the family life cycle, families will change their cohesion and adaptability to adapt to the stress.*

This hypothesis deals with change in the family system to deal with stress or to accommodate changes in family members, particularly as family members change their expectations. The Circumplex Model is dynamic in that it assumes that couples and families will change types and it hypothesizes that change can be beneficial to the maintenance and improvement of family functioning.

When one family member desires change, the family system must somehow deal with that request. For example, increasing numbers of wives want to develop more autonomy from their husbands (cohesion dimension) and also want more power and equality in their relationships (adaptability dimension). If their husbands are unwilling to understand and change in accordance with these expectations, the marriages will probably experience increasing levels of stress and dissatisfaction.

Another common example of changing expectations occurs when a child reaches adolescence. Like the wives in the previous example, adolescents often want more freedom, independence, and power in the family system.

The Circumplex Model allows one to integrate systems theory within family development, a proposal made more than two decades ago by Reuben Hill (1970). Building on the family development approach, it is therefore hypothesized that the stage of the family life cycle and composition of the family will have considerable impact on the type of family system.

It is first hypothesized that at any stage of the family life cycle there will be a diversity in the types of family systems as described in the Circumplex Model. In spite of this diversity, it is predicted that at different stages of the family life cycle many families will cluster together in some types more frequently than in others. For example, it would be predicted that premarital couples would tend toward the high range on cohesion (enmeshed and connected) and toward the higher range on adaptability (flexible and chaotic). In other words, they would fall into the upper left quadrant of the Circumplex Model.

The model is dynamic in that it assumes that changes occur in family types over time (Olson, Russell, & Sprenkle, 1989). Families can move in any direction that the situation, stage of the family life cycle, or socialization of family members may require. A look at a couple illustrates the dynamic nature of the model:

> Fred and Mary were married and developed a flexibly enmeshed marriage. Three years after their marriage they became parents and Mary resigned from her teaching job. Because of the dependency needs of their son, and their own desire for mutual support in this transition period, their family became *structurally connected.*
>
> However, when Mary and Fred's son became a teenager, their family moved from being connected to being more separated on cohesion. Mary started pursuing a career and both parents experienced a good deal of "consciousness raising" about sex roles through the media and through involvement in several growth groups. Because of their son's need for more autonomy at this age, as well as the their own separate career interests, they began operating at a lower level of cohesiveness.
>
> Furthermore, the family power structure shifted from being husband-dominant to a more shared pattern. They moved on adaptability from a structured type to a flexible type. Mary exercised much more control in the relationship than previously and the couple was struggling, almost on a weekly basis, to redefine the rules and role definitions that would govern their relationship. Although they occasionally yearn for the security of their earlier more structured relationship, both found the challenge in this more flexible relationship style. In short, their family could be described as *flexibly separated* at the adolescent stage of the family life cycle.

This brief case history illustrates the dynamic nature of the model that allows for movement within reasonable limits. It also seeks to recognize diverse values and to legitimize the diverse organizational ideals of families. None of the four balanced types in the inner circle is designated as "the ideal" at any given stage of the family life cycle—but all are more functional than the extreme types, especially with families at the adolescent stage.

Changes in a Family System Related to Physical Illness (Second-Order Change)

Although some hypotheses have been developed relating family systems described by the Circumplex Model and family stress (Olson, Russell, & Sprenkle, 1989), little research has been done that would help us understand the changes that take place in family processes related to physical and emotional illness. Short-term longitudinal studies are needed if we are better to understand the changes that occur in the family system, with comparisons between those individuals who recover more quickly and those who have difficulty recovering.

One hypothesis from the Circumplex Model is that balanced families, compared to extreme families, will do better because they are able to change their family system in order to cope more effectively with the illness of a family member. This is *second-order change,* because the family is changing its type of system to adapt to the major stressor.

An example of how the Circumplex Model can be used in both understanding and graphing the changes in family system over time is a family in which the husband has had a heart attack. In this family crisis, the husband, Peter (age 53), had a massive heart attack. His wife, Martha, was a homemaker and they had three teenagers living at home, one of whom was attending college.

The changes in this family system before and after Peter's heart attack are illustrated in Figure 2.3. Before the heart attack (point A), the family was structurally separated, which was generally appropriate for that stage of the family life cycle.

Once the heart attack occurred, however, the family quickly shifted to becoming a more chaotically enmeshed family (point B). Very high levels of closeness, characterized by enmeshment, occurred because the illness brought the family closer together emotionally. It also created chaos in the family because they needed to shift many of their daily routines dramatically.

From about the third to the sixth week, the family continued to be enmeshed but became more rigid in their structure. This rigidity was an attempt to stabilize the chaos by reorganizing some of the routines in their family system (point C).

Six months later, the family was functioning as a structurally connected family (point D). Some of the previous rigidity and extreme cohesion decreased, but they remained a rather close family with a more structured system because of Peter's disability.

In summary, because of Peter's heart attack, this family's system changed several times over the course of the following six months as they adapted to this family crisis. They started as a balanced system (flexibly separated), moved to two extreme types (chaotically enmeshed and structurally enmeshed), before ending up once again as a balanced system (structurally connected).

It is expected that family systems will change in response to a crisis. As hypothesized with the Circumplex Model, it is the balanced families that would have the resources and skills to shift their system in an appropriate way to cope more effectively with a crisis. In contrast, it is hypothesized

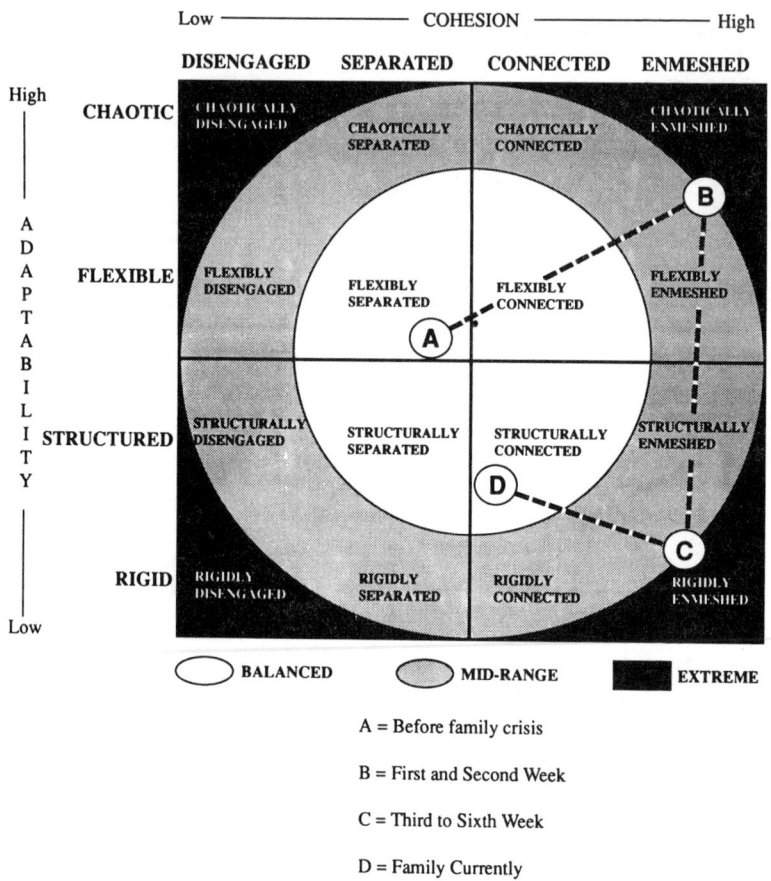

Figure 2.3. Family Change Before and After Husband's Heart Attack

that extreme families would not have the resources that are needed to change and, therefore, would have more difficulty adapting to a crisis. In other words, balanced families are higher in second-order change because they are able to alter their family system to adapt to family crises.

Studies Validating the Circumplex Model

Balanced Versus Extreme Families

A central hypothesis derived from the model is that balanced couples/families will function more adequately than extreme couples/families. This hypothesis is built on the assumption that families extreme on both dimensions will tend to have more difficulties functioning across the life cycle. This assumes a curvilinear relationship on the dimensions of cohesion and adaptability. This means that too little or too much cohesion or adaptability is seen as dysfunctional to the family system. However, families that are able to balance between these two extremes seem to function more adequately.

To test the major hypothesis that balanced family types are more functional then extreme types, a variety of studies have been done focusing on a range of emotional problems and symptoms in couples and families. A study by Clarke (1984) focused on families with schizophrenics, neurotics, families who had completed therapy sometime in their past, and a no-therapy control group (see Figure 2.4). Clarke used FACES II, a precursor to FACES III. In general, he found a very high level of extreme families in the neurotic and schizophrenic groups compared to the no-therapy group. Conversely, he found a significantly higher level of balanced families in the no-therapy group compared to the other groups.

Figure 2.4 illustrates the differences in the levels of cohesion and adaptability between these groups. While the percentage of extreme family types decreased dramatically from the symptomatic to the no-therapy groups (neurotic, 64%; schizophrenic, 56%; completed therapy, 38%; no therapy, 7%), the percentage of balanced families increased (neurotic, 8%; schizophrenic, 12%; completed therapy, 38%; no therapy, 48%) as hypothesized.

A study by Carnes (1989), using FACES II, investigated the family systems of sex offenders and found high levels of extreme family types in both their family-of-origin and their current families (see Figure 2.5). While 49% had extreme family types in their family-of-origin and 66% of their current families were extreme types, only 19% of the nonoffender families were extreme. Conversely, while only 11% of their family-of-origin and 19% of their current families were balanced types, 47% of the nonoffender families were balanced.

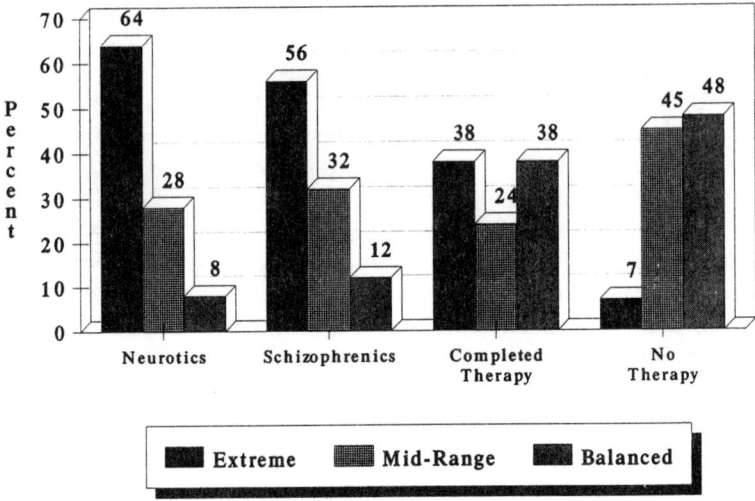

Figure 2.4. Problem Families and Circumplex Model

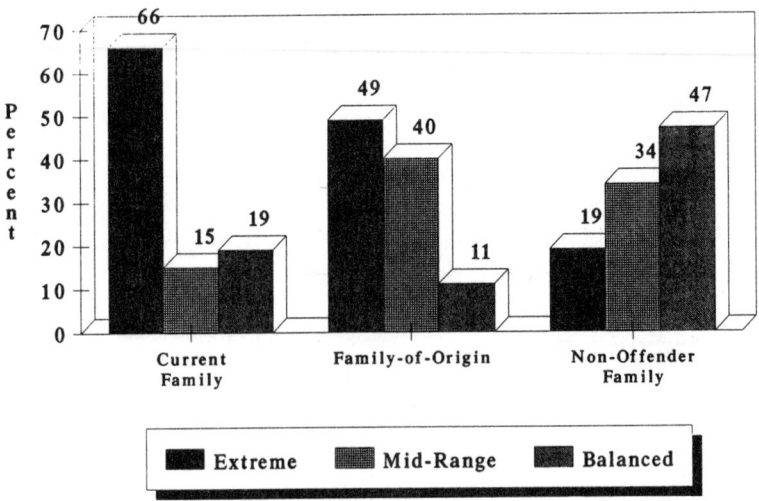

Figure 2.5. Sex Offenders and Circumplex Model

In summary, these studies of clinical samples clearly demonstrate the discriminate power of the Circumplex Model in distinguishing between problem families and nonsymptomatic families. There is strong empirical support for the hypothesis that balanced types of families are more functional than extreme family types. There is, however, a lack of evidence that any of these symptoms are specifically linked with a specific type of family system, such as chaotically enmeshed. This was the hope of early family research linking family symptoms (a schizophrenic offspring) and family systems.

In contrast to the curvilinear relationship found on these dimensions among problem families, there appears to be a linear relationship between cohesion and change (adaptability) in family functioning among "normal" families. More specifically, higher levels of cohesion and change seem to be associated with better family functioning.

These results were found in a national survey of 1,000 families across the life cycle and were reported by Olson, McCubbin, Barnes, Larsen, Muxen, and Wilson (1989). A primary reason for this finding is that normal families represent only a narrow spectrum of the range of behavior on these two dimensions. As a result, there are very few of the "normal" families that legitimately fall into the extreme types.

Balanced Families and Communication

Another hypothesis is that balanced families will have more positive communication skills than extreme families. Communication can be measured at both the marital and family levels. Using data from the national survey of 1,000 families, H. Barnes and Olson (1983, 1985) investigated parent-adolescent communication and family functioning. Using "nonproblem" families, the hypothesis that balanced families would have better communication skills was supported when relying on data from the parents. However, this hypothesis was not supported for adolescents. Future research is needed to test hypotheses at both the marital and family levels with both nonproblem and problem families.

In addition to testing the hypothesis regarding balanced versus extreme families reviewed earlier, Rodick, Henggler, and Hanson (1986) found strong support for the hypothesis that balanced families have more positive communication skills. Using observational measures of mother-adolescent interaction, they found that mothers in the balanced group had significantly higher rates of supportive communication, explicit information, and positive affect than did mothers in the extreme type with the majority of problem dyads (chaotically enmeshed).

Family Systems and Stress Across the Family Life Cycle

Empirically, this chapter builds upon and extends the findings from a national survey of nonclinical families described by Olson, McCubbin et al. (1989). However, the operationalization of family developmental stages, family stress and adaptation, family system types, and the analyses in the present chapter are updated from the results in the book. The overall sample comprised 1,251 families, with more than 100 families in seven family life stages and more than 200 families with adolescents. Data were collected from both spouses in each family and from adolescents in families that included adolescent(s) at home. The present analysis is based on responses of adults (husbands, wives).

The sample consisted of predominantly Caucasian, middle-class, Protestant families from both rural and urban areas. Husbands' ages ranged from 20 to 85 (mean = 46) and wives' ages ranged from 19 to 84 (mean = 43). Children's ages ranged from less than 1 year in preschool-stage families to more than 40 in retirement-stage families. A large variety of occupations was represented in the sample. Average family income fell in the $20,000 to $30,000 range. Data on education showed that 30% of the husbands and 20% of the wives had at least a college education. A more detailed description of sample characteristics is reported in Olson, McCubbin et al. (1989).

Measure and Scales

Family types. Families were classified into four system types by the Circumplex quadrants typological approach. Two scales were used to classify families: (a) Family Cohesion (10 items) measures the emotional bonding family members have toward one another; and (b) Family Flexibility (Adaptability) (10 items) measures the family's ability to change its structural relationships. Both scales were measured by FACES III (Olson, Portner, & Lavee, 1985).

Family life cycle. Although the sampling procedure yielded data from families at seven life stages (see "Sampling and Data Collection," above), data were collapsed into four family life stages in the present analyses to obtain a large enough sample in each stage: (a) Young couples without children; (b) Families with young children (oldest child is either preschool or school age); (c) Families with adolescents (oldest child is either an adolescent or has left home but there are other children living at home); and (d) Older couples (couples are either at an empty-nest stage or in retirement).

Family stressors. Family stressors were measured by a 10-item scale (H. McCubbin, Olson, Lavee, & Patterson, 1985). The scale lists events that represent family transitions (such as birth of a child, marriage, launching), work transitions, and nonnormative events (illness, death of a family member) that may have occurred during the past year. An event was considered to have happened in the family if either spouse indicated its occurrence. A family stressor score was computed as the number of events that occurred within the specific time.

Family strains. These were also measured by a 10-item scale (H. McCubbin et al., 1985). This scale lists changes during the past year in family interaction and role performance that represent increases in interpersonal strain, financial strain, and role strain (i.e., difficulty performing tasks). A change was considered to have happened in the family if either spouse indicated its occurrence. A family strain score was computed as the number of strain items indicated.

Family well-being (adaptational outcome). Family well-being was operationally defined as a composite index of three measures: (a) Marital Satisfaction (Olson, Fournier, & Druckman, 1986); (b) Family Satisfaction (Olson & Wilson, 1985); and (c) Quality of Life (H. Barnes & Olson, 1985). The three measures were factor analyzed and loaded on a single factor.

Family System Types Across the Family Life Cycle

Figures 2.6 and 2.7 represent the frequency of families at each of the four developmental stages classified by the Circumplex's main dimensions of cohesion (connected versus separated) and adaptability (flexible versus structured) families.

In terms of family cohesion, younger couples have the highest percentage that feel "connected" (71%) versus feeling "separated" (29%). The percentage feeling connected dropped to 63% in families with younger children and more dramatically to 40% in families with adolescents (see Figure 2.6).

As might be expected, younger couples felt their relationship was more "flexible" (62%) and this dropped to 37% in families with younger

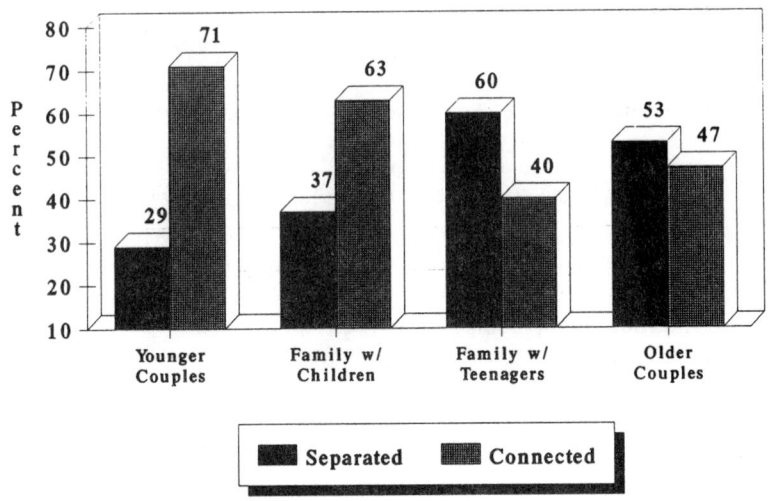

Figure 2.6. Family Cohesion Across the Family Life Cycle

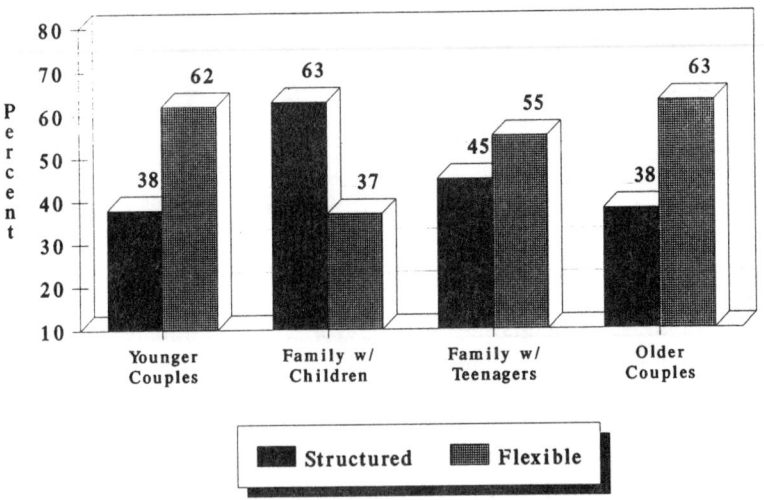

Figure 2.7. Family Flexibility Across the Family Life Cycle

children. As expected, the flexibility increased to 55% with families with adolescents and 63% with older couples (see Figure 2.7).

Family Stressors, Strains, and Well-Being Across the Family Life Cycle

This analysis examined the accumulation of stressors and strains and the level of family well-being across the family life cycle. The results of this analysis are graphically presented in Figure 2.8. There was very little difference in the accumulation of stressor events among the four family life stages. An analysis of variance indeed indicated no significant differences in the number of stressor events $[F(3) = 2.38, p > .10]$.

On the other hand, there was a significant difference among families' levels of strain at the four stages $[F(3) = 32.63, p > .01]$. The results in Figure 2.8 indicate that families with children, whether preschool and school age or adolescent, experience higher levels of intrafamily strain than do childless couples or families at the empty-nest stage and retirement stage. Furthermore, the results indicate that both younger and older couples have the lowest level of strain.

Couples at the first stage of family development (i.e., before children are born) and at the last stage of the family development (i.e., after all children have left home) are also more satisfied with their marriage, their families, and their quality of life than are those with children at home. Families with adolescents have lower levels of well-being than those families with younger children, despite having similar levels of stressors and strains.

Update on Inventories for Families Assessment

In order adequately to assess the three major dimensions of the Circumplex Model and other related concepts, Olson, McCubbin, et al. (1986) developed a variety of self-report assessment tools. These assessment tools were designed to provide not only an "insider's perspective" on one's own family system, but also an "outsider's perspective." The self-report instrument called the Circumplex Assessment Package (CAP) provides the insider's perspective, whereas the Clinical Rating Scale (CRS) provides the outsider's perspective. Both perspectives are useful and often provide conflicting data. Used together, however, they capture the complexity of marital and family systems (Olson, 1977).

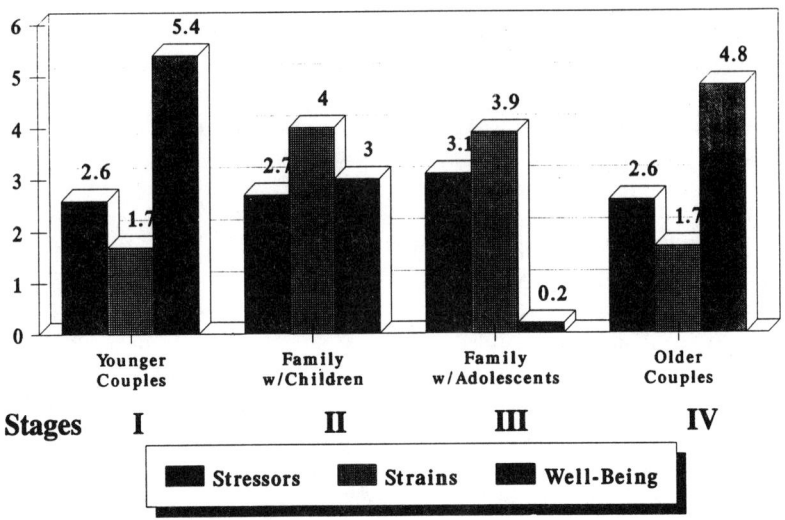

Figure 2.8. Stressors, Strains, and Well-Being Across the Family Life Cycle

Assessment Criteria: Multimethod, Multitrait, and Multisystem Levels

Multimethod assessment utilizes both self-report scales, which provide an insider's perspective on one's own relationship, and the therapists' or observers' ratings, which provide an outsider's perspective on that same system. Both clinical work and research with families have indicated that there is often a discrepancy between these two perspectives and related methodologies (Olson, 1986). Therefore, these two methodologies often provide an important rationale for why both approaches should be used in work with families.

If investigators rely only on their own perceptions of the system (an outsider's perspective), our data indicates that this will often differ in significant ways from one or more of the family members' perceptions. It is also problematic to rely on only one family member because family members often do not agree with each other in describing their family system (Olson, McCubbin et al., 1989). Assessment using multiple family members, therefore, provides a more complete picture of how each one views the system and the level of agreement or disagreement between them.

Multitrait assessment is based on the three central dimensions of the Circumplex Model: cohesion, adaptability, and communication. Although there are other traits that can be incorporated into couple and family assessment, these three dimensions provide the foundation and central core of these relationship systems.

Multisystem assessment ideally focuses on the individual, the marital system, parent-child system, and total family—including extended family relationships. One important question to ask family members is who they each consider to be members of their family. It is surprising to us how often family members disagree regarding who is currently in their family system. This raises important questions about boundary issues and who is psychologically and/or physically present in a given family system (Boss & Greenberg, 1984).

Circumplex Assessment Package and Clinical Rating Scale (CRS)

The Circumplex Assessment Package (CAP) is the latest in a series of self-report assessments that are developed based on the Circumplex Model. This assessment procedure is multidimensional in that it assesses the three Circumplex dimensions of cohesion, adaptability, and communication, as well as including a satisfaction dimension.

It is also multisystem level in that assessment procedures focus on both the marital system and the family system. More specifically, each of the four dimensions are assessed at the couple and family levels. Two-parent families (nuclear or blended) would complete both the marital and family scales. Single-parent families would complete the family scales and would complete the marital scales if the single parent had a significant other. Couples (married or cohabiting) would complete the couple scales.

FACES III is an acronym for Family Adaptability and Cohesion Evaluation Scales and MACES III is an acronym for Marital Adaptability and Cohesion Evaluation Scales. The communication dimension is assessed at the couple level using a subscale from the ENRICH instrument (Olson, Fournier, & Druckman, 1986) and family communication is based on the Parent-Adolescent Communication Scale (H. Barnes & Olson, 1983, 1985). The satisfaction dimension is assessed at the couple level using a subscale from the ENRICH instrument (Olson, Fournier, & Druckman, 1986) and the Family Satisfaction scale (Olson & Wilson, 1985) is based on the Circumplex dimensions.

The reliability of these scales has been assessed in a variety of studies. The most comprehensive summary is provided in *Family Inventories* (Olson, McCubbin et al., 1986). As indicated in Table 2.2, both the

Table 2.2 Circumplex Assessment Package (CAP): Reliability*

	Internal Consistency	Test Re-Test
FACES III (Family)		
Cohesion	.77	.83
Adaptability	.62	.80
FACES III (Marital)		
Cohesion	.79	.83
Adaptability	.73	.80
Communication		
Couple (ENRICH)	.82	.90
Parent-Adolescent	.88	.78
Satisfaction		
Couple (ENRICH)	.86	.86
Family	.92	.75
Average	.80	.82

*These scales are contained in the *Family Inventories* by Olson, McCubbin, et al. (1986).

internal consistency and test-retest reliability of these scales is consistently high ($r = .80$). In terms of validity, therapists and researchers have evaluated the items in terms of face validity and find them to meet acceptable criteria. The scales also demonstrate having discriminate validity in that they distinguish between clinical and nonclinical families (Olson, McCubbin et al., 1989).

The Clinical Rating Scale (CRS) was developed by Olson (1990) in order to do clinical assessment on cohesion, adaptability, and communication. It describes specific indicators for each level of the three dimensions. This scale is a useful training device for helping individuals learn more about the Circumplex Model and its value for family interaction assessment.

3

Gender Role Change in Families

A Macrosociological View

JOAN HUBER

The fact of gender role change in U.S. families is widely documented in sociological literature and reflected in mass media. The question for this chapter, however, is how to explain such change. Only if one understands what caused gender role changes in this century can one envision what may lie ahead in the next one.

A *role* involves expectations about appropriate interpersonal behaviors, beliefs, and feelings in various social arenas, a commonsense definition. To explain aggregate role change, one must first identify the factors that shape roles and make them vary by time and place. These factors include the macrolevel social and ecological conditions to which humans must adapt. Changes in these basic conditions elicit aggregate role changes.

I therefore first discuss the macrolevel causes of role change, drawing on one of the most important works on social stratification in this century. Gerhard Lenski (1966) demonstrated how the distribution of power and prestige is affected by the way that subsistence technology and environment constrain the division of labor. Lenski's book was the basis for

AUTHOR'S NOTE: This chapter was originally presented as part of the Family and Child Studies Center Lecture Series, Miami University, Oxford, OH, and has benefited from the comments of William Form.

the first sociology text to provide a theory about societal variation over time (the fifth edition is Lenski & Lenski, 1990). I outline this perspective below to show how it furthers the understanding of changes in family roles.

Human societies, which exist to enable individuals to satisfy needs, are adaptive mechanisms vital to our species's survival. A society must solve certain problems. It must be able to distribute goods and services, protect its members from dangers, control their behavior, and replace them across generations. A society must adapt to its natural environment (e.g., climate, terrain, and soil type) if it is to persist. Historically, these factors have changed slowly and have been difficult or impossible to bring under human control.

The environment is analytically complex because it includes social organizations that humans themselves create. One aspect is especially important because it is analytically separable from social organizations and especially because it can bring about rapid social change: technology, the way people produce the things they value (Preston, 1991). The analysis of technology will not explain everything about human history but it is a needed first step. One cannot explain why people think, feel, and act as they do without understanding the constraints posed by the tools they use and the conditions under which they use them.

Classifying societies by their dominant subsistence mode (e.g., foraging, the hoe, the plow, herding, or manufacturing) yields predictions about these societies such as population size, level of inequality in the distribution of goods, type of marriage, and gender stratification. Technological innovations, especially those that affect major subsistence tools, change the division of labor, thereby stimulating behaviors and beliefs that ultimately result in role changes. In the long sweep of human history, such inventions have been few. However, the rate of technological innovation rose exponentially after 1800 when the interdependent events now called the Industrial Revolution occurred in northwestern Europe and the northeastern United States. Today the speed with which new inventions appear makes it hard to understand what is going on and even harder to predict what lies ahead.

The strategy in this chapter is first to outline a theory of family gender roles. Then I apply it to foraging, hoe, herding, and plow societies and discuss industrialization's effects on family roles by ethnicity and class. Last, I point to aspects of contemporary family roles in which change seems probable.

Preindustrial Tools, Work, and Child Rearing

In any society the distribution of power and prestige is largely determined by the work people do. Those who produce have more power and prestige than those who consume; those who control the distribution of goods beyond the family have the most power in any society (Friedl, 1975; see also Blumberg, 1978; Chafetz, 1990). The basic question is, therefore, what factors determine which persons or groups have the chance to do the most rewarding work? Below, I show how these principles explain gender stratification in societies dominated by several types of subsistence technology.

Men's and women's roles tend to be shaped by the way the daily work that sustains individuals and groups meshes with pregnancy and lactation. In foraging societies men hunted large animals, which provided enough food to distribute beyond the family. Women gathered nuts and berries and killed small animals. Thus, even though women's activities may have contributed a higher proportion of the calories in daily diets, their work did not enable them to distribute the food they produced beyond their immediate families as men's hunting activities did. Then why didn't women also hunt large animals? Basically because tracking them required days away from camp, which made nursing impossible. Since women were pregnant or nursing during their most vigorous years to offset high death rates, the need for population replacement precluded their doing the work that yielded the most prestige and power (Huber & Spitze, 1988).

In hoe cultures women's contribution to food production tended to equal men's; a nursing mother could also tend a garden plot. Women's contribution to the food supply raised their status and also resulted in a high divorce rate since divorce little affected the subsistence of either spouse or their children. Among the hoe peoples of Sub-Saharan Africa, the ancestors of many contemporary Americans, women typically supported themselves and their children. "Populist polygyny" was common (Huber & Spitze, 1988). Nearly everyone married but women married young, men married old, and a high death rate helped to even the sex ratio.

Herding societies, technologically between hoe and plow societies, occurred where low rainfall, a short season, or rough terrain precluded growing crops. Water and grazing needs made warfare common; one group was always intruding on another's turf. Since warfare and herding animals far from home mesh poorly with nursing, women do not become major food producers. A great surplus can be amassed (e.g., Genghis Khan's) and a tiny political elite may become wealthy. "Elite polygyny" (only rich men can have many wives) may occur (Huber & Spitze, 1988).

In plow societies women's relative contribution to food production dropped and with it, their status. The plow was used further from home, which interfered with nursing. More important, the plow made land the chief form of wealth (Goody, 1976). Crops could be grown repeatedly in the same place. Hoe peoples had to move every few years when soil was exhausted. Since land is an impartible inheritance (with a given technology, it can support only a given number of persons), heir production had to be controlled. Since monogamy regulates heir production more efficiently than polygyny, monogamy came to dominate Eurasian plow cultures. Women's sexual behavior was constrained in order that a man could know a child was his.

Constraints on women were possibly greater in Asia than in Europe, an unanticipated consequence of the Roman Catholic Church's efforts to increase its landholdings (Goody, 1983). After 325 C.E. the Church introduced measures that reduced a person's supply of close relatives (banning adoption and cousin marriages, for example) in order to tempt the faithful to leave their property to the Church. However, some of these measures also improved women's status. For example, polygyny was condemned; mutual consent was required for valid marriage, thereby decreasing the probability that little girls would become pawns to family interests. Such measures may help to explain why European women did not suffer the worst horrors of plow cultures, such as foot binding in China and suttee in India, but to date no one has systematically explored this possibility.

American Colonial Family Roles

Following the theoretical scheme outlined above, one would expect to find three family types in colonial America. However, two of them did not survive industrialization. First, native Americans in the Eastern Woodlands tended to have the role patterns of foraging or simple hoe cultures, in which women were typically less subordinated than in plow or herding cultures. In the West, however, the introduction of the horse made buffalo hunting a significant factor in subsistence, thereby lowering women's relative status. Over time, most native Americans were killed by the diseases and guns of European settlers. Survivors tended to adapt to class and ethnic variants of dominant patterns.

Second, the Africans who were forced to migrate as slaves were socialized to Sub-Saharan patterns but "populist polygyny" gave way to slave patterns. The Emancipation put black families at the bottom of a caste system. Later urban migration after industrialization was well advanced and did little to improve their lot.

Third, immigrant Europeans carried with them the role patterns adapted to plow societies. The doctrine of coverture made a married woman her husband's property, obliged to serve and please him. Doubtless women's status relative to men's varied with living conditions. On the frontier, which was open until about 1880, women and men alike led hard lives but, in contrast with immigrants and native-born in Eastern cities, pioneers probably benefited from the independence derived from land ownership. However, as the frontier moved west, pioneer societies resembled herding cultures in that pregnancy and lactation mesh poorly with herding cattle and fighting off rustlers.

Consequently, women tended to be excluded from roles that yielded the most power and privilege. The typical Wild West film illustrates women's importance in frontier life. The cast included thousands of cattle, hundreds of cowboys, dozens of rustlers, a sheriff or two, and the hero. Often, the only woman in this sea of cattle and men was a prostitute with a heart of gold. Sometimes there was no woman at all and the hero rode off into the sunset on his horse.

In sum, gender roles in hunting and gathering, hoe, plow, and herding societies were strongly influenced by women's contributions to major subsistence tasks that, in turn, varied with the way those tasks meshed with pregnancy and lactation. However, in all of these preindustrial societies, gender roles were similar in four important ways. These similarities should be understood in order to grasp the enormous effect that industrialization had on family roles.

Preindustrial Role Similarities

The most important role similarity in preindustrial societies stems from that fact that in all of them a baby's survival depended upon its access to a lactating woman. Only after 1910, when safe methods of artificial infant feeding were invented, was breast-feeding not a critical factor in rates of infant mortality. In plow societies, rich women could hire wet nurses. Poor women had little choice. Sometimes a poor woman nursed another woman's baby because her own had died. Sometimes she needed money so desperately that she tried to nurse two babies, which was not easy on a poor diet (Sussman, 1982). Thus the bonding of the biological mother with her child significantly affected population maintenance.

A second similarity is that in all of these societies the work to be done was such that children could do some of it. In hoe societies, for example, older children typically looked after younger ones, freeing the mother to tend the garden. Since each additional child could often increase its family's level of subsistence, macrolevel needs for population maintenance paralleled microlevel incentives for child rearing. The economic value of children's labor decreased when machines became too complicated for children to operate. Early on, young children were employed in the mines and the textile mills. Industries with high demand for child labor sharply reduced a child's future wealth position. Families transferred few bequests to compensate children for lost schooling and future earnings. Instead, parents sold cheaply their children's future income streams to use for current consumption (D. Parsons & Goldin, 1987).

Third, people in all these societies faced the terrible problem of having enough but not too many children. Married couples had to rear enough children to ensure security when the parents were too old or too ill to work but they had to avoid having too many children for the available food supply. Achieving the right balance was difficult in the face of war, pestilence, famine, fire, and flood, especially because no reliable contraceptive techniques were available and abortion was dangerous (Himes, 1970).

Fourth, most persons in these societies learned adult roles mainly through informal socialization. Formal instruction, as in training for the priesthood in Eurasia, tended to be an elite privilege. Not until about 1880 was some schooling made compulsory in Europe and North America.

The opportunity for mass upward social mobility appeared only with industrialization. Before then, informal socialization taught people to do the work that their grandparents or great grandparents had done before them.

These four similarities indicate the constraints that affected family gender roles in all preindustrial societies. In trying to have enough but not too many children, our ancestors confronted terrible uncertainties in dealing with birth and death. In all of these societies women had to be near their babies, and, owing to high infant mortality, they had to devote much more of their adult lives to reproduction than is needed today. If a group was to reproduce itself, the great mass of women had no choice but to devote their most active years to work that could be managed with a nursing baby. Depending on which subsistence technology was dominant, women were variably excluded from the work that yielded greatest prestige and power. Individual women on rare occasions attained lofty positions in some preindustrial societies and a rare woman held great prestige in an industrializing society. However, until bottle feeding became possible after 1910, it was not feasible for the mass of women to strive for equality with the mass of men, and family gender roles reflected this fact. Even today some persons feel that women cannot compete for the best jobs because of the requirements of rearing children, but this belief ignores the fact that men and women alike can now perform the needed tasks of child rearing.

Industrialization

Although its beginnings could be seen earlier, the transformation of agricultural to industrial production accelerated about 1800 with the development of the textile industry in Northwest Europe and Northeast United States. Industrialization is the application of inanimate energy to the major productive and service sectors of a society (Form, 1979). Early on, it transformed erstwhile European, African, and Asian peasants, serfs, and slaves into urban wage workers. The process's beginning in Northwest Europe tended to give the descendants of the people who lived there a great advantage over folk who had chosen their ancestors with less care. Relatively well-educated Northwest Europeans were citizens of nations that had the most sophisticated industrial and military hardware.

By changing the nature of daily work and child care, industrialization altered family roles in unprecedented fashion. Five macrolevel events that tended to occur in sequence were especially important. Their effects differed significantly over various socioeconomic and ethnic status groups. In particular, the effects on Americans with any noticeable trace of African descent have been screened through a heavy filter of racism. These successive events also triggered waves of a women's rights movement (Rupp & Taylor, 1987).

Men Become Wage Workers

First, men shifted from agricultural to wage work, migrating to burgeoning cities. As Preston (1991) puts it, the process of urbanization shows how technological change becomes the dominant source of economic change and, in turn, social change. Millions of Americans moved to cities despite the Jeffersonian ideal of the yeoman farmer and a national political system that favored rural interests. They were driven, instead, by technological changes that reduced the prices of farm products relative to manufactured goods and reduced the proportion of income spent on food.

At first, whole families worked in the mills because men's wages were so low. Over time, as more efficient machines were invented, wages rose, but women and children (and, later, blacks and Asian immigrants) were barred from using the most efficient machines whose operators earned the highest wages. Consequently, a white male father's position as major provider was not at risk (Smelser, 1959). Husbands took pride in being able to keep their wives at home to care for the children.

Mass Education

Second, the spread of mass education was crucial in making a large family economically unappealing (J. Caldwell, 1980). Mass education destroyed traditional family patterns of obligation that had encouraged wealth flows from children to parents. Schooling saddled parents with out-of-pocket costs and also taught children skills that they could use to improve their lot if they left home. A child became an economic liability. Mass education also induced a shift to nuclear family living. In plow societies two generations lived under one roof oftener than today. The older generation controlled the land and therefore received large amounts of child services (D. Parsons, 1984). Thus did declining infant mortality and the spread of mass education reduce microlevel incentives to rear children.

Even after the Civil War, however, relatively little was spent on black (segregated) education, especially in the rural South. Consequently, blacks were poorly prepared to take advantage of opportunities for higher waged jobs that required ever higher levels of educational preparation, thereby illustrating the incremental nature of institutionalized racism.

The Demographic Transition

These two trends, accompanied by rapid economic growth, spurred a third, a transition to fertility more or less at population replacement level (or so it was implicitly assumed). Between 1860 and 1910 real income doubled. Economic growth triggers demographic change because a rise in real income fuels ambition, opens opportunities, and makes people feel more independent. In turn, the economic calculus of later generations responds to new preferences (Lesthaeghe, 1983). Fertility follows alterations in the value of children in the class-specific family economy (Greenhalgh, 1990).

Black fertility also declined in this period (Tolnay, 1987) but neither as far nor as fast as the fertility of the more highly educated and more urban white population. Black children's poor educational opportunities thus affected them directly and also indirectly through the effect of education on family size. Children reared in larger families develop less adequate cognitive skills than those in smaller families (Blake, 1989).

Early on, the fertility decline resulted from the use of methods that required self-discipline or physical risk: for men, coitus interruptus; for women, abortion (Kirk, 1968; Mohr, 1978). Less heroic methods appeared after a method to vulcanize rubber was invented in 1844, resulting by 1880 in an effective (but costly) condom (Frisch, 1978). U.S. physicians opposed contraception as degenerate. It first appeared in the *Reader's Guide* in 1909 under "race suicide" (Hart, 1933).

The factors that induced lower fertility also increased child-rearing responsibilities in several ways. The introduction of the germ theory of disease after the 1880s made child rearing more arduous (Preston, 1991). Before then, the sources of disease were thought to lie outside the home. The germ theory located the principal sources inside: bottles, hands, flies. Mothers were urged to become warriors against filth and they accepted this view of their duty. The Children's Bureau pamphlet *Baby Care* became the largest selling document in the history of government printing. Things changed somewhat after immunization and antibiotics moved responsibility for child health to the medical establishment (Preston & Haines, 1991).

New opportunities for upward mobility also made more work for mothers. They had to dress their children well enough to pass, starched and ironed, with stockings neatly mended. This may not sound like much to someone who has never used an old-fashioned iron, the kind one can find today in collectible shops. The iron was set on the cook stove until it was hot. If it was taken off too soon, it wouldn't work. If it was left on too long, it would scorch or burn the garment. Only the ironer's instinct told her when hot was hot enough.

Mothers also had to see that the children had enough baths lest they smell too ripe and offend their teachers and little friends. Standards of personal cleanliness had been low in England ever since the Romans left. Early standards were therefore easy to meet but they rose over time as improvements in the water supply and heating made winter bathing less of an ordeal. For a long time, each generation of American children was better washed and wore cleaner clothes than the preceding one. About as fast as technology made it easier to keep clean, the standards rose so that a mother's work hours remained about the same.

Artificial Methods of Infant Feeding

The fourth trend concerned infant feeding. By 1910, techniques of sterilization permitted babies to be fed safely with bottled formula. This breakthrough is little celebrated or even noted by feminists. Perhaps the inattention to this invention results from highly educated women's current ideology of maternity, which requires a mother to breast-feed for a period although, if techniques of sterilization are understood, breast and bottle babies are equally likely to live long enough to reproduce.

Women's Labor Force Participation

The fifth trend to affect family life was women's and especially married women's steadily increasing rates of labor force participation during the 20th century. Decreased fertility, bottle feeding, and mass education set the stage. The immediate impetus was the expansion of the service sector and the rise in women's wages relative to men's. In 1900, agricultural and manufacturing workers dominated the labor force. By 1986, 3% of the labor force was in agriculture, 22% in manufacturing, and 75% in the service sector, nearly triple the fraction in 1900 (U.S. Bureau of the Census, 1989b).

In 1900, women comprised 20% of the U.S. labor force. Most of them were young and unmarried or very poor women whose menfolk were unable to work, were unemployed, or whose wages were too low to support a family. Forty years later women's share had risen only to about 30% and the typical woman worker was still young, unmarried, or poor (Oppenheimer, 1973). Participation had increased slightly during World War I and again during the 1930s, when rising rates of male unemployment drove poor women to seek paid work. The first 40 years of the 20th century left family roles largely unscathed. But pressure for change was building up.

The rise in women's labor force participation affected families of varying socioeconomic status so differently that it is misleading to speak of effects on "the" U.S. family. I discuss two broad family types; first, families that were relatively well educated and predominantly white. Then I discuss effects on families who were poorly educated and often of minority status, especially blacks, who bore the added burden of housing segregation.

Post-1940 Effects on Advantaged Women

The year 1940 was a watershed for economic growth (Spitze & Huber, 1980). Real earnings per employee, having risen only 22% from 1920 through 1939, rose 215% from 1940 through 1959 (computed from U.S. Bureau of the Census, 1976). The young men who entered the labor force from the forties to the mid fifties had another advantage. They were better educated than their predecessors. High school completion rates had jumped from 29% in 1930 to 49% in 1940 (U.S. Bureau of the Census, 1976), and a postwar federal subsidy gave veterans, mostly men, unprecedented opportunity to attend college. Women's college completion rates relative to men's fell sharply. Young men's relative affluence lowered the age of marriage, thereby increasing fertility (Easterlin, 1980), which further disadvantaged women relative to men in the labor market. At first, the benefits of economic growth seemed to go disproportionately to men.

The postwar baby boom made family togetherness a 1950s catchword. In practice, this meant that mommy stayed home with the kiddies all week and did things with the kiddies and daddy on weekends. But the baby boom, a blip in a 200-year fertility decline, was caused by a unique historical confluence of factors all of which tend to decrease fertility: the delaying of births from the Depression and War years and young men's postwar affluence, which had lowered the age of marriage.

Despite the baby boom, women's labor force participation rose steadily after 1940. From 1940 to 1960, the largest increase occurred in the 45- to 54-year age group because the better educated younger women were attending college or at home having babies. After 1960, the largest increase was among women aged 25 to 34. Black women's typically higher rates began to converge with white rates from 1955 to 1976 (U.S. Department of Labor, 1977). Although persistent job segregation has kept women's wages low relative to men's (B. Reskin, 1991), most families can dispense with women's wages only by radically reducing their standard of living (J. Smith, 1987).

All analyses of national survey data on gender roles reflect trends toward approval of women's full participation in society. Firebaugh (1990) reports that by 1988 only 20% disapproved a married woman's working for pay and only 12% would not vote for a qualified woman as President. This opinion shift involved cohort replacement, not just an opinion shift in a given population. Despite speculation about antifeminist backlash in the late 1970s and early 1980s, K. Mason and Lu (1988) report a significant increase in profeminist views among both men and women.

Opinions of housewives and employed wives may come to diverge (Glass, 1990). In 1972, they were not easy to distinguish except that housewives were more likely to have preschoolers at home. By 1986, housewives were older than employed wives, reflecting the tendency for younger cohorts of wives to work for pay. Even adjusting for the age difference, housewives had less education, more children, and lower family incomes in 1986. These demographic differences, rather than employment per se, have widened differences between employed wives and housewives in their views on political issues such as abortion, women in politics, and the effects of maternal employment on children's well-being.

Post-1940 Effects on Disadvantaged Women

Since the 1940s, racism interacted with technological and economic change to dim black prospects. During World War II, blacks migrated from the South to find jobs in a tight labor market. In 1949, machine-harvesting of corn and cotton was introduced in the South. By 1950, the need for unskilled labor fell to one-tenth its former size. But when poorly educated blacks migrated to Northern cities in the 1950s, they were at the bottom of the labor queue. Demand was growing only for well-educated workers. The best jobs were moving to the suburbs, leaving central city blacks with the poorest jobs (Fusfeld, 1973). Even at that time, the white-nonwhite income gap was substantial for children (Kraly & Hirschman, 1990). Matters have worsened since then.

Black housing segregation led to a dramatic rise in the concentration of urban poverty. In turn, increases in poverty transformed urban neighborhoods into deteriorated areas of high crime, poor schools, excessive mortality, and welfare-dependent female-headed families (Massey, 1990; Massey & Denton, 1987).

Most scholars see male joblessness as the critical factor in the rise in the number of out-of-wedlock births and welfare dependency (Schoen & Kluegel, 1988; Wilson, 1987).

What male joblessness tended to do to black marriages was done to white marriages by the rise in female labor force participation. Black women tended to be driven into the labor force by low male wages while white women tended to be lured by rising female wages. But the outcome for both groups was much the same. The decreased level of economic dependence on husbands has decreased both black and white women's propensity to marry and remain married.

The Decline of Marriage as a Social Institution

The seventh trend is the decline in marriage as a social institution, as indicated by postponement, fewer persons ever marrying, a lower proportion of the life span spent in marriage, and shorter marital durations (Espenshade, 1985). Between 1940 and 1960 these indicators changed very little. After 1960 the time spent in first marriages declined sharply for both black and white women but it started earlier for blacks. Remarriage became increasingly common due to the larger number of divorced persons, not to an increasing propensity to remarry (Espenshade, 1985).

Time spent as a spouse is far less than it could be. If 1800 marriage patterns obtained with 1980 mortality, years married would increase from 27 to 45 years. The actual figure is 35 years (Watkins, Bongaarts, & Menken, 1987). Recent rates of divorce imply that about two thirds of all first marriages will end in divorce or separation (T. Martin & Bumpass, 1989). The proportion of black families maintained by married couples fell from 56% in 1980 to 51% in 1988 (U.S. Bureau of the Census, 1989a).

Below Replacement Fertility

The eighth trend (in the West) is a fertility decrease below replacement. In the United States the total fertility rate fell from 3.60 per 100,000 in 1960 to 1.83 per 100,000 in 1977, a halving in 17 years (Tabah, 1980). An increase in childlessness (Houseknecht, 1987; Jacobson, Heaton, & Taylor, 1989) is expected to continue (Watkins et al., 1987). In a strict sense, this trend is not new. With a few exceptions like the blip of the baby boom, U.S. fertility has been declining for 200 years. But a drop below replacement makes a qualitative difference. A norm of two-plus children per woman yields a stable population, consonant with a social climate in which people expect to marry and rear children. Now the West seems to be experiencing a population implosion (Bourgeois-Pichat, 1987).

For more than a decade the marital fertility rates of blacks and whites have been identical. Blacks are now a low fertility population despite high but declining rates of teenage childbearing (Farley, 1988). Because of the decline in marital fertility, the proportion of the total represented by nonmarital fertility has increased for both blacks and whites. After 1974 whites' (low) rate of nonmarital fertility increased markedly but blacks' (high) rate decreased. In 1986, 61% of black and 15% of white fertility was nonmarital; about one of every four U.S. children was born to an unwed mother (L. Bumpass & McLanahan, 1989).

Nonmarital teenage fertility thus appears to be an exception to the recent decline in fertility rates. For blacks, the lack of economic opportunity for teenage girls is a significant factor, much stronger than the effect of welfare (Duncan & Hoffman, 1990). For both blacks and whites, a critical factor appears to be the lack of assistance in avoiding pregnancy and laws that deny teenagers confidential access to birth control (Jones, 1986). The U.S. teenage birthrate was increasing in the 1970s while it was decreasing in a number of European countries. U.S. black teenagers had birthrates twice as high as U.S. white teenagers but U.S. white rates were twice as high as European rates although U.S. teenage sexual activity was no greater. It seems likely that providing better educational and economic opportunities for teenage girls and more adequate information about pregnancy avoidance will tend to make rates of teenage nonmarital fertility converge toward those of marital fertility.

An increasing number of studies reveal that children negatively affect parents' psychological well-being. Some time ago, Monahan (1955) noted that the widespread belief that children make for greater marital happiness was at odds with studies of the relationship of marital adjustment and childlessness. Other exhaustive literature reviews later reported similar findings (Hicks & Platt, 1970; McLanahan & Adams, 1987; G. Spanier & Lewis, 1980). Only in the 1980s, apparently, did such findings become part of the received wisdom about U.S. families.

Future Family Role Change

Let us stand back from these eight trends set in motion by technological and economic developments in the past century and examine strains on contemporary family roles in order to assess possibilities of change. I use as backdrop T. Parsons' (1943) theory of complementary marital roles, which now seems ethnocentric and timebound. Marriage worked best (i.e., lasted, in itself a timebound idea) if one partner brought home the bacon while the other cooked it. This is a theory of middle-class marriage uniquely suited to a period of time in which middle-class wives were basically consumers, not producers, and therefore much more dependent on husbands than vice versa. Parsons apparently assumed that wives' economic dependency would last. He never asked what might happen if both spouses brought home bacon, especially if there were no children around to eat it.

And this is just what I ask now. What will family roles look like if both spouses bring home earnings over 30 or 40 years, if children are few or absent, if most first marriages are put asunder not by death but by the court, and if the number of very old people increases substantially?

However, one must also ask what family roles will look like if men's earnings are low or uncertain, if women's low wages are supplemented by welfare, and if children's educational and economic prospects are bleak. Below, I point to areas where pressure is building up.

Caring for the Old-Old

Mortality declines increasingly affect old people. Between 1900 and 1976 the number of persons who lost a parent before age 15 dropped from one in 4 to one in 20 while the number of middle-aged couples with two or more living parents increased from 10% to 47% (Uhlenberg, 1980). Various retirement programs provide more or less well for most of this population. But there are terrible gaps, especially with regard to the skyrocketing medical costs that result from technical innovation. Many legal and ethical questions need to be addressed. The Hippocratic oath, which put the saving of human life above all goods, no longer seems adequate. Should life be prolonged no matter what its quality? Who should decide?

What kind of care do grown children owe elderly parents? The answers are unclear. Religion offers limited help. Religious norms developed in societies in which generational wealth transfers went from children to parents. Today old people dislike being dependent on their children. Research on generational contact, typically descriptive and seldom based on probability samples, rarely includes two major factors in generational exchange: women's employment patterns and divorce (Huber & Spitze, 1988). In the past, women did most of the actual caregiving. Will employed women abandon this role? What does a fully employed woman, recently remarried, owe her aging ailing new mother-in-law? Such problems will put great stress on marital roles.

The Household Division of Labor

For middle-class families, one might expect that, as women increase their hours of paid work outside the home, men would increase their hours of unpaid work inside it; Americans typically opt for the ideal of a level playing field. For example, respondents to a 1979 national survey overwhelmingly agreed that if both spouses worked full-time for pay, housework should be equally shared (Huber & Spitze, 1983). Housework is more an issue when it is combined with child care. Today the majority of mothers with children at home also work outside the home. In 1987, 59% of children under age 15 had employed mothers; 3% had mothers enrolled in school (U.S. Bureau of the Census, 1990).

Wives' and husbands' labor force participation rates are converging, from 87% of men and 32% of women in 1947 to 77% of men and 54% of women in 1984 (Blau & Ferber, 1986) but their housework hours continue to differ greatly. The wife's market hours do affect the husband's household hours but not by much (Giele, 1988; Spitze, 1985). Using evidence from U.S. time budget surveys in 1965, 1975, and 1985 and U.K. surveys in 1961, 1974, and 1984, Gershuny and Robinson (1988) report that women in the 1980s did substantially less housework than women in the 1960s. Men were doing a little more but still much less than women. These changes resemble changes in Canada, Holland, Denmark, and Norway, countries that also have historical time budget evidence.

In the future, the housework issue will probably become more divisive in middle-class families, white or black. A 1979 national survey reported that the more the husband worked around the house, the less likely was the wife to have considered divorce (Huber & Spitze, 1983). A later study reports that the wife's work hours outside the home increase the probability of divorce (Spitze & South, 1985). Hoffman's (1989) literature review also reported that the father's increased participation in housework and child care was related to marital discord. Hochschild (1989), studying employed spouses with children, sees the current family scene as a stalled revolution. The tired wives she observed talked about sleep the way a hungry person talks about food.

Perhaps the issue may come to be settled more on a pragmatic than an ideological basis (Spitze, 1988). Increases in shift work may increase men's household hours. The five occupations with the largest predicted growth 1984 to 1995 were those that involved the most shift work (cashier, registered nurse, janitor and cleaner, truck driver, waiter and waitress). Shift work is attractive to couples who need low-cost child care (Presser, 1988).

Acrimony over the division of household labor may highlight a major cost of child rearing. I predict that men will be under growing pressure to carry their fair share. Fathers' full participation in housework would throw into relief the life-style differences between those who rear children and those who do not.

Effects of Remarriage on Children

Remarriages are as satisfactory as first marriages except when both spouses are remarried and there are step children (L. White & Booth, 1985). In 1985, 53% of divorces involved children (U.S. Bureau of the Census, 1989c). A fifth of all children living with their mothers share homes with step-siblings (L. Bumpass, 1985). It is difficult to describe parents' and children's roles in such families because no standard names yet exist for step relationships. What, for example, should a child call its mother's third husband and what are the mutual role obligations? The answers will take time to work out.

Effect of Single Parenthood on Children

Most one-parent families are headed by women. Children land in them by two routes: Their parents have divorced or they never married. As McLanahan (1991) notes, children's and women's interests in preserving a marriage may vary. Although divorce decreases women's income (S. Hoffman & Duncan, 1988), it improves women's well-being. Women are much more likely than men to report having wanted a divorce and the overwhelming majority of women report substantial improvement in their postdivorce social and sexual relationships. However, children who live apart from one or both parents are more likely to drop out of high school, marry and reproduce in their teens, and form single-parent families themselves through marital disruption or nonmarital births. Such outcomes increase the risk of long-term poverty and economic dependence (McLanahan, 1991).

The major disadvantage of the single-parented child is not the absence of the father but the absence of male earnings (Cherlin, 1981). This could be addressed by macroeconomic policies but the problem of using federal programs to stabilize families is that society does not know how to ensure family stability, cannot buy it, and cannot know when it is worth preserving and when dissolution is better for everyone. It would make more sense to focus on macrolevel policies that tie benefits directly to children (Steiner, 1981).

Conclusion

This chapter, by highlighting the effects of technological and economic change on family role obligations, has thrown into relief the need for social inventions to deal with generational obligations on a societal level. The problem of caring for the very old cannot be solved without external support. The household division of labor calls for considerable change in men's level of participation; it also calls for external support for households that include children. The entire society benefits from generational reproduction but the actual parents bear most of the cost. Finally, external support is most needed to prepare the children of poor parents for productive adult work roles. Collectively, we are letting far too many U.S. children grow up without adequate preparation for both work and parenting, the core family roles.

PART 2

Challenges to the Family

4

The Transition to Marriage

Network Supports and Coping

JUDITH L. FISCHER
DONNA L. SOLLIE

As individuals undergo life transitions, the difficulty or ease of the experience may be mitigated by the social network of the individual as well as by coping techniques or coping mechanisms. Various studies have pointed to the importance of social support in aiding individuals to cope with stresses (Boswell, 1969; Tolsdorf, 1976). The major focus in this chapter is on two elements: (a) the effects of support mechanisms provided by the social network, and (b) the effects of coping strategies that are used by the individuals experiencing the transition to marriage.

Certain transitions are expected during the young adult years, including the completion of formal schooling, obtaining a full-time job, getting married, and starting a family (Modell, Furstenberg, & Hershberg, 1976). These transitions may be experienced as stressor events, even though they are "normal" stresses in that most adults in this society experience

AUTHORS' NOTE: This chapter (research grant 5 R01 HD 15864) was supported by the National Institute of Child Health and Human Development from September 1, 1981 to August 31, 1985. Support was also received from the Texas Tech College of Home Economics Research Institute. The authors wish to thank Sharla McLaughlin for her library assistance. This chapter was originally presented as part of the Family and Child Studies Center Lecture Series, Miami University, Oxford, OH.

these transitions during the young adult years (H. McCubbin & Figley, 1983; Modell et al., 1976). Normative stresses and transitions occur as individuals and families change in the course of normal physical, psychological, and social development across time. Perhaps the fact that such transitions are normal or expected has lead to a dearth of information on their impact. Nonetheless, only six life events are considered more stressful than getting married (Rahe, 1981). Some of the stresses encountered in the transition to marriage include decision making and conflicts surrounding the wedding itself, adjustment to in-laws, meshing of individual life-styles, friends, and preferences with a couple life-style, and work, economic, and residential changes. It may help to have understanding friends who are available to provide validation and support, an unbiased viewpoint, and a "safe" outlet for possible negative reactions to change and conflict.

Models of stress emphasize the contributions of perceptions of the events, resources (such as social support), and coping techniques in the adjustment to stress (M. McCubbin & McCubbin, 1989a). This chapter examines resources, in the form of friendships, and coping, including use of family, religion, and activity, as part of the adaptation of individuals to the normative stress of marriage.

The Transition to Marriage

The stage of a person's romantic involvement is significantly related to his or her social network involvement (M. Johnson & Leslie, 1982; Milardo, Johnson, & Huston, 1983). Generally, as romantic relationships develop, less time is spent with significant members of the social network, particularly those who might be perceived as threatening to couple closeness. However, relationships with closer network members are still valued and may even become increasingly important as peripheral network members are dropped. At issue is the extent to which friendship relationships provide a buffer to stresses accompanying normative life transitions, such as the transition to marriage.

Although recent studies on early marriage have appeared in the literature (cf. Atkinson & Huston, 1984; Greenblat, 1983; Parmelee, 1987) none of these have employed a comparison group. Furthermore, only a small number of prospective, longitudinal studies have been reported (e.g., E. Kelly & Conley, 1987; Markman, 1981); all of these were concerned with predicting marital satisfaction. In general, these studies have found that neuroticism, conflict, and communication deficits in early marriage predicted marital distress. None of these reports examined the role of the social network across the transition to marriage. As an exception, Fischer, Sollie, and Leslie's (1990) longitudinal study involving comparison groups, reported that newlyweds changed the structures of their kin networks and the composition of their friend networks without changing the overall interactions and social exchanges with kin and friends. These authors suggested that future work examine effects of the social network on adjustment during the transition to marriage. Those with more supportive social networks would be expected to fare better over the transition to marriage than those with less supportive networks.

The present chapter employs a cross-sectional as well as longitudinal design in examining the transition to marriage. Three groups are compared: those who remain single (singles), those who remain married (already marrieds), and those who make the transition from single or engaged to married (newly marrieds). Since the study encompasses nonmarrieds, measures of adjustment include those that are applicable regardless of marital status, such as personal well-being and loneliness, and measures applicable only to marrieds, such as marital adjustment.

Social Support and Coping

The stress and coping model indicates that individuals have or develop resources and coping techniques that vary in helpfulness in dealing with stresses and strains (H. McCubbin, Boss, Wilson, & Dahl, 1981). Having resources includes having social network members who are available. Coping techniques include engaging in activities such as utilizing social network members, turning to religion, volunteering in the community, and using various escape mechanisms.

S. Cohen and Wills (1985) reviewed the issues of stress, buffering, and social support, and concluded that social support acts both as a "main effect" and as a "buffer" depending on a number of circumstances. "Pure" buffering effects are described where there are group-by-support interactions such that a group undergoing a stressful event differs in its adjustment to that event depending upon the strength of the buffer. A group experiencing stress will be as adjusted as nonstressed groups if there is a high degree of buffering. But a low degree of buffering should result in less adjustment for the stressed group.

"Main effects" of the support variable in the absence of a significant interaction with group membership indicates that a variable has directly affected adjustment in similar ways for all groups, regardless of stresses experienced by the groups. Thus all highly supported groups would be more adjusted than all poorly supported groups. According to S. Cohen and Wills, *buffering effects* have been found with respect to perceived *availability* of social resources and *main effects* of support have been seen when there is integration or *embeddedness* in a social network. This chapter examines the effect of both embeddedness (i.e., the extent of social exchanges with social network members) and availability of social resources (i.e., number of friends, duration of friendships, frequency of seeing friends, and commitment to friends) on adjustment.

It is predicted that effective coping techniques at Time 1 would be related to adjustment at Time 2; that is, there should be a main effect of coping. Buffering, or interaction, effects are hypothesized when measures of availability of social network members are used. Thus, number of friends, frequency of seeing friends, duration of friendships, and commitment to friends should be helpful when a group undergoes stress. If the transition to marriage is stressful, then buffering effects should be seen in the newly married group. Finally, main effects are hypothesized where measures of embeddedness in the social network are employed. In other words, high levels of social exchanges with friends in the social network should be related to greater adjustment regardless of the level of stress.

Methods

Sample

From a random sample of 1,600 seniors and recent graduates of a southwestern university, using gender and major as delimiting criteria, 422 young men and women volunteered for a longitudinal study of life transitions and social support. The design for this study called for two levels of gender and three levels of marital status with subgroups of equal size. Therefore the first 20 men and 20 women in the data set who met the criteria for each subgroup were selected for analysis. The three subgroups were (a) a group who included respondents who were married before the first interview (already married); (b) a group of respon-

dents who became married after the first interview (newly married); and
(c) a group of respondents who remained single from the first interview
to the second (single). Although some groups had more than 20 participants who fit the description, choices were made based on the following criteria: (a) not a parent, (b) insofar as possible, nonmissing data,
and (c) cohort membership and interview timing matching that of the
newly married group. Mean time between the first (Time 1) and second
(Time 2) interviews was 10 months.

In the present study all participants in the newly married group were
part of an ongoing study and were not selected because they were
engaged or had specific plans to marry. They were followed not just in
the early months of marriage, but measures were obtained before they
married, and in some cases, before they even planned to marry.

Demographic and other characteristics of the participants may be
summarized as follows: mean age of both respondents and their spouses
was 24 years at Time 2; the newly marrieds were married a mean of 6
months and the already marrieds a mean of 31 months at Time 2.
Forty-five percent in each group were in professional jobs at Time 1
and 65% in each group were in professional jobs at Time 2. Participants
were overwhelmingly white, Protestant/Christian, came from small
towns and cities in Texas, and had college majors that were in proportion to those of the university as a whole. While equivalence across
groups on all demographic variables was desirable and matchings were
made to ensure equivalence as described above, there was a significant
difference in income. The already married group's higher income differed
significantly at Time 2 from both their Time 1 income and the Time 2
incomes of the newly married and single groups. In addition, men earned
more than women regardless of group membership. Income was not used
as a covariate in the analyses because correlations of income with the
variables of the study found only a few significant correlations at Time 1
and a few different significant correlations at Time 2.

Longitudinal studies are subject to dropouts of participants, which
may affect the results. A comparison of Time 1 scores on all variables
(including some not reported in this study) of dropouts with nondropouts found few significant differences, and these (such as masculinity scores) were related to the differential dropout rates of men (46%)
compared to women (29%) (Sollie & Fischer, 1988). Only nondropouts
were included in this study.

Procedures

Both a self-report questionnaire and an interview format were used in this research at both Time 1 and Time 2. Questionnaire variables included the usual demographic questions requesting age, marital status, religion, race, and occupation, as well as questions about when important transitions had occurred. In addition, the self-report questionnaire contained a number of scales; scales of well-being, loneliness, marital adjustment, and coping were utilized in the present study. At the end of the questionnaire participants were asked to list up to 50 adult social network members following Tolsdorf's (1976) criteria (the person is known by name, is one with whom there is a personal relationship, and the person is seen at least once a year). Participants were asked to list spouse or fiancé first and then close relatives and friends and then others. Respondents were requested to indicate the frequency of contact, the duration of the relationship, their commitment toward continuing the relationship, and the type of relationship held with each network member. Friends comprised one type of relationship or network sector, and kin another type. Although identical information was available for both kin and friends, only friend relationships were examined in this study in detail. This decision was based on two factors: coverage of kin was accomplished in that one of the coping scales specifically asked about turning to family for support; and some kin, more so than friends, might have been sources of stress (e.g., in-laws), which could potentially confuse the interpretation of results.

To explore the social exchanges sustained in each relationship, respondents were provided with a list of eight possible items (see Fischer, Sollie, Sorell, & Green, 1989) representing affective (comfort and affection), instrumental (activity and information), and practical exchanges (money, gifts, opinion, and evaluation). In the interview, respondents were asked to identify which items were presently given and received within each of the first 20 network relationships listed. Respondents were asked to reply to this question based on their perceptions of what was actually given and received in each relationship and to avoid answering based on their perceptions of how they might want these items to be exchanged or their perceptions of the network member's expectations for exchange. Following completion of both the questionnaire and interview, participants received $5.00.

The reliability of the interviewing and coding procedures is described in Fischer et al., 1989. Acceptable test-retest and internal consistency reliabilities were reported. This procedure has shown a 2-week test-retest reliability of .91 (Fischer et al., 1989).

Measures

Two general categories of social network characteristics were assessed: (a) availability and (b) embeddedness characteristics. *Availability* referred to the extent to which network members were around and accessible for interaction. Measures of availability in this study include: number of friends, duration of the relationships with friends, frequency of contact with friends, and commitment to friends. *Embeddedness* measures referred to the extent to which there was sharing and exchanges with social network members. Measures of embeddedness included affection exchanges, instrumental exchanges, and practical exchanges. For purposes of analyses, social network and coping variables were split at their respective medians into high and low support/coping categories.

Availability Measures

Number of friends. The size of the network was the number of individuals listed by the participant in response to the instructions to list up to 50 social network members. The *size of the friend network* was determined by calculating the number of network members who were explicitly identified as friends. Fiancés and potential mates were excluded from the definition of *friend.* Number of friends was used as a divisor for the other network variables of duration, contact, commitment, and exchanges.

Friendship contact. Contact with social network members was determined by asking respondents in the interview how often they had seen each network member during the past year. The average yearly frequency of *contact with friends* was computed by dividing the total friendship contact sum by the corresponding measure of friendship size.

Friendship duration. The duration of relationships was obtained by asking respondents in the interview how many months they had known each network member. An average *friendship duration* was computed by dividing the total sum of friendship months known by the appropriate measure of friendship network size.

Commitment. In the interview, respondents were asked to identify on a 6-point scale, from 1 = not at all to 6 = extremely strong commitment, how committed they were to remaining in each relationship. *Friend commitment* levels were obtained by dividing the total score for relationships labeled "friend" by the corresponding measure of friend network size.

Embeddedness Measures

Affectionate exchanges, which included both verbal and nonverbal expressions of affection and shared confidences or sympathy, were designated by combining the gives and receives in the areas of affection and comfort. *Instrumental* exchanges included giving and receiving factual information and engaging in any activities together. *Practical* exchanges were the giving or receiving of money, tangible goods, opinions, and evaluations or feedback.

Behaviors with network members were described for only the first 20 such network members since earlier work (Fischer et al., 1989) revealed minimal changes in behaviors beyond the 20th social network member. For each of the first 20 network members the respondent indicated which behaviors were given to the other and which were received from the other in that relationship. A score of 1 was recorded for each give and a score of 1 was indicated for each receive. These gives and receives were summed across network sector members and divided by the network sector size, so that different network sizes were controlled. For example, friend affection exchanges were calculated as instances of friend comfort and friend affection behaviors given and friend comfort and friend affection behaviors received divided by friend size. Instrumental exchanges and practical exchanges were computed in a similar fashion. Scores on affection and instrumental exchanges could range from 0 to 4 and scores on practical exchanges could range from 0 to 8.

Measures of Coping

The Family Coping Inventory contains 70 items of potential coping behaviors (H. McCubbin et al., 1981). The items are answered on a 4-point scale from 0 = not helpful to 3 = very helpful. Although the inventory has been factor analyzed these factors have been sample specific and may not be appropriate to explain coping in young adults. For the purposes of this study, the 70 items at Time 1 were factor analyzed with principal components factoring and varimax rotation. The rotation matrix failed to converge, therefore, the unrotated factor loadings and the correlation matrix were examined and items that did not relate or load on factors (less than .30) were eliminated. Thirty-one items were refactored with nine factors extracted having eigenvalues greater than 1.00. The screen test revealed three significant factors. The same three significant factors were replicated in factor analyses across the testing times and core items that appeared at all times were included in the final set of factors. The final factors were: *Family:* 6. Doing things with the family, 12. Trying to maintain family stability, 53. Seeking encouragement, guidance, and support from my parent(s), 66. Participating in gatherings and events with relatives (internal consistency reliability, Cronbach's alpha = .69); *Religion/community:* 7. Involvement in religious activities, 43. Believing in God, 44. Doing volunteer work, 60. Engaging in club work (church, PTA, etc.) (alpha = .75); and *Activity:* 51. Going shopping by myself, 59. Remodeling or redecorating the house, 63. Going shopping with friends (alpha = .70).

Adjustment Measures

Three measures of adjustment were used in this study: loneliness, well-being, and marital adjustment. Marital adjustment applied only at Time 2 and only to those who were in the newly married or already married groups.

UCLA Loneliness Scale. Loneliness was measured using the revised UCLA Loneliness Scale (Russell, Peplau, & Cutrona, 1980). The scale includes 20 statements about loneliness, 10 worded in a positive direction and 10 worded in a negative direction. For this study the answer choices ranged from 1 = strong agreement to 6 = strong disagreement. A higher score on the summed items indicated greater loneliness with items reverse scored as necessary. Cronbach's alpha was .92.

Well-being. The Personal Well-Being Scale is a 9-item semantic differential scale with 5 points separating the bipolar items (Campbell, Converse, & Rodgers, 1976). The items were scored for the positive direction such that higher scores indicated greater well-being. Cronbach's alpha was .78.

Marital Adjustment Test. Married and engaged participants completed the short form of the Marital Adjustment Test (MAT) (Locke & Wallace, 1959). The MAT has 15 items scored in the positive direction and measuring degree of marital happiness, agreement or disagreement on several marital issues, and beliefs about being married. Cronbach's alpha was .75.

Results

Analyses examined the main and buffering effects of both network and coping style on personal and relationship adjustment. The analyses for main and buffering effects were 2 (high vs. low coping/support) × 3 (single vs. newly married vs. already married) × 2 (male vs. female) multivariate and univariate analyses of variance on the Time 2 dependent variables of well-being and loneliness. In addition, to control for the possible effects of Time 1 scores on Time 2 scores, multivariate and univariate analyses of covariance were computed for well-being and loneliness with Time 1 scores on well-being and loneliness as the covariates where appropriate. Significant F values that occurred for both the multivariate analyses of variance and covariance are recorded in Table 4.1 (two values of p were marginal in the multivariate analyses of covariance, but are indicated in the table). Figures 4.1-4.4 depict significant buffering effects found in these analyses. No analyses of covariance were run on marital adjustment (MAT) scores because there were insufficient participants who answered the MAT at Time 1. The analytical approaches employed here are similar to those reported by Holahan and Moos (1986) in their longitudinal study of stress resistance, wherein results of both MANOVAs and MANCOVAs were reported. All the analyses involving loneliness as a dependent variable produced group effects, namely, the single group was more lonely at Time 2 than the newly marrieds or the already marrieds. These group effects are not repeated below. Follow-up multiple mean comparisons employed Tukey's procedure with p set at .05. Only significant mean differences are described.

Effects of Coping

The first prediction was that more effective coping at Time 1 would be reflected in greater adjustment at Time 2. As seen in Table 4.1, buffering effects, rather than main effects (group by gender by coping), were found when religion/community was the coping technique. In follow-up univariate analyses, these effects were seen on both loneliness and well-being (Figure 4.1). Already married men low in religious/community coping were lower on well-being than men high in religious/community coping. Single men low in religious/community coping were more lonely than people in any other group. To summarize,

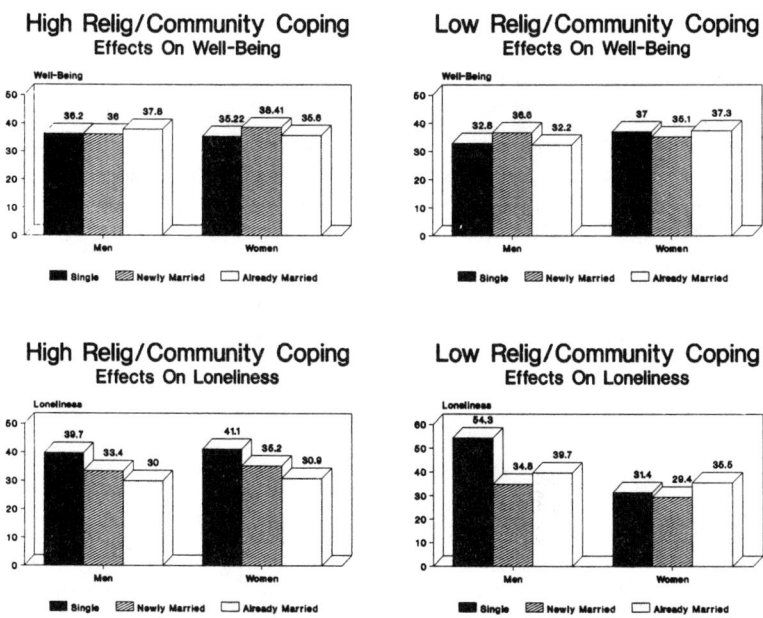

Figure 4.1. Effects of Religious/Community Coping on Well-Being and Loneliness

buffering effects were found, but not in ways that demonstrated buffering for newly marrieds.

Religion/community was involved in a three-way interaction with group and gender [$F(1, 72) = 9.92$, $p < .002$] on marital adjustment. There were no differences within the groups of men, but there were differences within the groups of women such that newlywed-low religious/community coping women were significantly lower on marital adjustment than newlywed-high religious/community coping women (see Figure 4.2), thus religious/community coping served as a buffer for newlywed women. There were differences within the high religious/community coping groups such that newlywed men high in religious/community coping were significantly lower on marital adjustment than newlywed women high in religion/community. Among those low on religious/community coping, already married men were lower in marital adjustment than already married women. Apparently low religious/community coping was detrimental to the marital adjustments of newlywed women

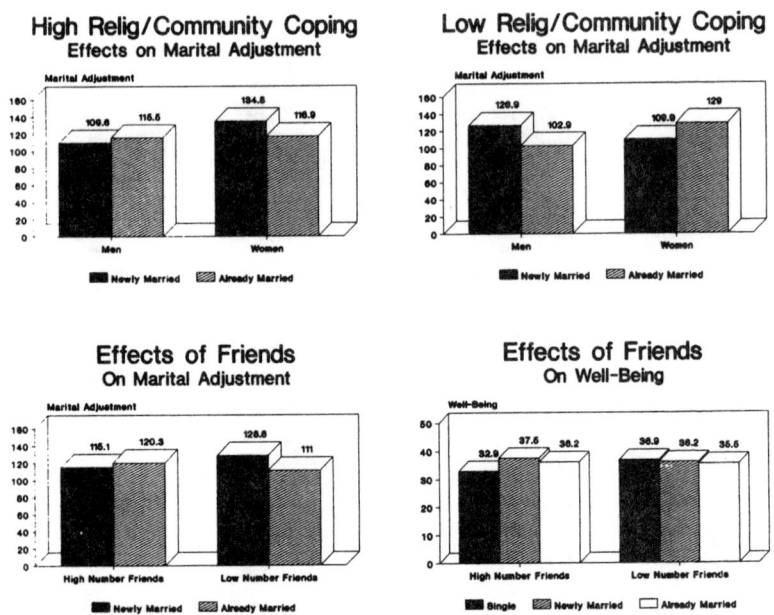

Figure 4.2. Effects of Religious/Community Coping and Number of Friends on Marital Adjustment and Effects of Number of Friends on Well-Being

compared to other women and already married men compared to already married women. Thus the hypothesis of a main effect of coping received no support, and buffering effects were found that at times benefited or failed to benefit members of all three groups.

Effects of Availability

It was hypothesized that there would be buffering effects for variables involving availability: network size, contact, commitment, and duration. As seen in Table 4.1, there were significant buffering effects for network size and commitment with group by support interactions, and duration with group by support by gender interactions. In follow-up univariate analyses, network size as a support was seen on well-being; commitment and duration were buffers for both well-being and loneliness.

Pure buffering effects for loneliness and well-being were found in the significant group by support by gender interaction when friendship

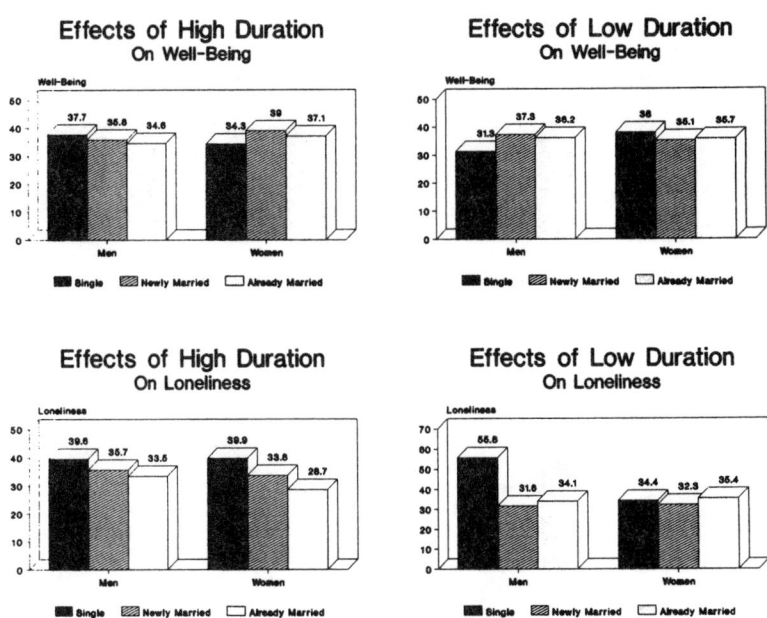

Figure 4.3. Effects of Duration on Well-Being and Loneliness

duration was the support available (see Figure 4.3). Contrary to expectations that buffering would be found for newlyweds, overall, singles were more lonely than those in other groups; in particular single men with low durations of friendships were more lonely than men in other groups or conditions. Similarly, for well-being, single men in low duration friendships reported less well-being than others.

Group-by-support interactions occurred for commitment and for number of friends. The single-low commitment condition was related to less well-being and more loneliness (Figure 4.4). Contrary to this pattern, singles who had more friends at Time 1 were less well off at Time 2 than other groups who reported fewer friends at Time 1 (see Figure 4.2). These findings run counter to the prediction of buffering for newlyweds.

Turning to marital adjustment as the dependent variable, pure buffering effects were found for number of friends (Figure 4.2). Number of friends interacted significantly with group $[F(1, 72) = 5.27, p < .025]$. In comparing means, those low in number of friends and newly married were higher on marital adjustment than those low in friends and already

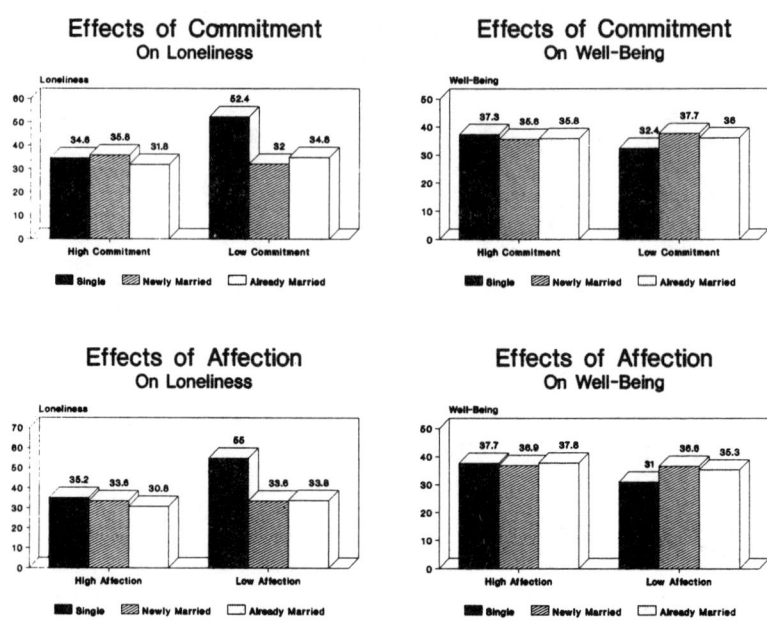

Figure 4.4. Effects of Commitment and Affection on Loneliness and Well-Being

married. Newlyweds and already marrieds high on number of friends were nonsignificantly in between on marital adjustment (Figure 4.2). It would appear that newlyweds benefited from fewer friends whereas already marrieds benefited from greater numbers of friends.

To summarize, the predicted buffering effects were found; however, these were found for people in the single group and not for newlyweds. Low levels of support left the single group more vulnerable to loneliness and distress. Surprisingly, a smaller social network provided buffering effects for singles and seemed to be helpful to the marital adjustments of newlyweds.

Effects of Embeddedness

It was predicted that there would be main effects of embeddedness variables (affection, instrumental, and practical social exchanges with friends). These variables were thought to be important to adjustment regardless of group membership. Such effects were found (Table 4.1)

Table 4.1   Significant Results of Multivariate Analyses of Variance and Multivariate Analyses of Covariance With Loneliness and Well-Being Time 2 as Dependent Variables (and Loneliness and Well-Being Time 1 as Covariates)

Independent Variables	df	*MANOVA* F	p	df	*MANCOVA* F	p
COPING						
Religion/community	4, 212	2.80^c	.05	4, 208	2.84^c	.05
AVAILABILITY						
Number of friends	4, 212	2.51^b	.05	4, 208	2.26^b	.06
Commitment	4, 212	3.28^b	.01	4, 208	2.40^b	.05
Duration	4, 212	3.45^c	.01	4, 208	2.32^c	.06
EMBEDDEDNESS						
Affection	4, 210	3.67^b	.01	4, 206	3.07^b	.05
	2, 105	7.30^a	.001	2, 103	4.81^a	.01
Instrumental	2, 105	3.77^a	.05	2, 103	3.41^a	.05
Practical	2, 105	8.52^a	.001	2, 103	4.26^a	.05

NOTE: In both Manova and Mancova analyses, the independent variables were group, gender, and support (the particular support variable varied as indicated in the table). There were significant group effects regardless of support variable in all the Manova and Mancova results (see text).
a. Support (Main Effect);
b. Group × Support (Buffering Effect);
c. Group × Gender × Support (Buffering Effect).

when instrumental, practical, and affection exchanges were considered. In the case of affection, there were also buffering effects found.

In all cases where there were significant main effects of support, low support was associated with greater loneliness than high support. Specifically, those with low practical support were more lonely than those with high practical support (means = 41.47 vs. 32.00). Similarly, those with low instrumental support were more lonely than those with high instrumental support (means = 38.73 vs. 34.23). The interaction of group with affection support on loneliness produced the following: the singles with low buffering were significantly more lonely than any of the other groups (Figure 4.4).

Mixed buffering effects were found for affection exchanges on well-being (Figure 4.4). A significant main effect of affection exchange was modified by a group-by-exchange significant interaction. Once again the findings for well-being paralleled those of loneliness. The single-low support group was significantly lower on well-being than all of the other groups (Figure 4.4).

There were no main or buffering effects when marital adjustment was the dependent variable. In summary, the predicted main effects of embeddedness were found, with greater embeddedness at Time 1 related to later distress, particularly to later loneliness. The main effect of affection on well-being and loneliness was modified by a buffering effect in that singles, but not newlyweds, with low affection exchanges were less well off at Time 2.

Discussion

According to S. Cohen and Wills (1985), effects of social support vary according to the kind of variable examined. Variables indicative of embeddedness in a social network should produce main effects of support whereas variables indicative of availability of social network members should produce buffering effects. In general, the findings of this study followed these predictions, particularly with respect to buffering. Well-being was affected by availability of social network members in terms of levels of commitment, number of friends, and friendship duration. Buffering effects, however, were found for singles, not newly marrieds. There were mixed main and buffering effects of the embeddedness measure of affection on loneliness and well-being. Marital adjustment was influenced by number of friends and religion/community as a coping technique (perhaps the latter variable reflected the perceived availability of a higher power).

The findings for number of friends ran counter to predictions in that a low number of friends in certain situations was related to higher well-being and higher marital adjustment. Singles with fewer friends at Time 1 reported higher well-being than those singles who reported more friends. Newlyweds with fewer friends indicated greater marital adjustment than those low in friends but who were already married. The transition to the newlywed stage may be a critical time for devoting oneself to the romantic partner and to spending less time with friends— such an observation is consistent with the dyadic withdrawal hypothesis. In the newlywed situation more friends probably would not provide greater support but, rather, greater competition for such resources as time and affection.

The situation for singles is puzzling—more friends should reflect the greater availability of support, and hence, there should be greater, not lesser well-being. Perhaps the timing of measures is important. The number of friends was measured at Time 1 and well-being was measured at Time 2. Approximately half of all friends at Time 2 were new. Perhaps for those in the singles group critical old friends were lost and not replaced. The importance of longer duration friendships was seen in the effects of this variable on the dependent variables. At Time 1 male singles whose friendships were of shorter duration were more lonely and reported less well-being at Time 2 than those with longer duration friendships.

Exploring further the situation of singles brings out another explanation. A large number of friends could preclude developing the kinds of relationships with a core few who would contribute to greater intimacy and exchanges of resources. Indeed, the singles with low exchanges in affection reported more loneliness and less well-being than those high on such exchanges.

This study found little evidence that the passage of time or an event such as marriage is stressful, at least in terms of loneliness, well-being, or marital adjustment. It was thought that utilizing social network support and coping techniques could have buffered the effects of a stressful transition in that high support could negate the effects of stress. It is possible that by only looking at friendship networks we have overlooked the role of kin. However, the measure of coping that involved turning to family members to cope found no effects on the dependent variables, suggesting that the young adults who married needed neither friends nor kin to negotiate the transition to marriage. These findings suggest several possibilities. First, although the transition to marriage is presumed to be a stressful life event, it is generally a positive experience. Ascertaining perceptions of the situation, as suggested by the stress and coping model, would clarify this point. The support of friends may not be necessary if a stressful situation is not perceived. W. R. Gove, Style, and Hughes (1990) recently reviewed a body of literature that suggested that marriage was positively related to well-being. Confiding, intimate relationships with a spouse appeared most important to well-being (Kessler & Essex, 1982).

Compared with the situation for newly marrieds, those who remained single appeared particularly vulnerable to the availability of friends (seen in commitment and friendship duration), the "availability" of a higher power (seen in religious/community coping), and to their embeddedness in their social networks (seen in affection exchanges). Perhaps for these young adults singlehood is more stressful than marriage, hence buffering effects are more likely to be found. With the current generation postponing marriage from early young adulthood to later young adulthood, a prolonged period of singlehood is likely for many. Those who experience the positive benefits of singlehood appear to be those plugged into a small, but significant, social network of friends.

It would be too easy to suggest that single young adults who experience loneliness and distress should marry. Those most vulnerable to distress were those with large, loose, and unavailable social networks. It may be that personal characteristics of these young adults precluded their developing close social networks; such personal characteristics would be likely to carry over into marriage, creating for these marrieds conflict and distress (W. R. Gove et al., 1990). Additional research on these lonely young adults would help to develop a stronger basis than that provided in this study for assisting them in life adjustments. In order to ameliorate the distress of these young adults, it may be that social skills need to be developed, or structural constraints could be removed (such as changing aspects of jobs that encourage isolation), or religious/community involvement should be enhanced, or one close relationship (perhaps, but not necessarily, marriage) could be encouraged. It may be that all of the above should be implemented. Future research designed to evaluate these alternatives should illuminate appropriate courses of action.

5

Supporting Parent-Child Relationships in the Early Years

Lessons Learned and Yet to Be Learned

DOUGLAS R. POWELL

In the past two decades, diverse sectors of American society have demonstrated intense and growing concern about the quality of parent-child relationships, especially in the child's early years. Changing demographic characteristics of families and communities have contributed to widespread interest in the nature and consequences of eroding sources of help for parents with young children. Through direct experience and media reports, most Americans encounter daily reminders of the loss of extended families and neighborhoods as traditional sources of support for parenting, and home environments that fail to facilitate children's optimal development.

Concern about the quality of parent-child relations has led to a variety of initiatives aimed at supporting parents. The bulk of activity has been in the form of parent education and support programs designed to improve the quality of parent-child relationships. At national, state, and local levels, there has been dramatic growth in the development and expansion of educational support programs targeted at parents of young

AUTHOR'S NOTE: This chapter was originally presented as part of the Family and Child Studies Center Lecture Series, Miami University, Oxford, OH.

children. A good deal of talk—but considerably less action—has occurred surrounding initiatives that expand the amount of time parents spend with their children (e.g., flexible work hours).

In view of escalating interest in efforts to support parents during the early years of child rearing, this is an important time to take stock of what is known and not known about appropriate ways to facilitate the development of healthy parent-child relationships in the early years. Toward this end, I summarize what has been learned and what remains to be learned about programmatic approaches to parent education and support during the early years of a child's life. The summary is based primarily on investigations of parent functioning and on research regarding the processes and effects of parent educational support programs. To provide a context for current interest in the quality of parenthood, the chapter begins with a brief description and explanation of renewed societal attention to parenting.

Society's Renewed Interest in Support Systems for Parents and Children

Contemporary concern about the quality of parent-child relationships is an extension of earlier themes in America about the importance of parenting in the early years, especially by mothers. Our nation has a long and rich history of efforts to enhance the ways in which parents relate to their young children (Brim, 1959). Within all theories of child development is an assumption that lay persons need expert guidance in the rearing of young children (Kessen, 1979). One of the original purposes of the nursery school, for example, was to serve as a forum for educating parents about the nature and nurture of young children. Prevalent within the nursery school movement of the 1920s and 1930s was the notion that learning to become a parent through imitation and the trial and error method was glaringly inadequate. Nursery schools served as a laboratory to train parents in child development and appropriate child-rearing practices (Fein, 1980).

Some parents, especially those representing ethnic minority and low-income populations, historically have been deemed to be in greater need of expert child-rearing guidance than other parents, namely those representative of the dominant culture and family type. Hence, increased societal interest in supporting parents of young children has corresponded with major U.S. demographic shifts such as the influx of European immigrants in the 1890s and the growth of single-parent families beginning in the 1960s. This persistent theme of the parent education tradition has produced periodic debate about the ethics of imposing the child-rearing values and practices of one population on another (e.g., Laosa, 1983).

Indications of Growing Interest and Concern

Evidence of the increased interest in the parent-child relationship in the early years can be found in communities across the country. At a national level, the federal government has launched such efforts as the Comprehensive Child Development Program and Even Start, both of which are family-centered education programs aimed at helping parents assist their children in reaching their full potential as learners. At the state level, there are developments under way in a variety of states— including Kentucky, Minnesota, Missouri, South Carolina, Connecticut, Maryland, Florida, and Illinois—to support parents during the early years of parenthood. One of the oldest state initiatives is Minnesota's Early Childhood and Family Education program, which provides parent group discussions, home visits, child development classes, and other approaches to enhancing and supporting the competence of parents. At the local community level there are many grassroots programs aimed at parents, ranging from a program known as Family Focus in the Chicago area, which features a drop-in center approach to parent support, to *Avance* in San Antonio, TX, which is a parent support program involving Mexican-American families with very young children.

Attention to parenting responsibilities also is found in the workplace. A small but growing number of employers have generated programs and policies that seek to be responsive to the family needs of workers. These initiatives are in response to calls for more "family-friendly" work environments, and concerns about worker productivity, economic competitiveness, and, in some sectors, labor shortages. While the bulk of this response has focused on child-care needs, there also is a strand of workplace programs such as brown-bag lunches focused on parenting topics (Galinsky, 1991).

Popular movies of the past several years have explored various dimensions of parenthood, and a frequent subject of both broadcast and print media reports is the struggles of being a parent in today's complex society.

Why the Interest and Concern?

Several factors are responsible for the current zeitgeist surrounding parenthood. As noted earlier, a major force is the new family demographics. Professionals and lay persons alike are familiar with the litany of statistics on changes in the structure and function of families, including numbers of single-parent households, women in the paid labor force, divorce rates, and geographic mobility (National Commission on Children, 1991).

Many scholars view the rapid and complex societal changes as contributing to a decline in the resourcefulness of families for rearing children. For example, J. Coleman (1987) argues that over the past 25 years there has been an extensive erosion of *social capital* within families and communities for the proper rearing of young children. In the family, social capital includes the presence of adults and the range of parent-child exchanges about academic, social, and personal matters. In the community, social capital involves norms of social control, adult-sponsored youth organizations, and informal relations between adults and children that permit, for instance, an adult lending a sympathetic ear to problems not discussible with parents.

Policy analysts representing both liberal and conservative political ideologies have pointed to the limited capacity of families for optimal child rearing as a pressing public policy issue. A recent article in the conservative Heritage Foundation's *Policy Review* (Mattox, 1991) argues that a "parenting deficit" in America today is more pressing than budget and trade deficits. The article cites studies showing that parents, on average, spend 17 hours a week with their children, down from 30 hours a week in 1965. A monograph published recently by the more liberal Progressive Policy Institute made a similar point (Galston, 1990).

Recent indicators of child functioning also have contributed to a sense of alarm about the state of parent-child relations. The U.S. Department of Education continues periodically to unveil national data showing that American children's academic performance, as measured by standardized tests, is below that of widely held expectations as well as performance scores of children in cohorts of earlier eras and current-day cohorts in other countries. A recent report of Columbia University's National Center for Children in Poverty (1990) indicates that nearly one out of every four children less than 6 years of age lives in poverty, and that poor children are at greater risk of impaired health than are other children.

Proposed remedies for less-than-optimal child functioning often point to parents as a necessary target of intervention. The National Goals for Education, established in 1990 by the U.S. President and 50 Governors, call for parents to spend time with their preschool child every day, helping the child be prepared to enter school ready to learn. The goal statement indicates parents "must be more interested and involved in their children's education" (p. 2) and that "American homes must be places of learning" (U.S. Department of Education, 1990, p. 9). Similarly, the Columbia University report on poverty targets the family as an essential point of intervention, noting that many poor parents are less able than other parents to prevent their children's exposure to harm and to promote positive health and developmental outcomes.

The interest and concern regarding the parent-child relationship in the formative years also stems from a greater awareness of the ecological embeddedness of child development. Due largely to the influential scholarly work of Urie Bronfenbrenner (1979) and to changes in family and community demographic characteristics, there is greater understanding in society that children grow and develop within the context of families and their social networks, and that families in turn are engaged in a set of complex negotiations with a variety of environments. Programs traditionally focused almost exclusively on children now emphasize a family context, often including educational and social services aimed at parents and other adult family members. For instance, conceptualizations of child care as a family support system have been increasingly prevalent in the past two decades (e.g., B. Caldwell, 1985; Galinsky & Hooks, 1977). Early childhood intervention programs have undergone a similar change, with growing attention to the provision of family support as an integral part of efforts to alter a child's developmental course (e.g., Dunst & Trivette, 1988).

Also contributing to interest in parenting during the early years is research evidence indicating that educational programs for young children and their parents have long-term effects. Findings from the early education studies represented in the Consortium for Longitudinal Studies (1983), including the Perry Preschool Study, have left the widespread public impression that programs in the early years produce large benefits that in the long run more than repay the public's investment (Haskins, 1989). Especially important in highlighting attention to the parental role was Bronfenbrenner's (1974) review of early education programs, which concluded that early intervention was more effective when parents were involved. Against a backdrop of growing concern about child functioning and the child-rearing capacities of families, then, is research evidence interpreted as providing hope of improved circumstances if programmatic attention is given to parents and children in the early years.

Lessons Learned

The extant literature on parent functioning and educational support programs for parents points to four major lessons about appropriate strategies for supporting parents. Collectively the lessons provide an informative guide for decisions about program design and implementation.

Multiple Determinants of Parenting

An important lesson from research and program experiences is that *parenting is best understood and facilitated within the context of individual and environmental conditions.* Determinants of individual differences in parent functioning fall into three major domains: (a) psychological characteristics and resources of the parent, (b) sources of stress and support within the environment, and (c) characteristics of the child (Belsky, 1984).

Psychological characteristics and resources of the parent are partly a manifestation of a parent's developmental history. Perhaps the most frequently cited finding regarding the long-term effects of early experience is that parents who abuse and/or neglect their children are more likely to have been mistreated as a child than parents who are not abusive or neglectful. The causal linkages here are not well established, of course, but the correlational evidence suggests that one's past experiences with nurturance cannot be separated from the present (e.g., Parke & Collmer, 1975).

An example of a parent-child program that directly addresses a psychological resource or personal characteristic of the parent is the University of Washington's mental health approach to infant intervention, where program designers tested the assumption that a mother's *interpersonal competence* was a necessary condition for improving her child-rearing abilities (C. Booth, Mitchell, Barnard, & Spieker, 1989). A basis of this assumption was research showing that multiproblem mothers tended to have inadequate social skills. The program viewed personal resources as necessary for effectively mobilizing environmental resources. Improvements in a mother's social skills were expected to lead to a ripple or spillover effect on her ability as a parent to manage the environment. The program assumed a mother's ability to communicate effectively with other adults might facilitate her ability as a parent to obtain necessary services from health care providers and other professionals. The program further assumed that social skills were essential for establishing and maintaining close personal relationships that might help the mother gain support for parenting.

There is a rapidly growing body of research literature within the ecological tradition that points to the relation of environmental conditions to the quality of parent-child relations. For instance, a recent investigation discovered that minor daily hassles associated with parenting, conceptualized as irritating, frustrating, annoying, and distressing demands found in everyday transactions with the environment, were a more significant source of stress within the parent-child system than sources of major life stress. Moreover, the investigators found that mothers' social support served to moderate the influence of hassles on indices of maternal behavior (Crnic & Greenberg, 1990).

The salience of environmental conditions in parents' lives is demonstrated by longitudinal data from observations of open-ended parent discussion groups involving mothers of young children in a low-income neighborhood. Over a 12-month period there was a sharp decline in mothers' discussion of child rearing and parenthood, and a significant increase in the frequency of discussing topics related to the parent as person and as environmental manager. These topics included relations with the landlord, problems in accessing health and social services, the lack of public transportation to the neighborhood, and where to find a job. For instance, discussion of child rearing and parenting decreased from 44% in the first quarter to 18% in the fourth quarter of the program (Powell & Eisenstadt, 1988). There is reason to believe this pattern is not limited to low-income populations. In a study of long-term parent groups composed of highly educated, middle-class mothers and fathers, there was a pattern of parents initially discussing the implications for one's career of having a baby, the problems of finding good child care, how to curtail the good intentions of intrusive in-laws, and how to accommodate a child in the couple relationship. This content tended to be pursued by the parents prior to serious consideration of topics directly related to the ages and stages of child development.

Efforts to enhance the social context of parenthood represent an emerging direction in the field of parent-child programs (Powell, 1988a). Initiatives include attempts to strengthen parents' social networks, social support, and community ties as a buffer against stressful life circumstances and transitions. For example, the Family Matters program launched by Cornell University sought to strengthen parents' social networks, including interpersonal connections within the neighborhood, as a means of empowering parents for child-rearing responsibilities (Cochran, 1988).

The terminology used to describe programs for parents reflects the implications of an ecological perspective on the parenting process. Increasingly it is common to use the term *support* in addition to, or instead of, the more conventional term of *parent education*. The traditional parent education program assumes the dissemination of information to parents will affect behaviors and attitudes, whereas the parent support approach assumes the provision of social support will positively influence parent functioning. The support paradigm emphasizes interpersonal relationships and envisions a supported parent as a program outcome; the education paradigm emphasizes knowledge and skill acquisition, leading to an informed parent (Powell, 1988b). The programmatic interest in the social context of parenthood is not limited to the domain of parent education and support programs. Similar movement can be found in the fields of social work, public health, and medicine.

Some programs for parents view stability in personal and contextual factors as a prerequisite to the parent's ability to entertain information about children. That is, personal and/or environmental difficulties are thought to interfere with a parent's ability to attend to the child and to the information and suggestions of a program. The following words of a program worker in one such program provide an apt summary of this rationale: "If a mother isn't making it financially, and she's just had a fight with her boyfriend, and he's just split, there ain't no way I can say to her, 'OK, let's you and I go play a game with the child' " (Mindick, 1986, p. 83).

Representative of this perspective is the previously discussed University of Washington program, which proceeded in two steps: first, mothers worked with mental health nurses on interpersonal competence issues, and, as a second step, mothers were given child-rearing information. One of the interesting findings of the program evaluation was that mental health nurses found it difficult to provide social skills training independent of parenting issues; mothers' concerns about the parent-child relationship kept surfacing in the sessions designed to focus on social skill enhancement (C. Booth et al., 1989).

The third area of influence on parent functioning is characteristics of the child. A growing body of research points to the ways in which child attributes such as temperament relate to patterns of parental behavior and attitudes. The extent to which programs for parents actively incorporate attention to individual differences into program content and methods is not clear. There are reports in the literature of initiatives that train parents to read and respond to infant cues (Dickie & Gerber, 1980), for instance, but there also is a tendency for many programs to generalize about child functioning and to assume a one-way flow of influence, from parent to child.

Parents as Active Thinkers

A second key lesson is that *parenting is an active, cognitive process.* Until recently, there has been a tendency in child development research to give minimal attention to the complexities of parental functioning. Developmentalists have gone to great lengths to understand children's cognitive processes, for example, but typically attribute little cognitive functioning to parents. The image one gets from most earlier and many existing studies is that parents are simplistic black-box reactors. Yet recent data indicate that parents are far from being blank slates. Parents hold a variety of beliefs about children and parenting that have direct and multiple implications for the ways in which education and support programs work with parents.

Evidence indicates that parents hold beliefs of various sorts about children's developmental processes generally and about specific abilities. These beliefs often relate in predicted ways to actual child-rearing practices and to children's development (S. Miller, 1988). For example, both mothers' and fathers' beliefs that children learn by constructing information through experience rather than rote memorization or some other didactic means have been found to be correlated to the quality of the child's cognitive functioning (J. Johnson & Martin, 1985; McGillicuddy-DeLisi, 1985). What is more, new information about children and parenting is filtered and edited by parents' existing constructs (Goodnow, 1988) and sometimes by the powerful messages of members of a parent's social network, such as the mother of an adolescent parent (Stevens, 1984).

Studies of parenting also point to the active and highly cognitive tasks of parenthood. Galinsky's (1981) portrayal of six stages of parenthood, based primarily on interviews with 212 parents, shows the central role of parents' image-making to ways in which parents handle the many developmental tasks of parenthood. Consider, for instance, the image-making that expectant parents pursue while anticipating the birth of a child, and the process of adjusting these images once the baby is on the scene (e.g., reconciling the idealized baby with the real baby). Consider also the cognitive demands on parents of interpreting values and a worldview to ever-inquisitive youngsters who want to know why things happen the way they do.

Programs aimed at parents have implemented several practices that stem from a view of parents as active thinkers about their children's development. One practice is to adjust program content in relation to the parent's beliefs and values regarding child development. For example, home visitors in one program routinely asked parents to describe what they wanted to achieve in the program and what their expectations were for their own children. The program assumed that the success of parental involvement in the project depended on sensitivity to parents' goals. Home visitors discovered that mothers held divergent views about what was important for children. Some mothers were concerned about discipline, others had an interest in their child's peer relations and social skills, and still others wanted to know how to improve their child's academic or creative skills. The information proved to be helpful to home visitors in being responsive to individual parent concerns and interests (Segal, 1985).

This strategy reflects a larger principle in the educational and human services: "begin where the client is." It is an attempt to tailor services according to the parent's "inner world" of feelings, frustrations, and dreams regarding the child and family (Provence, Naylor, & Patterson, 1977).

Another practice designed to respect parental cognitions about children is the long-standing method of open-ended discussion. Principles of adult education have long recommended that programs have a strong experiential component. The adult education literature suggests that personal experience be used as a learning resource (Brookfield, 1986). Discussion provides an opportunity for parents to digest new information and insights in relation to existing constructs about children and parenting.

Research suggests that long-term parent discussion groups can be a powerful tool in facilitating change in parents. Slaughter (1983) found that low-income African-American mothers who participated in a two-year discussion group exhibited superior ego development, expressed social values, and exhibited maternal teaching style compared to mothers enrolled in a two-year structured home-based program. Slaughter has suggested the discussion group may have functioned as a new form of the extended family. While some authorities suggest that discussion is best when it occurs within a group (Brookfield, 1986), there is limited research to support the claim that the group format is a superior context for parent discussion. Under certain conditions a one-on-one dialogue within the context of a home visit may be a more direct and effective way to engage parents in discussion of child and parenting issues (Powell, 1990).

Programs as Adaptive Systems

A third lesson is that *effective programs for parents are responsive to parent and community characteristics.* Quite simply, one program size does not fit all. This lesson has been difficult to learn because of the prevalent notion that programs are "treatments" applicable to any population and transportable to any setting.

The lesson of responsiveness to community factors comes primarily from multisite demonstration programs of the late 1960s and 1970s involving Head Start and similar interventions aimed at parents and young children. Investigators discovered that human service programs do not lend themselves to mass production. Rigid, cookie-cutter approaches to duplicating a model intervention represent a sad story in the recent history of human services in this country (Schorr, 1988). Effective programs naturally adapt to fit local circumstances, and often achieve greater impacts on children and families when they are tailored to their contexts. Thus each program initiative faces the challenge of learning how to provide new sources of support to a population without supplanting or tearing down existing ones (Halpern & Larner, 1988).

This lesson of responsiveness was relearned in the 1980s in efforts to provide programs for ethnic minority parents. It was discovered that effective programs for non-Anglo populations require more than simply extending existing service models. Programs also need to be culturally responsive to patterns of learning and interpersonal relations among children and parents of different backgrounds (Tharp, 1989). Thus it cannot be assumed a parent program or policy that has been effective with one population will be equally effective with another population. In the absence of proper evidence, it is dangerous to assume that impressive model programs will yield similar results when implemented without regard to the conditions that made them successful at the original demonstration site (Laosa, 1990).

Unfortunately, there is only a thin base of empirical data on population characteristics that can guide decisions about the design of specific program methods and content. Needed is research on the parenting needs and program preferences of population groups defined in ways that transcend global population categories (e.g., Hispanics). For example, a recent study found significant differences between low-income Mexican immigrant and Mexican-American mothers regarding preferred methods and content of a parent education program. Mexican immigrant mothers were more likely than Mexican-American mothers to prefer a program with group and home visiting modes than a program with group as the only mode, to indicate concern about interpersonal aspects of group participation, to prefer attendance of spouse and extended family members at all program meetings, and to indicate interest in program content related to family-environment relations (Powell, Zambrana, & Silva-Palacios, 1990).

At the root of program responsiveness is a stance of the program staff to respectfully accommodate the parent's agenda as defined by the parent. In programs exhibiting high levels of adaptiveness, both parent and staff member work together to generate an understanding of the parent's interests, strengths, and needs. In contrast, programs exhibiting low levels of adaptiveness expect parents to accommodate the content and structure of the program, including assumptions about parent needs and goals as well as activities for reaching goals.

The concept of *parental empowerment* often is used to describe program adaptiveness (Cochran, 1988). While many definitions of *empowerment* can be found in the literature, a common element is the assumption that hope and self-respect are the crux of competence and that an individual's location in the social structure influences the development of competence through the provision of opportunity, respect, and power. As M. Brewster Smith (1968) observed many years ago, "when opportunities are offered without a sharing of power, we have paternalism, which undercuts respect and accentuates dependence" (p. 313). Operationally, collaborative relations between parents and program staff provide a structural mechanism for helping programs be sensitive and responsive to the needs and cultural norms of the population to be served. Such relations involve shared decision-making control over the nature of parent participation, including program method and content (Powell, 1984).

Opportunities to maximize program responsiveness are evident in the policies of state-supported family education and support programs. A descriptive study of four state initiatives shows there is local discretion regarding the structure and content of programs. Missouri's Parents as Teachers program allows local schools to use materials other than the state-provided program curriculum if they can be shown to have the same features. Minnesota's legislation for the statewide Early Childhood Family Education Program specifies a set of general services for parents and children, but allows considerable local choice with respect to specific programming and materials. The two other states in this study (Connecticut and Maryland) entertain locally developed proposals for program services, thus permitting a proliferation of models at local community level (H. Weiss, 1989).

This lesson has contributed to a change in views of effective strategies for supporting parents. It is clear that a unidirectional model, wherein the presumed flow of influence is from program to parent, does not exist in reality. Rather, programs entail an interaction between parent characteristics, program resources, and outcomes. Thus the same program can be experienced in different ways by different parents (Eisenstadt & Powell, 1987).

A paradigm shift in views of programs is reflected in the metaphors used to describe programs and evaluations. There has been movement from metaphors involving machines to metaphors of a biological nature to describe the essence of supporting parents. The mechanistic view of a program as a static entity that transforms inputs into desired products or outcomes has given way to a perspective of a social program as a complex, dynamic system engaged in active transactions with multiple parts of its environment. In this latter view, programs have a developmental life course, with growth and change determined largely by the nature of adaptations to the community context, which of course includes the target population.

Images of parent programs as adaptive, open systems also has led to greater differentiation and complexity in the type of evaluation questions being asked today. Increasingly, the question of whether a given program is effective is replaced by this question: What type of program is effective for what population and under what conditions? Answers to this latter question hold great promise of enriching our understanding of the conditions under which programs are effective, and ultimately will help us make informed choices about the types of strategies that are likely to be effective with different populations.

Intensity of Support

A fourth key lesson is that *the magnitude of program effects is greater when programs are intensive.* Meaningful support of and change in parents cannot be done on the cheap. The parent-child relationship is far too complex to assume that brief encounters between a program and parents will dramatically alter or strengthen the pattern of parenting and ultimately improve child outcomes.

Findings of studies with both middle- and low-income populations support this lesson. In a review of outcome studies of 20 early intervention programs targeted at some aspect of family functioning, Heinicke and his colleagues (Heinicke, Beckwith, & Thompson, 1988) concluded that more pervasive and sustained effects are likely to be realized when the intervention includes 11 or more contacts over at least a three-month period. The investigators suggest that a certain duration of contact is needed to permit the development of a trusting relationship between family members and program staff. The 20 programs included in this review were initiated at some time in the period from pregnancy to the first three months of the baby's life, and included a range of socioeconomic populations. Another approach to program intensity is the comprehensiveness or range of services a program offers. In a review involving 11 infancy intervention programs, it was found that a child's intellectual development was improved most significantly when a high-quality child-care program was offered in conjunction with other family services. Home visits alone were not found to increase IQ by age 2, and home visits plus medical and educational intervention or parent-oriented training had moderate effects on IQ. The strongest effects involved these family services plus a high-quality child-care program (Ramey, Bryant, & Suarez, 1985).

Indirect support for this lesson is found in results of research on efforts to enhance the parent-infant relationship in the first few days of the infant's life. The Brazelton Neonatal Behavioral Assessment is a frequent strategy for attempting to heighten parental awareness of newborn competencies and hopefully promoting sensitive parenting and interactional synchrony. The better designed studies of this minor intervention indicate there are no effects on parent-child interaction. In one well-designed investigation, families assigned to one of four treatment groups were compared at 1, 3, and 9 months to examine the effects of a neonatal intervention using the Brazelton assessment tool. In half of the families mothers and fathers were the target of intervention, and in the remaining half of the families mothers were the sole target of intervention. The intervention consisted of active or passive exposure to the Brazelton Assessment; the active exposure group elicited responses from their newborn under the direction of a facilitator, and the passive exposure group listened to a detailed verbal description of their infant's performance on the examination. The experimental intervention was found to have no effects on mother-infant, father-infant, and husband-wife interaction across groups (Belsky, 1985). While the Brazelton assessment procedure may be an important means of entry into the developing parent-infant system, by itself this minimalist intervention does not appear to lead to effects on parent-infant interaction.

Lessons Yet To Be Learned

The four lessons summarized in this chapter provide the beginnings of a framework for designing initiatives that are likely to be effective in supporting parents engaged in the early years of child rearing. Yet there is much to be learned if major advances are to be made in designing programs that match the needs and characteristics of parents in an increasingly diverse society. Three areas warrant special attention.

Balancing Child, Family, and Institutional Needs

Designers of parent support initiatives need to learn how to balance the needs of child, parent, and third-party institutions. The need stems from a view of parenthood within the context of individual and environmental conditions. As described in the first lesson, programs cannot isolate and then alter parenting without regard for its direct linkages to other aspects of the parent's functioning. Programs, then, need to address a range of content. Yet in doing so there is a tendency for child development matters to be ignored or overshadowed by pressing parent issues. This pattern is especially evident in initiatives involving parents living in highly stressful circumstances. It also is present in programs serving dual-worker families where parents are preoccupied with work-family tensions and problems in finding affordable, high-quality child care. Program time and staff may become primarily focused on the resolution of parent and family issues. Research reports on such efforts suggest, however, that the consequences for the child may not be favorable.

Informative here are the evaluation results of the Child and Family Resource Program, which may be interpreted as suggesting that family circumstances but not child functioning were improved by the program, because the content of home visits focused almost exclusively on family needs. This innovative program used home visitors who worked with parents to develop a family action plan. With the worker, the family generated realistic goals to improve their living situation. The evaluation results showed the program contributed to improved family situations; there were increased parental feelings of personal efficacy and awareness of their roles as educators of their child. There also was improved coordination of community services, and movement of parents into jobs, school, or vocational training. However, there was no measurable effect on children's development at age 3, as measured by various scales of social and cognitive functioning (Travers, Nauta, & Irwin, 1982).

An inherent tension is established when the content boundaries of parent programs are broadened to include attention to a range of individual and family issues. Yet not to do so runs the risk of seriously limited program effects because multiple forces that impinge on the parent-child relationship are ignored. Programs need to contend with a social environment that often works against rather than for the best interests of children and parents.

The agendas of third-party institutions that sponsor parent education and support programs also require attention. Increasingly, programs for parents and young children are being launched to partly meet the needs of these institutions. Workplace initiatives aimed at family needs, for instance, typically are created with the aim of improving worker productivity and corporate competitiveness (Friedman, 1990), and school-sponsored educational programs for parents of young children typically seek to improve children's school readiness via parental influence, thereby reducing the need for classrooms to accommodate a wide range of student readiness levels (Powell, 1991). A problem occurs when these institutional agendas overshadow or limit a fundamental interest in the optimal development of the child and parent *independent* of their roles within or contributions to the sponsoring agency. For instance, the parent education approach that closely matches the expertise and interest of schools is to conceptualize parents as teachers. The home becomes an extension of the classroom, with suggested or prescribed parent-child activities approximating teacher-student exchanges (Powell, 1991). Aside from the obvious ethical issue of imposing the school culture on the family, a potential programmatic problem is that the school's agenda for the parent may not match the parent's agenda.

Mechanisms for Making Programs Adaptive

Parent education and support programs need tested procedures on how to tailor content and methods to the needs and characteristics of particular populations. The second and third lessons, pertaining to parents as active thinkers and programs as responsive to family and community characteristics, are difficult to implement without concrete guidelines on how to adapt program resources.

Key questions to be addressed here include the following: What aspects of child and parent functioning are to be used to alter program content and methods? To what extent will formal and/or informal procedures be used to determine needed program directions? In what ways, if any, will parents be involved in making decisions about the content and method of programs in which they are involved?

Parent programs that rely on home visits offer a special opportunity to examine these questions because home visiting lends itself to individualization. A review of studies and descriptions of home visiting programs indicates that individualization procedures typically rely on informal staff judgment to tailor program services, often without the aid of systematic data-gathering tools or specific program guidelines on how to individualize the session (Powell, 1990). Hence, much work remains to be done.

Families can be viewed through a variety of theoretical windows, and at present there is no consensus in the parent education and support field about what dimensions of family functioning are important to assess. Potential areas include the family's strengths, needs, resources, current functioning, coping strategies, and styles of parent-child interaction (Krauss & Jacobs, 1990). Especially needed are procedures to generate a valid understanding of the family that is free of cultural and class biases.

For programs and policies governing parent support, the challenge here requires a superordinate decision about relationships between program staff and parents. Is the relationship to be a collaborative one, with equal decision-making power regarding program content and methods, or a more traditional parent-professional relationship where staff members' judgments prevail in decisions about program adaptation? In short, whose standards—the program's or the parent's—of desired child and parent functioning are to be used to determine needed program directions?

There has been considerable endorsement of the collaborative or partnership model of parent-staff relationships in parent programs, stemming largely from the aforementioned empowerment perspective. Formal family assessment tools, which usually require a conventional professional posture, run contrary to the collaborative model, which assumes that parents are capable of articulating their own needs. In a genuine partnership between parents and program staff, it is inappropriate for the staff member to assume a superior role in interpreting family needs assessment data or to engage in clinical appraisal of the family through techniques other than direct responses to questions (Krauss & Jacobs, 1990).

Extending What Is Known

There is a need to reduce the disparity between what is known about effective practices with parents versus what is typically done to support the parent-child relationship. Few programs of support for parents embody the lessons learned about exemplary practices. There are numerous instances of programs (a) ignoring personal and contextual factors affecting parents, (b) assuming parents are blank slates, (c) attempting to implement predetermined "treatments" with diverse communities and populations, and (d) providing limited program resources for brief periods of time. The reasons are many and familiar, including a lack of communication among professionals in the field, weak or nonexistent linkages among disparate institutional settings sponsoring parent programs, a program staff need or desire to "reinvent the wheel," and seriously limited funds for program operations.

Increased attention to staff training is one piece of a solution to this problem. No other topic comes closer to the heart of a parent program than personnel preparation. The essence of program services rests directly with staff behaviors and attitudes. Much work needs to be done here. Leaders need to determine what educational content and methods best prepare individuals to work with parents, including minimum staff education requirements. Minnesota's statewide Early Childhood Family Education program has one of the most well-developed staff credentialing systems in the country, while most other initiatives have policies that imply an ambivalence about the contribution of formal education to the preparation of personnel in parent education and support programs.

Concluding Comments

In spite of a long history of efforts to support parents with early child-rearing responsibilities, the field of parent education and support programs has yet to reach a mature state of development. Primarily, this is a reflection of a U.S. culture that has assumed families should rely on their own resources for parenthood and child-rearing responsibilities, with societal supports offered when a family is unable to do so. Parent education and support programs have never been a core part of mainstream educational and human services. The field's peripheral status in society may be undergoing alteration, however. In response to the consequences of rapid social and economic changes, increasingly there are arguments that all families need some type of support for child rearing (see Dokecki & Moroney, 1983). Family capacity for nurturing the optimal development of children is deemed by many to be compromised beyond reasonable limits. It remains to be seen whether parent programs eventually will emerge as an element of a social infrastructure, with universal entitlement for all families. For the present time, growing societal concern about family environments for children provides an opportunity to work toward widespread adaptation of what is known about essential parameters of support to parents, and to pursue research and development activities that contribute to program advances at conceptual and operational levels.

6

Work and Family Relationships

PATRICIA VOYDANOFF

In recent years interest has grown in the work/family interface and its implications for the quality of work and family life. The assumption that work and family life are separate spheres has shifted to a recognition that work and family roles are interdependent and to a need to understand the nature and implications of this interdependence. Although recent research has described the elements of the work/family interface, it is just beginning to address the mechanisms and processes involved. This chapter will address some of these processes by examining how men and women combine and coordinate work and family roles over the life course. It will also address institutional coordinating mechanisms and their implications for gender equality.

Context for Viewing the Work/Family Interface

Before beginning this analysis, it is important to set the context. In 1988, traditional families in which the husband, but not the wife, is in the labor force accounted for one fifth of all families compared with more than three-fifths in 1940 (Hayghe, 1990). In 1988, 65% of married mothers were in the labor force, up from 40% in 1970. The percentage of married women with children under 6 who are in the labor force

AUTHOR'S NOTE: This chapter was originally presented as part of the Family and Child Studies Center Lecture Series, Miami University, Oxford, OH.

increased from 30% in 1970 to 57% in 1988. Sixty-seven percent of women maintaining families with children under 18 were in the labor force in 1988; the comparable figure for women with children under 3 is 54% (U.S. House of Representatives, 1989).

The trend toward increasing female employment is expected to continue. By the year 2000 it is predicted that 80% of women ages 25-54 will be employed outside the home (Shank, 1988). This trend has two major implications for the work/family interface. First, the provider role, the traditional mainstay of men's participation in family life, will be increasingly shared by women. Most women in two-earner and single-parent families work because of economic need; many families cannot be supported solely by a man working outside the home. Earnings from the paid employment of women are critical to the maintenance of an adequate standard of living in many families. In 1981, employed married women contributed, on average, 26.7% of total family income (B. F. Reskin & Hartmann, 1986). Women working full time year-round in 1978 contributed 40% of family income (B. Johnson, 1980). These percentages are higher among families with the lowest income levels. In other families, women's paid employment makes the difference between having a working-class or a middle-class life-style in terms of home ownership and material possessions.

Second, increased wife employment means that a growing majority of families will have no adult in the home full time. This development has significant implications for many aspects of "women's work." Women generally are expected to be the "emotional glue" of a marriage and family. They are responsible for maintaining ties with extended kin and serve as the major family representative in the local community. They are major caretakers of young children and other family members needing care, such as elderly parents and the ill and disabled. Today women can expect to spend more years caring for an aging parent than for a child (S. K. Wisensale & Allison, 1988). We have barely begun to address these issues. Attempts to deal with the most obvious issue, child care, are still in the early stages.

These trends mean that the basis for both men's and women's participation in work and family life is changing. Men are no longer the sole economic providers and women are no longer home to care for their families full time. It is important to recognize that these changes affect both men and women. It is not sufficient to view work/family issues as women's issues that affect men only as husbands of working women. The analysis of work/family linkages must move beyond an examination of women's roles and assume a broader perspective in which work/family issues are recognized as relevant to both men and women. This can be done most effectively through a multiple role perspective.

The Constraints of Work and Family Roles

Most individuals at some time perform the roles of worker, parent, and/or spouse. Often all of these roles are performed simultaneously. Each involves activities, identities, obligations, and relationships with others. The three roles are interdependent in terms of the time, energy, and commitment required for adequate performance. Under certain circumstances, this interdependence can result in role conflict, a situation in which participation in one role is more difficult because of participation in another role. Role conflict can be of two types, overload and interference. Overload exists when demands on time and energy are too great to be met adequately or comfortably. Interference occurs when conflicting demands make it difficult to fulfill the requirements associated with both work and family roles.

The expectations and demands of work and family roles place constraints on each other over the life course. Traditional work and family roles can be viewed from the perspective of a *career,* defined as a succession of related stages through which persons move in an ordered sequence (Wilensky, 1961). One formulation of occupational career stages includes preparation, novitiate, early career, middle career, late career, and post exit (Bailyn & Schein, 1976). The nature and intensity of work demands vary over these several stages. Some of the most important work influences on family life include amount and scheduling of work time, job demands, orientations to work, and intrinsic work-role characteristics (Voydanoff, 1987).

Families can also be described in terms of career stages such as establishment, new parents, school-aged family, postparental family, and aging family (Hill, 1964). As with work characteristics, several aspects of family roles may be associated with role conflict, for example, family structure (first married, single-parent, or remarried family); presence, number, and ages of children; and the presence of elderly parents needing care.

When individuals pursue traditional work and family role sequences simultaneously, these combined demands frequently result in overload and interference. For example, when individuals in early career stages are also the parents of young children, overload is high. In the early stages of a career individuals are establishing themselves as full members of their occupations, resulting in a relatively high involvement in work (Hall & Hall, 1979). At the same time young children are very demanding in terms of time, attention, and energy (Aldous, 1978). Members of families with young children are likely to experience job tension and a shortage of time (R. Kelly & Voydanoff, 1985; Voydanoff & Kelly, 1984). Interference tends to be high among families with school-aged children. Timing and scheduling become important as parents are expected to attend school and community functions at times that often conflict with working hours (Harry, 1976). Parents of school-aged children also report high levels of time shortage (Voydanoff & Kelly, 1984). In later career stages, work demands require relatively less attention and individuals often have more time for their families. By this time, however, some husbands and wives have developed separate interests and many children have left home (Aldous, 1978; J. Cohen, 1979; Pleck, 1977). Many middle-aged women seeking to establish careers after their children have grown find themselves responsible for the care of elderly parents (E. Brody, 1985).

These patterns of overload and interference have been documented among families in which the husband works outside the home and the wife is at home to care for the household and children. If both husband and wife pursue these traditional work and family career patterns, overload and interference are increased further, especially among women. In many cases working women maintain their traditional family responsibilities in addition to their employment outside the home. Until recently most husbands of working wives have spent little, if any, more time in family work than other husbands.

This overload and interference can be reduced on two levels: (a) by individuals and families coordinating their activities so as to limit their work and family role demands and (b) by changes in employment policies and the structure of work.

Individual Responses: Work/Family Role Coordination Over the Life Course

Sequential role staging and symmetrical role allocation are two major ways in which individuals and families attempt to reduce the conflicting demands of traditional work and family career patterns. Sequential role staging is used to alternate the work and family responsibilities of the husband and/or wife over the life course. Symmetrical role allocation is an attempt to reduce overload and interference by shifting the responsibilities of work and family roles between the husband and wife within various stages of the life course.

Sequential Work/Family Role Staging

Increases in wife employment have provided the major impetus for the adoption of sequential role staging and/or symmetrical role allocation. Sequential staging of work and family responsibilities is the modal type of labor force participation among women (Chenoweth & Maret, 1980). Relatively few women work continuously over their entire work history. The Panel Study of Income Dynamics indicates that 23% of women worked full time continuously between 1972 and 1976; 30% did not work at all. The remaining 47% either were involved in part-time work or worked only part of the time (Moen, 1985). Women also enter and leave the labor force more often than men, an average of 4½ times for women and 3 times for men (S. Smith, 1982). Most sequencing is oriented toward the accommodation of work-role participation to the responsibilities associated with family career stages.

Several types of sequential work/family participation have been documented: conventional, in which a woman quits working when she marries or has children and does not return to work; early interrupted, in which she stops working for childbearing early in her career development and then returns; late interrupted, in which she establishes her career, quits for a period of childbearing, and then returns; and unstable, in which she alternates between full-time homemaking and paid employment. These patterns may be contrasted with simultaneous staging in which women pursue work and family activities across work and family career stages with minimal interruptions for childbearing (J. Bernard, 1971; Elder, 1977; St. John-Parsons, 1978). These various career patterns depend on age at childbearing, age of children when women return to work, and the number and spacing of children.

The choice between early and late parenthood involves several trade-offs in the performance of work and family activities over the life course. Early parenthood may increase economic pressures on the family and create some difficulties in career establishment upon return. Many women, however, may find advantages in having children at an age more compatible with others. An earlier period of childbearing also gives women breathing room in order to formulate goals for a later career effort (Daniels & Weingarten, 1982).

Late parenthood may reduce the overload, interference, and economic pressures associated with early parenthood. It allows earlier career establishment with some advantages on return and involves parenting responsibilities when there is less pressure to advance in a career by both the husband and wife (Hall & Hall, 1979). However, some women find it difficult to interrupt a career once it has been established and others find childbearing difficult at a later age.

In addition, recent studies indicate that significant minorities of those caring for elderly family members, especially women, quit or consider quitting their jobs, rearrange work schedules, reduce work hours, or take time off without pay to care for elderly relatives (E. Brody, 1985; E. Brody, Kleban, Johnson, Hoffman, & Schoonover, 1987; Finch & Groves, 1983; Women's Bureau, 1986). Employed female caregivers continue to provide most of the help received by their disabled mothers (E. Brody & Schoonover, 1986). Being employed significantly reduces the hours of caregiving among sons but not daughters of elderly parents (Stoller, 1983).

Role staging has been used mainly by women to coordinate work and family roles. Women have adjusted the time of work, marriage, and childbearing to reduce overload and interference and to increase options within the constraints of traditional role allocation. However, the increasing numbers of women who are committed to working over the life course find it difficult to engage in extensive work/family role staging. Many of these women perform two full-time jobs—one at work and one at home. This situation prompts the perception that the division of work and family roles between men and women is unfair and stimulates calls for the husbands of employed women to do more family work.

Symmetrical Work/Family Role Allocation

The development of a more symmetrical division of labor is a second individual approach for reducing overload and interference in work and family roles. In a symmetrical pattern of role allocation, husbands perform more family work and women perform more work-role duties than in traditional role allocation. The difference between traditional families with some role sharing and symmetrical families with extensive sharing of tasks and responsibilities is one of degree rather than kind. The major difference is one of responsibility. Wives in symmetrical families are coproviders with major responsibility for contributing economically to the family. In addition, in symmetrical families, husbands move beyond "helping" their wives with family work and assume responsibility in this area. Both responsibilities and task performance are more symmetrical.

Symmetrical role allocation requires more accommodation to family needs by men and more accommodation to work demands by women than the traditional pattern. It also implies a more balanced commitment to both work and family careers by husbands and wives (Young & Willmott, 1973). Women's increased labor force participation reduces the strain associated with the traditional male provider role. Men whose wives share the provider role have more flexibility to pursue satisfying work and develop a broader range of interests, relationships, and identities. Recent data suggest a slight increase in the amount of time husbands of employed women spend in family work, although women still spend more time in family work than men. The major contributor to symmetry in family work is the decreased amount of time spent in family work by women (Pleck, 1983; Spitze, 1988; L. Thompson & Walker, 1989).

Work/family role staging is a more common individual response to role conflict than is a symmetrical division of labor. The most common pattern involves a relatively traditional division of labor in which both men and women work outside the home while women do the bulk of the family work. One can argue that role staging with its associated career disadvantages facilitates the maintenance of a traditional division of labor at home. Women remain supplementary earners rather than coproviders, since being a coprovider requires either simultaneous staging or a situation in which both husbands and wives use sequential staging at different times.

When families attempt more symmetrical role allocation, the need for structural changes in employment becomes apparent. When both husband and wife attempt to pursue demanding work over the life course, the development of symmetrical role allocation can reduce overload and interference for women. However, the total demands on both spouses may still be excessive. In addition, parents in single-parent families are unable to use role staging and allocation to reduce demands. For men and women to meet the demands of work and family in the coming years, the structure of work needs to change.

Institutional Responses: Policy Implications of Work/Family Linkages

Current employment policies and the structure of work are oriented toward the disappearing traditional family in which the husband works outside the home and the wife works in the home caring for the household and children and helping her husband in his career. These policies include "9 to 5" work hours, work located physically outside the home, nondiscretionary overtime, and career penalties for part-time work. Although these policies create strain among traditional families, their lack of fit with two-earner and single-parent families is even more evident.

Alternative employment policies are being developed that attempt to address sources of work/family conflict, namely amount and scheduling of work time and caring for children and elderly family members. Policies dealing with amount and scheduling of work time include family leave and alternative work schedules. Policies and programs that address the need for family members to care for children and elderly relatives take several forms including information and referral services, on-site care, and providing financial resources and tax credits to support the purchase of care. These policies and programs have varying effects on work/family conflict over the life course and gender equality.

Family Leave

Patterns of employment before and after pregnancy and maternity leave arrangements have changed considerably for women from the early 1960s to the 1980s. Among women having their first births in 1961-1965, 60% had worked six or more months continuously before the birth of their first child; the comparable figure for 1981-1985 first births was 75%. In the early 1960s, 16% of women received maternity or paid leave with the assurance that they could return to their jobs. Sixty-three percent quit their jobs during their pregnancy or shortly after giving birth. In the early 1980s, 47% received maternity benefits and only 28% quit their jobs. Eighty-one percent of those taking maternity leave received cash benefits; however, only about one-half received full pay during their leave (O'Connell, 1990).

Women also were more likely to return to work following the birth of their first child in the 1980s than in the 1960s. Among those having their first birth in 1961-1965, 17% were working by the 12th month following the birth compared to 53% in 1981-1984. Those most likely to return to work within six months had worked until the last month of pregnancy and had received maternity benefits during or after their pregnancy (71% in both groups) (O'Connell, 1990). Part of the increase in maternity benefits can be attributed to legislative changes. The Pregnancy Discrimination Act of 1978 amended Title VII of the 1964 Civil Rights Act to prohibit discrimination in employment on the basis of pregnancy, childbirth, or related medical conditions, and required that "women affected by pregnancy, childbirth, or related medical conditions shall be treated the same for all employment-related purposes, including receipt of benefits under fringe benefit programs" (Bureau of National Affairs, 1986, p. 102). Thus only women working for employers with disability insurance benefits were covered by this legislation.

In recent years the Family and Medical Leave Act expanded the concept of maternity leave for working women to include unpaid leave for women and men upon the birth or adoption of a child, serious illness of a child or parent, or serious health condition of the employee. Although this bill was vetoed by President George Bush in 1990, 14 states passed similar legislation between 1987 and 1989 (Gilbert & Benokraitis, 1989; Institute for American Values, 1989; S. K. Wisensale & Allison, 1988).

Although a minority of companies offer paternal leave comparable in length to maternal leave following childbirth, very few fathers make use of it. Fathers rarely use formal paternal leave because it is unpaid and because of employers' negative attitudes. However, many fathers do take short informal leaves following childbirth by using personal leave or vacation time (Pleck, 1989, 1990). Thus at the present time family leave to address family responsibilities is used much more by women than by men.

Alternative Work Schedules

Several alternative ways to schedule work are available other than working from 9 to 5, five days a week. These include reducing work hours by working part time or adjusting the scheduling of work through flextime or shift work.

These alternative work schedules generally were not initiated to accommodate family responsibilities. They have often been established by corporations to meet their own needs, for example, part-time workers are needed for peak hours in banks and retail establishments; shift work is necessary for continuous process and assembly-line operations; and flextime reduces commuting time, conserves energy, uses expensive equipment more efficiently, and keeps businesses open longer hours to meet customer needs.

Part-time work. Women are more likely to work part time than are men. In 1985, 27% of women were working part time compared with 10% of men. In addition, men work part time for different reasons than women do. Men do so because they are in school or are unable to find full-time employment. Male part-time work is concentrated among younger and older age groups. Women are more likely to work part time during their child-rearing years and because of family responsibilities (Nardone, 1986; Voydanoff, 1987).

Because the number of hours worked is associated with work/family conflict among both men and women (Voydanoff, 1987), part-time work may be a viable means of reducing this conflict. Much part-time work, however, is found in traditionally female jobs, such as retail trade and services. These jobs are often characterized by low pay, few benefits, and little opportunity for advancement.

Flextime. Under flextime, employees vary the times they begin and end their work day from the standard schedule beginning at 8 or 9 a.m. and ending at 5 p.m. Nearly all flextime plans involve a core time period during which all employees are at work, with variable beginning and end times surrounding the core. The amount of flexibility in beginning and end times varies, ranging from 30 minutes to three hours or more. In 1985, 13% of men and 11% of women were on flextime schedules (Mellor, 1986).

Despite expectations to the contrary, flextime generally does not relieve work/family role strain among parents. It also is not related to men spending more time in child care and housework, although men on flextime schedules do spend more time playing with their children than do other men (Christensen & Staines, 1990; Voydanoff, 1987).

Shift work. Higher percentages of workers are involved in shift work than flextime. In 1985, 18% of men and 13% of women worked other than a day shift, that is, they worked afternoon shifts (generally from 3 p.m. to 11 p.m.) or evening shifts (generally from 11 p.m. to 7 a.m.).

Approximately three fourths of those involved in shift work are not doing so voluntarily but because the job requires it (Mellor, 1986).

In one third of dual-earner couples with children less than 6 years old, at least one spouse works a nonday shift. Eighteen percent of mothers and fathers have no overlap in the hours they work. Twenty-six percent of fathers are not working one or more days a week when their wives are working. These fathers provide child care during the hours that their wives are working and they are not. However, less than 8% of fathers who worked nonday shifts gave child care as the reason compared with 42% of mothers. Another 11% of women cite care of other family members as a reason for shift work (Presser, 1989). Thus, although men care for children when they are home and their wives are working, it is the wives who establish the schedules that permit this care.

Thus gender differences in work patterns are greatest for interrupting labor force participation and part-time work. Few gender differences exist in flextime and shift work. Men, however, are more likely to participate in alternative work patterns because of job and economic demands while women are more likely to do so in response to family responsibilities.

Dependent Care

As large numbers of women have become employed outside the home and have increased their long-term attachment to the labor force, the need for child care and care for other family members has become more evident. The National Research Council concluded recently that "existing child care services in the United States are inadequate to meet the current and future needs of children, parents, and society as a whole" (Hayes, Palmer, & Zaslow, 1990, p. 290). This inadequacy occurs in terms of availability, affordability, and quality. Employed parents also report specific problems regarding the care of sick children, before- and after-school care, illness of a care provider, transportation, and school holidays (Bureau of National Affairs, 1986).

Families report diverse patterns of child care. Approximately one fourth of preschool children are cared for in more than one arrangement. In 1987, 47% of preschool children of employed mothers were cared for *primarily* by a relative, 22% in family day care, 6% by a sitter in the home, and 24% in day-care centers (O'Connell & Bachu, 1990). Half of the relatives caring for children are mothers (9%) or fathers (15%).

This finding reinforces the importance of alternative work schedules such as part-time work and shift work so that a parent is available for child care. Expanded parental leave policies also would contribute to parental care of infants.

Studies also reveal increases in the numbers of workers, especially women, who are combining employment with the care of elderly family members. Employee surveys indicate that approximately one quarter of employees are actively involved in caregiving. Caregivers are more likely than other employees to take time off from work and experience work/family conflict (Scharlach & Boyd, 1989).

The Family and Medical Leave Act is the first national policy that has explicitly addressed the work/family conflict involved in caring for elderly family members. Efforts to provide assistance to caregivers or alternative sources of care are sporadic at best.

Implications for Gender Equality

An implicit assumption underlying many of these institutional responses to work/family conflict is that they will increase gender equality (Bohen, 1984; Haas, 1990). To examine the extent to which this occurs, it is necessary to operationalize gender equality. In this chapter I will use three criteria: (a) the ability of men and women to be economically self-supporting with pay equity, (b) work and family roles with comparable social value for men and women, and (c) equity between men and women in work loads at home and at work.

The ability of men and women to be economically self-supporting with pay equity. To the extent that work/family policies enable women to work outside the home, they do reduce the economic dependence of women on men. However, women's use of sequential staging and policies such as parental leave and part-time work do not facilitate women becoming coproviders as opposed to supplementary earners. Alternative work patterns used more by men, flextime and shift work, are less likely to affect labor force participation or wages and thus have less bearing on economic self-sufficiency.

Work and family roles with comparable social value for men and women. For this criterion to be realized, work/family policies must be perceived as appropriate for both men and women. When work/family issues are treated as women's issues, women's employment opportunities are limited. For example, part-time jobs created for women allow many women to work and maintain their traditional family responsibilities;

however, part-time work is generally low-paying, lacking in benefits, and limited in advancement opportunities.

When policies and programs are designed to meet the traditional family needs of women and to attract women employees, only women will use them. Women will continue to be at a disadvantage at work in terms of occupational segregation, pay, and opportunities for advancement. In addition, men will not assume more family work when women limit their work role to accommodate these family responsibilities.

However, men do use these alternative work patterns, but for different reasons; for example, they interrupt careers to return to school or they work part time or nonday shifts because the job requires it. When these patterns are used to advance a career or to meet employer needs, they mean something different from when they are used, or assumed to be used, to accommodate family responsibilities. In addition, when men do adjust their work to accommodate family needs, it may be called something else; for example, men frequently take time off following the birth of a child through personal days, vacation, or sick leave rather than "parental leave."

If the use of policies that reduce work/family conflict is associated with women's work or with career penalties, men and women wanting both career advancement and children will continue to be placed in a very difficult situation requiring extensive individual and family accommodation. Hunt and Hunt (1982) have suggested that two classes of workers may emerge: work-oriented nonparents and family-oriented parents. This would impose unpleasant choices on individual families and lead to economic difficulties among families with children that are similar to those now experienced by working mothers.

In the context of current career definitions, gender equality will not be furthered if only women take advantage of family-oriented policies and men don't—or do, but call it something else. However, providing alternative work policies without penalties for both men and women would benefit both family life and the workplace. Women and families would no longer suffer career penalties and men would have more options for combining their work and family roles. In addition, the productivity of a broader segment of the population would be available to the labor force and the economy.

Equity between men and women in work loads at home and at work. Work/family policies generally help women combine work and family roles in the context of traditional work and family structures. Alternative career paths and work schedules enable women to adopt a work role in the traditional structure while still maintaining major responsibility for family work and child rearing. The greatest change in family work occurs with the amount of child care men do in families engaged in shift work. This is not intentional, however—at least on the part of men.

It appears that most of the policies and programs discussed in this chapter are oriented toward furthering women's economic participation without challenging the traditional career model or family division of labor. Many women seem to prefer this accommodation; others, however, are challenging the "superwoman" aspect inherent in this approach.

Therefore, gender equality requires changes that go beyond incorporating women in the work world while accommodating traditional work institutions and family roles. It is necessary to challenge the "male career model" and traditional division of family work by increasing work/family flexibility for both men and women. This flexibility must be built into career paths and organizational structures rather than having employers accommodate specific groups, such as parents of young children and adult children of elderly parents. This could take the form of flexible life scheduling in which work alternates with several other activities such as sabbaticals and increased education as well as leave for childbearing or the care of elderly relatives (Best, 1980).

Conclusion

This chapter analyzes mechanisms involved in the work/family interface by examining individual and institutional responses to work/family constraints. Most individuals perform work and family roles that must be coordinated with each other over time. Both work and family roles consist of careers with several stages that vary in their activities, obligations, identities, and relationships with others. The combined demands from these activities and relationships may result in role overload and interference. Mechanisms used by individuals to construct workable patterns of activities and relationships include work/family role staging and work/family role allocation. Institutional responses to work/family conflict include changes in employment policies and associated norms. The balance between individual and structural accommodations to the changing nature of work and family responsibilities and their contributions to gender equality will be a major issue in this decade.

7

Families and Marital Disruption

MARILYN COLEMAN
LAWRENCE H. GANONG

Demographic Trends in Family Disruption

More than 9 out of 10 Americans get married (Norton & Moorman, 1987). In fact, the United States has the highest marriage rate of any industrialized society. It also has the highest divorce rate.

Recent estimates indicate that a majority of marriages (60%) will end in divorce (L. Bumpass, 1990). More than half will involve children (Bane, 1979). Despite this high dissolution rate, it does not appear that the number of marriage failures (i.e., divorces) leads to disenchantment with marriage. More than 60% of women and 75% of men who divorce remarry, usually quickly; the average time between divorce and remarriage is less than three years (Furstenberg, 1990; Norton & Moorman, 1987).

Samuel Johnson referred to remarriage as "the triumph of hope over experience," and it appears that hope isn't enough in many cases. The estimated divorce rate for remarriages is slightly higher than that for first marriages. About half the children whose parents divorce and remarry will experience a second parental divorce (L. Bumpass, 1984).

The recent increase in cohabitation (i.e., first marriages preceded by cohabitation increased from 8% in the late 1960s to 49% in the mid-

AUTHORS' NOTE: This chapter was originally presented as part of the Center Lecture Series, Miami University, Oxford, OH.

1980s; L. L. Bumpass & Sweet, 1989) complicates our understanding of family disruption. The "informal divorces" that occur when cohabiting couples break up depress the reported divorce rate, which means the rate of family disruptions far exceeds the reported divorce statistics.

Because approximately half of the increasing number of cohabiting couples have children (L. Bumpass, Sweet, & Cherlin, 1989), many children are involved in family disruptions that do not move through the legal system and do not show up in divorce statistics. There is no way, at this time, of calculating the number of children who are affected by multiple family disruptions. It is obvious, however, that this number is already large and growing rapidly.

There is a widely held assumption that marriages and families used to be more stable (Goode, 1963, refers to this as the "world we have lost"). However, the overall rate of marital dissolution has remained approximately the same for more than 100 years; it is the precursor (now most commonly divorce, rather than desertion and death) that has changed.

Although the rate of marital dissolution has remained stable for 100 years, the rate of divorce has been steadily increasing. The only exceptions include a plateau in the 1950s and a recent plateau that may be due to the increase in cohabitation and changing demographics (L. Bumpass, 1990).

Reasons for Disruption

Why are family disruptions so common? What do family disruptions mean to the individuals whose lives are being disrupted? Perhaps the answer to that question comes at the other end of the process. Why do people marry?

Historically, marriage was primarily an economic and procreative partnership. In fact, adults had few alternatives to marriage for security and subsistence. Emotional satisfaction from marriage, although often an expectation, was only one of many.

As marriage began to be seen more as a personal relationship designed to fulfill needs and ensure happiness and less as an institution necessary for survival, divorce became more common. Divorce has come to be viewed as a solution to an unhappy relationship that is not meeting at least one partner's needs. This increasingly has become the case as women enter the marketplace and earn enough to survive outside of marriage. In fact, the more hours a wife works (and presumably the more money she makes), the more likely she is to divorce (South & Spitze, 1986).

Among those assuming that marriages used to be more stable, social changes such as the liberalization of family law are blamed for the increasing divorce rate. It should be noted, however, that the changes in divorce laws came considerably after the increase in divorce, *not* before. Also, the influx of women into the marketplace followed rather than preceded the increased divorce rate.

Rather than viewing the family as a previously stable, fixed form that has recently undergone massive disruption, the institution of the family could more accurately be described as a constantly changing entity. Normative expectations for families (the "shoulds" and "oughts") lag far behind behaviors, the ways we actually live.

Defining Disruption

Often divorce is seen as a specific event, and perhaps legally it is. However, most researchers and clinicians now consider divorce as a process rather than an event. This process may include years of marital conflict, separation, the legal divorce, and family reorganization after the legal divorce. Bohannon (1970) refers to six overlapping experiences or stages of divorce:

1. *The emotional divorce* centers around the problem of the deteriorating marriage. The couple are withholding bonding emotions and communication from the relationship and undermining each other's self-esteem through betrayals of various sorts.
2. *The legal divorce* is based on grounds and represented by a court action. The primary purpose of the legal divorce is to dissolve the marriage bond so that emotionally divorced spouses can legally remarry. The legal divorce tends to focus on the *day* of the divorce. Unfortunately, the illusion is created that the day of the divorce is the end of negotiation and relationships (J. Bernard, 1981).
3. *The economic divorce* deals with dividing money and property. Alimony and child support also are part of this.
4. *The coparental divorce* deals with custody and visitation and is often cited as the most difficult aspect of divorce.
5. *The community divorce* relates to the changes of kin, friend, and community relationships. When people marry they usually replace single friends

with "couple friends." When they divorce, couple friends may be reluctant to become involved in conflicts over allegiances, and new friends must be sought.

6. *The psychic divorce* refers to problems of regaining individual autonomy and no longer being part of a couple. To be successful, Bohannon says a psychic divorce requires a period of mourning. Eventually, the ex-partners must take responsibility for their own part in the end of the relationship, forgive themselves, forgive the partner, and move on with their lives.

All of these divorce experiences are of interest and concern to family professionals, but the most problematic and on-going is the coparental divorce. When a childless couple divorces there may be few complicating factors. The relevant stages are quickly executed and life goes on. When a couple with children divorce, however, they remain "united" through their children. The quality of this postdivorce parental tie becomes crucially important to the emotional and often financial well-being of the children. The "common knowledge" is that divorce is extremely stressful and quite harmful to children's development. However in a recent review of research, Demo and Acock (1988) cautioned that, "it is simplistic and inaccurate to think of divorce as having uniform consequences for children. . . . Characteristics of families, on the other hand, are critical to youthful well-being" (p. 643).

Characteristics of Postdivorce Families

Divorcing and postdivorce families vary widely in ways that undoubtedly affect children's development and well-being. Ahrons and Rodgers (1987) have identified five styles or types of postdivorce relationships that create distinct emotional environments for children.

Type 1 was labeled "Perfect Pals." These postdivorce couples continue to relate to each other as close friends. They have a great deal of mutual respect for each other as people and as parents. Perfect Pals are likely to continue celebrating holidays together with the children and to keep in touch with each others' extended family. Their decision to divorce may have occurred over a long period of time and may relate to life-style decisions. Children of Perfect Pals keep in close touch with both parents and are unlikely to feel abandoned. A former student, obviously a child of Perfect Pals, shared with her incredulous college classmates that her parents, stepparents (both her parents had remarried), sister, and step-sister rent a ski lodge each Christmas and spend the holiday together.

Type 2 couples were "Cooperative Colleagues." They did not de-scribe themselves as good friends, but they were able to cooperate successfully as parents. They managed conflict well and kept it from escalating into huge power struggles. Custody was usually flexible but clearly spelled out, and boundaries were clear between the two house-holds. Cooperative Colleagues would be highly unlikely to spend holi-days together but could cooperate in such a way that their children would not feel torn loyalty and guilt about their holiday plans.

A third category, "Angry Associates," would present greater challenges to family life professionals. These postdivorce couples maintain resentful feelings about the marriage and the actual divorce process. They function similarly to hostile marital partners and often engage children in their struggles. Parenting is parallel rather than integrated and major life events such as birthdays, weddings, and graduations are big stressors. The children experience ongoing loyalty conflicts. Holidays often end up as power struggles over who gets to spend the most time with the children.

An even more explosive group, "Fiery Foes," have almost no ability to coparent and they neither respect or accept each others' parenting rights. Legal battles over custody and child support are likely to con-tinue, and power struggles pervade the entire family. Often with this group as well as the Angry Associates, the father controls the money and the mother controls the children; he withholds child support and she withholds visitation. Because children get caught in the middle, they often take sides with one parent, usually the mother. Contact with the father typically diminishes over time, and the parents blame each other for this. These children may feel abandoned by at least one parent and very angry with them. This anger often carries over to stepparents whom the children may believe were responsible for the divorce.

The last category, "Dissolved Duos," do not maintain postdivorce relationships. One spouse usually leaves the geographic area and does not maintain contact. Children most certainly feel abandoned by the geographically distant parent. Furstenberg and Nord (1985) found that nearly half the children in their study had not seen their noncustodial parent in the past year. In the case of remarriage, the stepparent may adopt the child of Dissolved Duos and attempt to establish a nuclear family model. If all family members are reading from the same "script," if *all* family members agree they are going to ignore previous family ties and live like a nuclear family, it may work. If even one family member is unwilling to do this, the attempt to replicate a nuclear family likely will not be successful.

It is important for family practitioners to investigate parents' post-divorce relationships and not assume that children of divorce have much in common other than the fact their parents are divorced. When parents are Fiery Foes and absolutely unable to communicate about anything, counselors may want to suggest utilizing the extended kin network (e.g., grandparents) as go-betweens (Andresen, 1990). At the least, this may enable parents to communicate information concerning the children. Nonadversarial techniques such as mediation are also recommended to keep hostility to a minimum and focus on what's best for the children.

Effects of Family Disruption on Children

In spite of cautions such as those expressed by Demo and Acock (1988) about drawing conclusions regarding the effects of divorce on children, family professionals remain quite concerned, especially about the effects of serial marriage on children (G. Brody, Neubaum, & Forehand, 1988). The diminished parenting quality likely to occur when marital disruption has precipitated intense emotional pain and upset in one or both parents is particularly troubling.

However, staying together for the "sake of the children" is probably ill-advised. Results from J. Block, Block, and Gjerde's (1986) longitudinal study suggest that many of the behavioral problems boys exhibit at the time of divorce and after are present as many as 11 years before marital disruption actually occurs. These predivorce behavioral problems were not evident in girls. J. Block et al. hypothesized that girls may respond internally (e.g., withdraw or perhaps be very well behaved) to family discord. Zaslow (1989), after reviewing the research on sex differences in children's response to parental divorce, concluded that "boys do indeed respond more negatively to parental divorce, both immediately and over a period of years, *if* they are living with an unremarried mother; whereas in post-divorce families involving a stepfather or father custody, girls fare worse" (p. 136).

Kurdek (1986) was one of the first to consider divorce from a developmental or life-cycle perspective. After reviewing the limited research, he formulated the following guidelines for age-related responses to divorce. Keep in mind, however, that the age of the child at the time of the divorce is often confounded by such things as parental hostility levels and length of time between separation and divorce (R. Emery, 1988).

Three months to two years old. Very young children may have attachment problems. Higher levels of separation anxiety and regressive behavior may be evidenced. Children may show reactions to extreme tension, especially in the mothers. Because children this age lack language skills, nonverbal cues must be examined for signs of distress.

Three to five years old. Preschoolers more likely focus on the fact that one parent is physically leaving home than on the poor parental relationship. Developmentally at a more egocentric stage, they may see themselves as central to the break-up. They may view the parental separation as temporary and think that if they are good the noncustodial parent will return home. These children are often sad, frightened, and bewildered. The primary vehicle for feelings of mastery is play, and there is evidence that songs, puppets, and story telling can increase children's understanding of family disruptions (Griffin, Weeks-Kirk, & Coleman, 1985). Rossiter (1988) recommends helping children practice activities such as saying goodbye and hello to their noncustodial parent, packing suitcases, using the phone, and distinguishing the difference between a hope and a wish.

The mothers of children this age also need support. It is crucial, for example, that day-care providers understand potential divorcing and postdivorce dynamics so they can comfort the child and support the mother. Suggestions for supportive practices can be found in Gray and Coleman (1985).

Six to eight years old. Children this age may begin to be aware of parent conflict and incompatibility as contributing to the divorce. By this age children are less likely to blame themselves for the divorce but they may worry that their behavior will add to parental stress (and it probably does). Although children in this age group wish their parents would reconcile, few believe they will. Those in highly conflictual homes may view the reduced conflict as a positive aspect of divorce but see the reduction in contact with the noncustodial parent as a definite loss. Few children this age willingly discuss divorce with their friends, even though such discussions might be quite helpful to them. However, there is a direct linkage between children's divorce adjustment and children's social support. Interventions involving parents and peers are advised (Kurdek, 1987).

Nine to twelve years old. The cognitive ability of children this age usually enables them to understand that internal changes and incompatibility can lead to divorce. They rarely blame themselves for the divorce and may feel strongly ambivalent toward one or both parents. Children in this age range whose parents remarry may feel disloyal to their biological parent if they like their stepparent. These loyalty conflicts may create anger. One former student shared that she hated her stepmother because she was warm and expressive, always hugging her. Her mother was reserved and somewhat cold. This young woman obviously found it easier to hate her stepmother than to face her conflicted feelings about her mother's style of interaction.

Thirteen to nineteen years old. Formal operational thought enables children of this age to think abstractly about their situation. They tend to interpret divorce in terms of incompatibility and may regard their parents' decision to divorce as mature and sensible. Many will relate that divorce instigated positive personality changes in both parents.

Children this age seldom feel responsible for marital disruption (with the exception of divorce in remarriage) and often attribute their sense of self-reliance, responsibility, and independence to the divorce. There is little evidence that experiencing divorce has a negative impact on marital aspirations, although children of divorced parents have a more positive attitude toward divorce than those from nuclear families (Ganong, Coleman, & Brown, 1980).

Ironically, in stepfamilies the onset of formal operational thought in the adolescent may cause an unanticipated upheaval. As children become able to think abstractly, they may begin to think about what their life would be like if their parents hadn't divorced (or in the case of families disrupted by death, what life would be like if their parent were still living). Roles and relationships may have to be renegotiated at this time.

It is crucial that researchers, clinicians, and family life educators not make broad assumptions about children's reactions to divorce and that information about adjustment be collected from children as well as parents and teachers. Kurdek (1987) found that children, mothers, and teachers did *not* provide similar information with regard to children's divorce adjustment. Researchers report that teachers and others who know a child's family structure respond to the same behavior in different ways (Ganong, Coleman, & Mapes, 1990). For the most part, they tend to evaluate behavior of children they believe are from remarried or single-parent homes more negatively than the same behavior from children they believe live in a nondivorced, two-parent family. An example of how this personal bias might work in a classroom was provided by a teacher-turned-journalist who was interviewing one of the authors of this chapter. He shared that he could tell when a child in his class was from a divorced family because the child was always waving his or her hand in the air and trying to get attention. When one of the authors related that her two "children of divorce" were rather shy in the school setting, he quickly terminated the interview and never returned to finish it. A promising journalism career may have been ended by nailing this journalist-to-be about his rather naive hypothesis of family structure effects.

Young Adults and Parental Divorce

Little research has been done on the effects of parental divorce on offspring who are older than age 18 (Kitson & Morgan, 1990). A common assumption seems to be that parental divorce does not have a major impact on offspring who are adults at the time of the divorce (Cooney, 1988). However, the evidence from some recent, small-scale studies of white, middle-class respondents is that young adults may have difficulties adapting to recent parental divorce (Cooney, 1988; Cooney, Smyer, Hagestad, & Klock, 1986). Divorce may disrupt parents' ability to support their offspring, who are encountering the developmental challenges of young adulthood.

At a time in their lives when they may feel uncertain about their own future, parents' divorce can be emotionally overwhelming for some young adults. Sadness, anger, guilt, feelings of vulnerability, and general emotional distress are not uncommon reactions when parents end long-term marriages (Bonkowski, 1989; Cain, 1989; Cooney et al., 1986). Offspring are often surprised by the news of their parents' divorce, even when their parents' marriage was conflictual (Cain, 1989), and consequently are ill-prepared for coping with the changes that ensue.

Some of these changes, such as parents moving from the family residence, reductions in parents' incomes, lowered ability of parents to provide emotional support, and increased needs of parents for emotional support, may contribute to rapid redefinitions in the nature of parent-child relations (Cooney, 1988). Some young adults feel responsible for their parents' well-being, particularly for their mothers or for the parent who did not initiate the separation (Bonkowski, 1989; Cain, 1989). Thus young adults sometimes find themselves being relied upon by parents.

Family relationships are affected in other ways as well. Some young adults and divorcing parents report feeling closer to each other following the divorce (Cooney et al., 1986), while others become more emotionally distant and are less frequently in contact with each other (Bonkowski, 1989). When one parent is blamed for the divorce, relationships with the "guilty" parent are strained and contact reduced (Bonkowski, 1989).

For those who are shocked and surprised by parental divorce, and for those who may have strained relationships with parents' postdivorce, the experience may facilitate rethinking their perceptions about the nature and quality of the parents' marriage and their beliefs about marriage and family life in general (Cain, 1989). Current love relationships are reexamined, and young adults wrestle with doubts about their own ability to have a lasting marriage (Cain, 1989). More careful scrutiny may not necessarily be a negative process, but it does make developmental transitions related to this aspect of adulthood more complicated.

It should be noted that these findings are based on a few studies conducted on a narrow segment of society. Larger studies with more representative samples may yield quite different results. It should also be noted that not all reactions to parental divorce by young adults are negative. Some are relieved by parental divorce (Cooney et al., 1986), some families are drawn closer, and, even among those who have difficult adjustments to parental divorce, the preponderance of evidence is that young adults continue to make progress achieving developmental tasks (Bonkowski, 1989). One young adult revealed being extremely relieved by her parent's divorce and quite resentful that it had not occurred sooner. Because her home life had been so dysfunctional, she said she spends enormous amounts of time watching families, trying to figure out how "normal" families behave. She is unsure of her ability to ever establish a normal family, since she has never lived in one. On the positive side, however, she does approach relationships with more maturity and thoughtfulness than many of her peers.

Young adults do not tend to seek therapy or other professional help for support when dealing with parental divorce (Cain, 1989). It may be that, since society in general assumes that young adults are less affected by their parents' divorce than minors, the young adults themselves are reluctant to admit problems.

Divorce Effects on Older Adults

Prevalence

Although the elderly divorce at a lower rate than other age groups, the rate of divorce for older people has increased in the past few years (Thornton & Freedman, 1983). This rate will probably continue to increase somewhat (Uhlenberg & Meyers, 1981). A larger population of older individuals, greater economic freedom for women in later life, and reduced social stigma attached to divorce likely will contribute to increased numbers of late life divorces in the future (Lloyd & Zick, 1986). An increasing number of older adults already will have experienced divorce and remarriage, and thus may be less hesitant to divorce again (Hennon, 1983).

Effects

There has been little research on the effects of divorce among older adults (Brubaker, 1990b; Cooney, 1988; Hennon, 1983). There are, however, a few conclusions that may be drawn about the effects of divorce in later life on psychological, social, physical, economic, and familial adjustment.

Psychological effects. Anger, self-blame, sadness, increased feelings of helplessness (Weingarten, 1988), loneliness, guilt, a sense of loss, anxiety, and decreased self-esteem (Cain, 1988) are psychological reactions of recently divorced older persons. These reactions certainly are not unique to older individuals (Kitson & Morgan, 1990), and some of these feelings are similar to the feelings of those who are widowed in later life (Hennon, 1983). It has been argued, however, that older persons are particularly vulnerable to negative psychological effects, since they may be facing other stressful life transitions at the same time (DeShane & Brown-Wilson, 1981). On the contrary, however, W. Gove and Shin (1989) found that older divorced persons had *better* psychological well-being than did younger divorced individuals.

There is some evidence that older men and women differ in their psychological reactions to divorce (Chiriboga, 1982; Gander & Jorgensen, 1990). There has not been enough research on gender differences, however, to draw conclusions about the specific nature of these differences (Brubaker, 1990b).

Social consequences. Older persons who divorce report reduced social contacts (Cain, 1988; Keith, 1986). Divorce in later life is still unusual enough that a divorced older person may have relatively few peers who can understand and empathize with them, and thus their social network may be limited (Hagestad & Smyer, 1982). For many older persons, social contacts are already reduced due to phenomena related to aging, such as illness, moves made after retirement, death, and reduced mobility as a result of physical limitations; divorce is just one of several reasons for having fewer friends available to them. The social stigma of divorce has also been identified as a reason for the withdrawal of friends (Cain, 1988).

Physical health effects. The physical well-being of divorced adults is worse than that of the married and widowed (Keith, 1986; Kitson & Morgan, 1990). Their physical health may be reduced due to several factors: (a) loss of the stress-buffering effects of social support as a result of the reduction in the size of the social network; (b) lower income and greater financial stresses, which may result in poorer health care and lower living standards; (c) the pile-up of stressors due to changes in daily routines and other changes related to the loss of a marriage partner; and (d) lower psychological well-being, with the resultant reduction in the ability to cope with stressors.

Economic consequences. Older divorced persons are economically disadvantaged in comparison to married and widowed individuals and are less satisfied with their economic situations (Hennon, 1983; Uhlenberg & Meyers, 1981). There may be gender differences in the financial positions of divorced older people (Keith, 1986), but both sexes are financially harmed following divorce (Fethke, 1989).

Family relationships. It is reasonable to assume that divorce in later life will have an effect on relationships with family members (DeShane & Brown-Wilson, 1981). However, the ways in which the quality and quantity of contact with kin are affected is likely to be quite variable, depending in part on such factors as family members' perceptions of the divorce, geographic mobility, emotional closeness between kin prior to the divorce, and the gender of both the older individual and their adult offspring. Unfortunately, few researchers have examined the influence of late life divorce on family relationships, and the studies that have been done yield mixed findings. For example, Hennon (1983) concluded that divorced women were less integrated into their extended family systems than widows; Keith (1986) found that divorced women had similar amounts of contact with family as did widowed and never-married women; and Cooney (1988) reported that a higher percentage of recently divorced women resided with their adult offspring than did married, widowed, and long-divorced women.

For many older persons, divorce will reduce contacts with family; men are especially likely to be isolated from family following divorce (Keith, 1986). It is also likely that contacts with former spouses are reduced, as are contacts with relatives of the former spouse (Cain, 1988). The loss of these potentially important, long-term relationships may add stress to the older person's life.

The types of resources exchanged between older persons and their kin may be affected (Hennon, 1983). For example, the exchange of financial advice and assistance may be diminished (Hennon, 1983), or children may provide increased financial assistance and a place to live (Cooney, 1988). Emotional support may be sought from adult offspring and even grandchildren, particularly if friends have withdrawn from contact (Cain, 1988; Gander & Jorgensen, 1990).

Interventions. Langelier and Deckert (1980) offer counseling guidelines for older divorced women, based on a study of 204 late divorcing Canadian women. They suggest there are six life adjustment areas that should be focused on: emotions, divorce grounds, finances and budgeting, children, life-style changes, and autonomy. For example, older women need pragmatic assistance in such areas as budgeting, finding jobs, and understanding their legal rights. Support groups to reduce the sense of isolation, and psycho-educational groups, such as those designed to teach assertive communication skills or relaxation techniques, are also recommended. Certainly individual and family therapy are needed for some older divorced persons, but many elderly are reluctant to pursue therapy as an option, and there is some evidence that the divorced are not open to more traditional therapeutic approaches (Weingarten, 1988).

Divorce by the Children of Older Adults

Another way that older adults are affected by divorce is when their children dissolve their marriages (Cicirelli, 1983; C. Johnson, 1988). An increasing number of older adults will witness the dissolution of their offsprings' marriages, thus experiencing what Hagestad (1988) referred to as a *countertransition,* a transition that occurs as a result of a change in someone else's life. How are these older individuals affected by the breakups of their children's marriages? How are generational ties affected?

Contact With the Older Adult

The amount of contact (visits, phone calls, letters) between older adults and their divorced children appears to be unaffected by divorce (Ahrons & Bowman, 1982; Anspach, 1976; Spicer & Hampe, 1975), although in some families contact increases for a period of time immediately after the divorce (Ahrons & Bowman, 1982; C. Johnson, 1988). However, contact with former in-laws does decrease (Ahrons & Bowman, 1982; Ambert, 1988; Anspach, 1976). It follows, then, that contact with grandchildren following divorce is related to where the grandchildren reside; those who live with the older adults' offspring remain in contact with grandparents at levels similar to before the divorce, and those who live with the ex-in-laws of grandparents are less often in contact (Ambert, 1988; Gladstone, 1988). There is evidence that custodial parents, particularly mothers, make some attempts to encourage their children to remain in touch with their former spouse's parents (Ambert, 1988). If nonresidential parents do not provide a link between their parents and their children, however, contact is likely to be infrequent (Anspach, 1976).

Given what is known about the relatively infrequent contact between many noncustodial parents and their children following divorce (Furstenberg & Nord, 1985; J. Seltzer & Bianchi, 1988), it is not surprising that the parents of noncustodial adults also lose contact with their grandchildren. Not all grandparents accept this situation with ease, however, and the past decade has seen a tremendous increase in legislation and legal decisions that allow postdivorce visitation rights for grandparents (Derdeyn, 1985).

Exchange of Support

Generally, support provided for offspring by older adults does not diminish following divorce (Ahrons & Bowman, 1982; Anspach, 1976); in fact, emotional and financial support from parents may increase immediately after the divorce, but decline gradually over time (C. Johnson, 1988). Few older individuals provide support for their former in-laws (Ambert, 1988), however, nor are they likely to receive any assistance from them.

Patterns of interaction and resource exchange vary with how families reorganize and redefine themselves following divorce (C. Johnson, 1988). In an in-depth study of 52 grandmothers, C. Johnson found three general approaches to postdivorce reorganization: some custodial parents emphasized ties with their blood kin, reducing contact with the former spouse's kin; a second group drew boundaries around the household (divorced parent and child); and the final group included extended kin, non-kin (former spouse's kin), and the household. Further study is needed to examine how these, and perhaps other, patterns of family reorganization are related to adaptation and adjustment.

More also needs to be known about what kinds of family support are most helpful. There is evidence that certain kinds of support may benefit divorced mothers, while their children may respond better to other types of support from grandparents (Isaacs & Leon, 1986). It should be noted that not all support has positive effects on the recipients, and that support for divorced offspring may be offered for a variety of reasons (e.g., obligation, concern).

What about support provided to the elderly from their divorced offspring? Marital disruption appears to impair the ability to provide support to older parents (Cicirelli, 1983; C. Johnson, 1988). It is not known if this situation changes over time, nor are we sure if such impairment is limited only to certain kinds of support. More information about the exchange of postdivorce support within families and across generations is needed, particularly given the increasing amount of marital disruption in American society.

It is doubtful that a magical solution to family disruption will be found. Normative expectations of marriage are phenomenally high, almost ensuring disappointment and divorce. Does this mean the end of the family? No. It does mean, however, that many of us will be living in new, more complex families. In these new families, roles, rules, and responsibilities may have to be negotiated rather than taken for granted as is typical in more traditional families. This new American family was captured in the following essay by a University of Missouri journalism senior, Dan O'Keeffe (December 6, 1990 *Columbia Missourian*). To some of us what he's describing is threatening, even frightening. To others, Dan is merely describing the changes that have been taking place in this country for more than 100 years.

> My parents told me when I was 6 that they couldn't live with each other anymore. They were getting a divorce. The news hurt at the time, but as I grew up listening to them argue constantly over the phone, I realized their decision to separate was for the best. Although they still exchanged words, I

rarely had to witness it with both of them in the room. My sister and I learned to ignore their squabbles. I knew from my time spent with each of them that they both l0oved us, despite their own differences. They had spared themselves the misery of living with each other. I became comfortable with the situation.

Following the divorce, I lived in Ohio with my mother. During the summer, my sister and I would travel to Florida to live with my father. I moved to Orlando permanently during high school. This constant shuffling of suitcases and addresses became routine. I didn't necessarily like the situation, but then again, I didn't know what I was missing. To this day, I rack my brain every holiday season trying to decide where I want to, or should, spend Thanksgiving and Christmas.

About three years ago, my father divorced his second wife, whom my sister and I had grown to love as part of our family. I now have a new stepmother, so to speak, and a 13-month-old half brother.

The second divorce left me feeling a little empty. I missed my first stepmother and I felt deprived of a family member and a friend. But the feelings passed and now I look forward to spending time with my father's new family, as well as visiting my mother and sister.

Divorce and separation, subjects on which I consider myself to be an expert, are carving a neatly defined and increasingly accepted niche in today's society. Experts have predicted that 50% of today's marriages will end in divorce. The children of tomorrow may grow into extended families comprised of stepparents, stepbrothers and stepsisters, or half brothers and half sisters. Consequently, these children may find themselves adjusting to their situations with few difficulties. The massive sense of guilt will not overwhelm them as it does many of today's children. Eventually, they may become the norm, as opposed to the traditional nuclear family of the past.

Whether this development is morally or ethically right is not the question. More important, parents considering divorce must ask themselves what kind of life they want for their children after they separate and begin leading different lives. They must determine when the best time to break the news will be and then to do it.

Children see things in a different light than teenagers or adults. They possess an incredible ability to adapt to new situations. Divorce strikes teens and young adults as a crisis situation in which they see themselves as the cause. They fall into depressive states. Children react aggressively. They get hurt initially, but learn quickly to accept their situation. They grow as their family changes, instead of having change forced upon them in their later years.

As I look back, I have to thank my parents for being strong enough to face their problems and act on them. I know they did it for their children's benefit. I consider myself a stronger person because of it.

This Christmas, I'll find myself playing with my little brother on the floor, trying to teach him to say my name. Between goos and gaas, I'll make a few telephone calls to my family and friends in Ohio. I'll spend time with my father, his wife and my relatives from Clearwater, Florida. Then I'll steal away to visit my stepbrother and his wife, my 13-month-old stepniece and my first stepmother. And if I have the opportunity, I'll call my former stepgrandparents. I'll spend a lot of time on the telephone and a lot of time on the road this Christmas. I'll be busy, but it will be worth it. After all, they are my family.

8

Abuse in the Family

An Ecological, Life-Cycle Perspective

SALLY A. LLOYD
BETH C. EMERY

Abuse in the family, although present since ancient times, has only recently been intensively scrutinized by scholars and professionals. Beginning with the article "The Battered Child Syndrome" in 1962 by Kempe, Silverman, Steele, Droegemueller, and Silver, the problem of child battering was hurtled into the forefront of American social problems. Over the next three decades, scholars documented the existence of abuse in virtually every type of relationship, from husband and wife, to courting couples, to adult child and elderly parent. Ultimately it became clear that abuse was a family legacy that affected all generations of family members, from the child to the elder.

The purpose of this chapter is to review the literature on family abuse from both life cycle and ecological perspectives. Within the life cycle perspective, abuse is examined as it occurs across various family relationships and life stages. Particular attention will be paid to the impact of abuse on the subsequent life course.

The ecological perspective is utilized as a framework for understanding the dynamics of abuse in the family. This perspective emphasizes the interplay of individual, family, social, and cultural factors (Tan, Ray, & Cate, 1991). Belsky (1980) discusses an ecological framework that contains four levels of influence. At the *ontogenetic* level, the individual characteristics that both abuser and victim bring with them to the family setting are considered. The *microsystem* is the immediate family setting within which abuse takes place; here interaction in the family system is examined. The *exosystem* represents those systems that surround the family microsystem, including the social network, community, and economic sector. The *macrosystem* represents the cultural norms/values that foster abuse through their influence on the other systems. This ecological model emphasizes the interdependence of the levels; an examination of any one of these levels alone is insufficient to understanding how abuse within the family is both fostered and maintained (Garbarino, 1977).

Physical Abuse of Children

Physical abuse of children has been defined and operationalized in a variety of ways. Straus and Gelles (1986) define *physical violence* against a child as "an act carried out with the intention, or the perceived intention, of causing physical pain or injury to another person" (p. 467). Their definition purposefully places spanking within the realm of violent actions, drawing attention to the fact that many "normative" behaviors are indeed violent and injury producing. Abuse of a child is defined as those acts with a high likelihood of producing injury (e.g., punching, beating, kicking, etc.).

Estimates of the incidence of physical maltreatment of children vary widely. In a national survey of 6,002 families, Straus and Gelles (1990) found the incidence of child abuse in 1985 to be 24 per 1,000 children ages 3-17, or approximately 1.5 million children. The National Center on Child Abuse & Neglect (1988) surveyed community professionals likely to encounter cases of child abuse, and found the rate of physical abuse to be 5.7 per 1,000 children. The lowest figures for the rate of child abuse come from the American Association for Protecting Children's (1988) report of official child abuse cases substantiated by state protective services: 3.5 cases of physical child abuse per 1,000 children for the reporting year 1986.

The Ontogenetic Level

A great deal of research has examined the individual characteristics of both perpetrator and victim. Initial research on child abuse characterized the abuser as pathological; however, current work emphasizes that only 10% to 15% of abusing parents have a psychiatric condition (Ammerman, 1990). Child-abusing parents are subject to a host of stress-related symptoms that are likely to lower parental competence, including low frustration tolerance, inappropriate expression of anger, health problems, and emotional distress (Wolfe, 1987). Abusing parents may perceive their environment to be unpredictable; their response to stress has been described as hypersensitive (W. Bauer & Twentyman, 1985). They have poor parenting skills, poor problem-solving ability, unrealistic expectations of their children, extremely high standards for themselves as parents, and a tendency to attribute malevolent intentions to their children (Ammerman, 1990; Azar, Robinson, Hekimian, & Twentyman, 1984; Crittenden, 1988). Some suffer from alcohol abuse (Leonard & Jacob, 1988).

Overall, child-abusing parents are low in adult psychological resources, which may be a result of their experience with troubled family relationships as a child. In particular, insecure, hostile, rejecting, or pathological relationships with their own parents as well as the experience of physical or psychological abuse as a child or witnessing parental violence characterize child-abusing parents more so than their nonabusing counterparts (Kaufman & Zigler, 1987; Vondra, 1990).

Characteristics of the child may also serve as risk factors for abuse (Belsky, 1980). Boys are more likely than girls to experience abuse (Wauchope & Straus, 1990). It is believed that young children are more likely to be abused; they do suffer the most serious injuries (Starr, Dubowitz, & Bush, 1990). Abused children are more likely to have been premaritally conceived or unplanned, to have been low in birth weight, to have difficult temperaments, and to suffer from developmental disabilities or mental retardation (Hamilton, Stiles, Melowsky, & Beal, 1987).

The Microsystem

One of the most consistent interaction patterns found in abusing families is a greater proportion of parental negative and aversive behavior toward their family members (Wolfe, 1987). Such aversive behaviors include yelling, threats, arguments, commands, and the reciprocation of negative behavior (Burgess, Anderson, Schellenbach, & Conger, 1981; Wolfe, 1985). The high proportion of negative behavior displayed by abusing parents is largely a result of their very low levels of positive interaction (i.e., low levels of facilitating behavior, tactile stimulation, auditory communication, and positive affect toward their children) (Wolfe, 1985).

Abusing parents tend to be controlling, intrusive, and insensitive to the child's cues, behavior that may actually increase the level of aversive child behavior rather than soothe the child. Alternatively, some abused children are compliant in an attempt to avoid the aversive reaction of the parent (Crittenden, 1988). Understandably, abused children display insecure attachment to their caretakers (Youngblade & Belsky, 1990). Negative interaction is not only directed at the abused child, but is characteristic of the parents' marital relationship as well, which is likely to be high in conflict (Wolfe, 1987). When physical abuse between husband and wife is present, the risk of physical abuse of the child is increased by as much as 150% (Straus & Smith, 1990). Thus child-abusing families are characterized by generally troubled interpersonal relationships (Vondra, 1990).

The Exosystem

The exosystem consists of those factors external to the family that serve either to enhance or debilitate the ability of parents effectively to nurture their children's development. Two exosystem factors consistently emerge: economic stress and a lack of social support. The majority of families reported to child protective services belong to the lowest socioeconomic sectors of our society (Vondra, 1990); this is partially a result of the socioeconomic bias inherent in who is reported to the authorities (Starr et al., 1990). Yet, even representative surveys demonstrate that child abuse does occur more often among families of low socioeconomic status (Straus & Gelles, 1990). The link between abuse and socioeconomic status may be attributed to the frustration and stress that are inherent in the struggle to survive under conditions of poverty and financial hardship (Ammerman, 1990). In addition, lower class families are characterized by authoritarian parenting and punitive discipline practices, which may increase the likelihood of physical punishment (Vondra, 1990).

Inadequate support relationships also characterize the child-abusing family. Although many abusing families have close contact with their families of origin, they are likely to find these relationships stressful and nonreciprocal. Their relationships with friends tend to be short-term and strife-ridden (Crittenden, 1988). Their neighborhoods are socially impoverished, with few connections between neighbors, a higher percentage of vacant housing, and a higher percentage of single-family dwellings (Zuravin, 1989). Abusive parents tend to be isolated from institutional supports such as churches and community centers (Garbarino, 1977). A context that fosters abuse may be present when severe physical punishment is advocated by the social network.

A lack of social support is related to child abuse in two key ways. First, adequate support is associated with increased parental well-being and ability to deal with stress. Such support may even provide "time off" from the parenting relationship if friends, family, and community are available for child care. Second, social support can also serve as a means of social control by providing appropriate role models for parenting and setting limits on parental behavior (Vondra, 1990).

The Macrosystem

Ultimately, in order for any type of abuse to occur in the family, there must be cultural justification for the use of force against family members (Garbarino, 1977). Cultural attitudes have historically supported the parental right to use corporal punishment. The right of parents to raise their children as they see fit is a deeply rooted belief in U.S. culture; children are, after all, the property of their parents (Vondra, 1990). The physical abuse of children is indirectly supported by the cultural norm of family privacy. We are loathe to intervene in private family matters, and may fail to intervene even when a child's life is clearly threatened. Such cultural attitudes, when coupled with social isolation, economic stress, psychological deficits in parents, and dysfunctional family patterns, mitigate against the adequate protection of our children (Garbarino, 1977; Vondra, 1990). Fortunately, the recent judicial trend toward the restriction of "absolute parental rights" may reflect a change in our attitudes toward the importance of intervention in cases of child maltreatment.

Implications of Child Physical Abuse for the Life Course

What is the impact of child abuse on later life? Abused children have a number of cognitive, social, and emotional deficits that are believed to be a result of both their experience of abuse and their development in a dysfunctional, socially impoverished environment (Gelles & Conte, 1990). Maltreated infants are at risk for insecure attachment to their caretakers (Youngblade & Belsky, 1990). Abused children show significantly more behavior problems and social incompetencies, including greater aggression, greater dependency, lower self-esteem, low compliance and persistence, less prosocial behavior with peers, and a tendency to avoid contact with familiar adults (Vondra, 1990; Youngblade & Belsky, 1990). Adults who were physically abused as children may show all or some of the following characteristics: low self-esteem, impaired identity formation, an inability to feel "grown-up," depression, trouble finding pleasure in their lives, anxiety, an increased risk of alcohol abuse, dissociation, somatization and suicidal ideation, and in some cases, borderline or narcissistic personality disorders (Briere & Runtz, 1988a; Steele, 1986).

The notion that "violence begets violence," that is, that those who experienced abuse as children have a greater likelihood of being violent as adults, is one of the most common beliefs about abusing parents (Widom, 1989). There are two components to this "intergenerational transfer hypothesis"—first, abused children will grow up to be violent criminals, and second, abused children will grow up to abuse their own offspring. Widom (1989) concludes that being abused as a child is significantly related to higher rates of violent crimes as an adult, particularly for males. She cautions, however, that the *majority* of abused adults do not have any record of adult crime.

In a comprehensive review of the hypothesis that adults abused as children will repeat the pattern of abuse, Kaufman and Zigler (1987) conclude that the best estimate of the rate of intergenerational transfer is about 30%. Widom (1989) concludes that less than 20% of parents repeat the pattern of abuse. These figures are both heartening and frightening. While clearly the majority of abused children are not doomed to repeat the pattern of abuse, the fact of being the child of a parent who was abused in his or her younger years raises the chances of experiencing maltreatment by as much as tenfold (Gelles & Conte, 1990).

Perhaps the most important question is what *prevents* the intergenerational transmission of abuse. Egeland, Jacobvitz, and Sroufe (1988), in a prospective study, found that mothers who had been abused as children who did not repeat the pattern were likely to report significant emotional support from other adults during childhood, participation in therapy at some point in their lives, and relatively stable, nonabusive, supportive relationships with their mates. Thus socially supportive interpersonal relationships appear to be a key factor in breaking the cycle of abuse.

Sexual Abuse of Children

Sexual abuse of children involves a wide variety of behaviors and perpetrators. In this review, we will concentrate on sexual abuse that is intrafamilial, that is, involving a perpetrator who is related to the child either biologically or through the adoption of a parental or familial role (Wolfe, Wolfe, & Best, 1988). Gelles and Conte (1990) define *sexual abuse* as "forced, tricked, or coerced sexual behavior between a young person and an older person" (p. 1050). Typically, definitions of sexual abuse emphasize the difference in age between perpetrator and victim, and the victim's inability to give consent to the sexual actions due to immaturity, lack of comprehension, or coercion (Wolfe et al., 1988). Sexual abuse may include fondling, oral-genital contact, intercourse, or penetration by an object (Gelles & Conte, 1990).

Official reporting data yield annual incidence figures that are very low: 0.7 to 1.4 per 1,000 children (Wolfe et al., 1988). However, lifetime prevalence figures, which assess whether sexual abuse occurred at some point during childhood, are much higher. Finkelhor, Hotaling, Lewis, and Smith (1990), using a random national sample, found that 6.2% of women and 1.8% of men had experienced childhood sexual abuse. Russell (1988) noted that 16% of women reported one or more incidents of intrafamilial sexual abuse by age 18.

The Ontogenetic Level

At the individual level of analysis, characteristics of the abusers and risk factors for the victims of sexual abuse have been extensively discussed. Upwards of 90% of abusers are male, which holds true for both male and female victims (Gelles & Conte, 1990). Stepfathers are more likely to abuse their daughters than are biological fathers; however, uncles are the most commonly reported perpetrator of sexual abuse (Finkelhor et al., 1990; Russell, 1988).

Sexual abusers may be emotionally immature and low in self-esteem; sexually abusing a child provides a sense of mastery and control. The majority of intrafamilial sexual abusers do not manifest a severe psychiatric problem; however, they are likely to exhibit symptoms of depression, anxiety, passivity, and dependency, as well as high levels of personal stress and alcohol abuse (Finkelhor & Baron, 1986; Williams & Finkelhor, 1990).

Sexual abusers also show signs of problems in their interpersonal relationships. They feel insecure, sexually anxious, lacking in social skills, and they may expect rejection from women (Finkelhor & Baron, 1986). In their family backgrounds, sexual abusers report troubled relationships with their parents, rejection by the father, and physical maltreatment. They may have had sexual contact with an adult early in life that predisposes them to be sexually abusive. Some intrafamilial sexual abusers are characterized by sexual arousal to children (Williams & Finkelhor, 1990).

What characteristics of the child increase the risk of sexual abuse? Females make up 85% of all victims of sexual abuse (Gelles & Conte, 1990). However, the incidence of sexual abuse of males may be vastly underreported, due to the stigma attached to sexual contact between males (Lusk & Waterman, 1986). The high-risk years for the onset of sexual abuse are ages 4 through 9. Socioeconomic status and race have not been found to be risk factors (Wolfe et al., 1988).

The Microsystem

The family system of the sexual abuser and victim is characterized by either rigid or chaotic enmeshment (Trepper & Barrett, 1986). The marital relationship may be distressed, containing high levels of conflict, and at times, wife abuse (Finkelhor & Baron, 1986; Truesdell, McNeil, & Deschner, 1986). Eventually, dysfunctional marital communication may lead to a pattern of avoidance between husband and wife, including an absence of sex (Trepper & Barrett, 1986; Waterman, 1986).

Trepper and Barrett (1986) describe four types of incestuous families. In *father-executive* families, the father is a strong authority figure, and the mother is emotionally or physically absent. As a result, the victimized daughter reverses roles with the mother. In *mother-executive* families, the mother is the sole executive. The father functions as one of the children; his sexual needs are met by a daughter who functions as a "generational peer." In the *third-generation* pattern, the mother acts as a grandparent, parenting the father and remaining removed from the children. In the *chaotic* family, there is no executive parent, and few boundaries/rules exist between parents and children.

Sexually abused daughters often report a poor relationship with their mothers, one that is characterized by either harsh, cold, and punitive parenting or by rejection and withdrawal (Finkelhor & Baron, 1986).

Sexually abusing males appear to lack a capacity for empathy with children; although they on the one hand enjoy a "special relationship" with the victim, this relationship is not a nurturing one (Williams & Finkelhor, 1990).

Several environmental characteristics of the family microsystem are related to intrafamilial sexual abuse. Sexual abuse may begin during a period of particularly high stress for the father (Finkelhor & Baron, 1986). The physical absence of the mother may serve to heighten the abuser's feelings of sexual deprivation, and may serve to decrease the likelihood of detection (Tierney & Corwin, 1983). Furthermore, environmental factors that make the child available to the abuser (such as crowded living arrangements, or the abuser being left to supervise the child) may enhance the possibility of abuse (Faller, 1990). Abusers may justify their sexual interaction with a victim in terms of educating her about sex, protecting her from sexual interaction with other males, or with the notion that the victim is "mature" enough to handle sexual interaction (Frude, 1982).

The Exosystem

In contrast to the physical abuse of children, social class does not appear to be related to the incidence of sexual abuse. Representative surveys indicate that there is no increase in prevalence of sexual abuse as a function of income or educational level of the perpetrator (Wolfe et al., 1988).

The social isolation of both the perpetrator and victim of sexual abuse emerges consistently in the literature. Sexually abusing fathers report few friends and few contacts with organizations (Williams & Finkelhor, 1990). Victims of sexual abuse also report few friends and little involvement in extracurricular school activities (Finkelhor & Baron, 1986). This isolation increases the opportunity for sexual abuse, since the family is afforded privacy, as well as decreases the probability of detection and the social inhibitions against sexual abuse, as outsiders are less likely to know of its occurrence (Frude, 1982).

The Macrosystem

The cultural attitudes that support the sexual abuse of children are particularly interesting since these attitudes are in direct conflict with the nearly universal "incest taboo." Although there are strong prohibitions against sexual contact between biological relatives, parental "ownership" of children and the right of family privacy contribute to a sociocultural milieu that fails to prevent sexual abuse (Faller, 1990). In addition, our cultural attitudes concerning patriarchy and sexuality contribute to the problem. Males are socialized to view themselves as authorities over women and children; other family members are to provide both sexual and domestic services to males (Breines & Gordon, 1983). In essence, patriarchy may give men "permission" to behave as they wish with their daughters (stepdaughters, nieces, etc). Several features of male sexual socialization may serve to reduce the incest taboo: males are socialized to see heterosexual success as highly important to their concept of masculinity, to remove sexuality from the context of a relationship (and instead to focus on sexual acts), to express dependency needs through sexuality, and to choose sexual partners who are smaller and younger than themselves (Finkelhor, 1982). These socialization patterns may particularly contribute to the sexual abuse of children at the hands of stepfathers and uncles, for whom the incest taboo is already weaker.

Implications of Childhood Sexual Abuse for the Life Course

The experience of childhood sexual abuse, particularly intrafamilial abuse, has serious consequences. In the short term, the sexually abused child demonstrates emotional consequences including fear, guilt, anger, hostility, shame, depression, a sense of powerlessness, feelings of grief and loss, and a sense of stigma (Browne & Finkelhor, 1986; Conte & Berliner, 1988). Sexual abuse takes a physical toll, as abused children are often noted to have changes in sleep patterns, increased nightmares, bed-wetting, and higher levels of somatic complaints (Mannarino & Cohen, 1986). The abused child may display inappropriate sexual behavior with adults and peers, including public masturbation, sexual curiosity, and exposure of the genitals (Browne & Finkelhor, 1986). Socially, the sexual abuse victim may exhibit increased aggressiveness, truancy, suicide attempts, isolation from friends, substance abuse, running away behavior, teenage pregnancy, and early marriage (Browne & Finkelhor, 1986; Butler & Burton, 1990; Singer, Petchers, & Hussey, 1989).

Adults who were sexually abused as children display greater incidence of depression, suicide attempts, dissociative symptoms, negative self-concept, symptoms of post-traumatic stress disorder, and bulimia (Briere & Runtz, 1988b; Bulik, Sullivan, & Rorty, 1989; Greenwald & Leitenberg, 1990). Interpersonally, female victims report difficulty in close relationships, fear of men, hostility toward their mothers, problems in parenting their own children, marital unhappiness, marital violence, and problems of sexual adjustment in adulthood (Browne & Finkelhor, 1986; Cole & Woogler, 1989; Wolfe et al., 1988). Male victims report fear of homosexuality, lower psychological adjustment, feelings of shame and self-blame, and self-destructive behavior (Mey, 1988).

Males who have experienced sexual abuse as children appear to have a heightened risk of becoming sexually abusing as adults (Mey, 1988). Yet, only about 20% of those abused as children will in turn become sexually abusive (Williams & Finkelhor, 1990). Females have a heightened risk of further sexual victimization as an adult, including increased risk of rape (Russell, 1988).

The impact of sexual abuse is mediated by characteristics of the child and family. More severe consequences of abuse are noted for older victims, longer duration of abuse, more severe sexual activity (e.g., intercourse versus fondling), multiple perpetrators, and a close relationship between abuser and victim (Conte & Berliner, 1988). The reaction of family and community to the disclosure of the abuse has a powerful impact; cases wherein the child is not believed, the nonabusing parent reacts negatively, and intervention is traumatic show worse outcomes for the child (Browne & Finkelhor, 1986). One of the more important factors in reducing the negative impact of sexual abuse appears to be the support of the nonabusing parent and siblings (Conte & Berliner, 1988).

Abuse in Courtship

Both physical and sexual abuse in courtship have been extensively studied. *Physical abuse* has been defined as "the use or threat of physical force or restraint carried out with the intention of causing pain or injury to another" (Sugarman & Hotaling, 1989, p. 4). The first study of physical abuse in courtship among college students reported a rate of 21% (Makepeace, 1981). Stets and Henderson (1991), using a nationally representative sample, found that 30% reported behaving abusively and 31% reported being the recipient of abuse during the past 12 months.

Reports of acquaintance or date rape (intercourse with a dating partner that occurs due to threats or force) range from 15% to 28% (Lane & Gwartney-Gibbs, 1985; Muehlenhard & Linton, 1987). When the definition is expanded to include other types of forced sexual contact, 50% to 75% of women report some type of sexual aggression in a dating relationship (Burke, Stets, & Pirog-Good, 1988; Muehlenhard & Linton, 1987).

Physical injuries (viz., bruises, black eyes, cuts, internal injuries, and unconsciousness) occur in three fourths of acquaintance rapes (Belknap, 1989).

The Ontogenetic Level

Although many research studies have examined the role of individual-level factors in physical abuse in courtship, as of yet no clear profile of abusers or victims has emerged. Some studies do find a significant relationship between sex role orientation and the male perpetration of physical abuse in courtship; however, there is some debate as to whether the male perpetrator is high in femininity or masculinity (J. L. Bernard, Bernard, & Bernard, 1985; Burke et al., 1988). Similarly, self-esteem is an inconsistent risk marker for physical abuse (Sugarman & Hotaling, 1989). The evidence on life stress events (e.g., being fired from a job, financial problems) is more consistent, with stress being related to an increased incidence of physical abuse in courtship (Makepeace, 1983).

The literature on sexual abuse in courtship does provide a fairly clear profile of the male abuser. Sexually abusive males tend to hold traditional beliefs about women, view their dating relationships as adversarial, and believe in rape-supportive myths (Koss, 1988; Muehlenhard & Linton, 1987). They also exhibit greater physiological arousal to rape scenarios, greater acceptance of physical violence, greater hostility toward women, and may use sex as a means of expressing anger or dominance (Burkhart & Stanton, 1988; Malamuth, 1981). However, female victims of sexual abuse in courtship differ very little from female nonvictims. There are no differences in self-esteem or other attitudinal or personality factors including assertiveness, feminist ideology, or belief in rape-supportive myths (Koss & Dinero, 1989).

Finally, there is some support for the intergenerational transfer hypothesis. Several studies report a relationship between premarital physical abuse and either experiencing child abuse or witnessing parental violence (G. Barnes, Greenwood, & Sommer, 1991; DeMaris, 1990; B. C. Emery, 1983). Recent studies on sexual aggression in dating relationships have also documented the link for females between child sexual abuse and later sexual victimization in a dating relationship (Lundberg-Love & Geffner, 1989).

The Microsystem

The precipitators of physical and sexual abuse include jealousy, anger, frustration, and sexual denial (B. C. Emery, Lloyd, & Castleton, 1989; Makepeace, 1981). J. M. Henton, Cate, Koval, Lloyd, and Christopher (1983) further note that aggressors and victims attribute physical abuse to confusion, anger, love, fear, and sadness. Physical abuse is more likely to occur once relationships have reached the serious stage or cohabitation; the risk of physical abuse increases with the length of the relationship (Cate, Henton, Koval, Christopher, & Lloyd, 1982; Stets & Pirog-Good, 1989). Similarly, sexual aggression is more likely to occur in long-term versus casual relationships; rape in particular is likely to occur at the hands of a well-known assailant rather than an acquaintance (Belknap, 1989).

Partners in physically abusive courtships exhibit more negative affect, conflict, verbal aggression, indirect styles of negotiation (i.e., withdrawal or crying), confrontation, blaming the partner, and expression of anger (Billingham & Sack, 1987; Bird, Stith, & Schladale, 1991; Lloyd, Koval, & Cate, 1989). These partners are also distinguished by their use of persistence as a negotiation strategy, high investment in the relationship, and the belief that the partner can be changed (Lloyd et al., 1989). Miscommunication about sexuality is cited as a risk factor for sexual aggression. Males tend to view females' behavior as more "sexual" than do females, which may result in the misinterpretation of petting as a signal that the female desires intercourse. The result is that males may feel that "she led me on" (Muehlenhard & Linton, 1987).

Men may use physical abuse to maintain their control over their partners and get their own way or as a tactic of intimidation and "striking fear" into the partner. Women, on the other hand, may resort to violence to regain some control over the abusive situation and the relationship, or in retaliation, self defense, anger, and frustration (B. C. Emery et al., 1989; Follingstad, Wright, Lloyd, & Sebastian, 1991; Sugarman & Hotaling, 1989). Sexual aggression is also viewed as a result of the power imbalance existing between men and women (Lundberg-Love & Geffner, 1989). Specifically, sexual aggression has been associated with male attempts to dominate, change, and impose one's will on the partner (Stets & Pirog-Good, 1990).

The Exosystem

A fundamental exosystem factor is the social support networks of dating couples and individuals. Victims and perpetrators of physical and sexual abuse are likely to be isolated or to perceive little benefit in disclosing their abuse. Most physical and sexual abuse occurs in private; even when others are present, intervention occurs in less than 50% of the incidents (Makepeace, 1981). Victims of abuse in courtship tell of their experience infrequently. When they do it is usually to friends, then parents, and lastly, teachers, counselors, physicians, or police (B. C. Emery, 1983; Koss, 1988). Social networks must also be acknowledged for their role in influencing the norms surrounding physical abuse and sexual aggression. Males who engage in physical and sexual abuse in courtship have been found to have peer groups that support or encourage the physical and sexual abuse of women (DeKeseredy, 1988). Thus physical and sexual abuse may be supported by the prevailing norms of the social network.

The Macrosystem

At the broadest level we must examine the values and belief systems that support sexual aggression and the use of physical violence in dating relationships. Physical abuse may be "legitimized" by the context; in particular, abuse is viewed as more legitimate when the perpetrator reports high levels of stress, when the abusive behavior is seen as "not too severe," and when the female initiates the abuse (B. Emery, Cate, Henton, & Andrews, 1988).

The romantic ideal (viz., love conquers all, love is blind, etc.) allows violence and sexual aggression to be downplayed and forgiven by attributing those behaviors to external factors rather than to flaws in the relationship itself (Billingham & Sack, 1987; J. M. Henton et al., 1983). Romanticism, then, acts as a constraining factor in courtship by encouraging couples to remain together regardless of negative interaction patterns (Lloyd, 1991). Burkhart and Stanton (1988) stress the role of patriarchy in both physical and sexual aggression in courtship. Men are socialized to be the aggressor in a culture that simultaneously maintains standards that emphasize his need for sex and sexual conquest, whereas women are socialized to be victims through societal emphasis on attractiveness, submissiveness, and passivity.

Implications of Abuse in Courtship for the Life Course

On a short-term basis, studies of physical abuse report that reactions vary from emotions such as anger and fear to responding with physical abuse itself (B. C. Emery et al., 1989; Follingstad et al., 1991). Reactions to sexual aggression and rape include anger, fear, sexual distress, and depression (Kilpatrick, Best, Saunders, & Vernon, 1988). Research has also revealed long-term effects of courtship abuse. B. C. Emery et al. (1989) found that women who had experienced physical abuse were wary of partners who tried to control them, had a "check list" of characteristics to avoid in potential partners, and were reluctant to trust males again. They reported either developing stronger self-concepts as a result of dealing with the abuse or harboring feelings of cheapness and embarrassment along with low self-concepts. In a study of the long-term impact of rape by a date, Kilpatrick et al. (1988) note symptoms of major depression, social phobia, and sexual dysfunction.

Does the experience of abuse in courtship predispose individuals to inflict or sustain such behavior in marital relationships as well? Recent longitudinal work by O'Leary et al. (1989) clearly confirms the carryover of abuse in courtship to the marriage.

Abuse in Marriage

Abuse in marriage can take many forms, from coercion and intimidation to beatings to rape. *Spouse abuse* is defined as the victimization of the spouse through physical violence, sexual aggression, verbal threats, and/or psychological degradation or intimidation (Geffner & Pagelow, 1990). Physical and sexual abuse in marriage are alarmingly prevalent. In the 1985 National Family Violence Survey, Straus and Gelles (1990) found the incidence of physical violence (including slap, push, kick, punch, beat, stab, threaten or use a weapon) to be 16.1%, or one out of every six married couples. Severe violence (kick, punch, hit with an object, beat, stab, threaten or use a weapon) occurred in 6.3% of couples. These figures may be twice as high among separated and divorced couples (Frieze & Browne, 1989).

The rate of sexual abuse in marriage is also high; Russell (1982) found that 14% of her sample reported marital rape or other forced sexual interaction, and Finkelhor and Yllo (1985) reported prevalences of marital rape of 10% in intact couples and 25% in divorced couples. About half of all marital rapes involve physical abuse as well (Frieze & Browne, 1989).

The Ontogenetic Level

Numerous investigations have examined the individual characteristics of both the abusing husband and the abused wife. Abusers are characterized as immature, dependent, and insecure (Dutton, 1988). Although they may value the traditional masculine model of "manhood," they feel inadequate in living up to the model. Abusers are also characterized by low levels of assertion with the spouse, alcohol abuse, low self-image, rigidity, conservatism, and high levels of stress (Hotaling & Sugarman, 1986; G. Kantor & Straus, 1990; Rosenbaum & Maiuro, 1990). The intergenerational transmission of violence, in particular witnessing parental marital violence, is associated with males' use of violent behavior in their own marriages (Rosenbaum & Maiuro, 1990).

There are several factors that raise the risk that the wife will experience abuse. The most consistent risk factor is having witnessed violence between parents; this may serve to legitimize her husband's use of force and make her less likely to resist or leave (Hotaling & Sugarman, 1986). Other risk factors include traditional sex role socialization (which may condition her to accept male domination), immaturity, and low self-esteem (Geffner & Pagelow, 1990). Abused wives report both objective dependency (i.e., they are less likely to be working and are more likely to have young children) and subjective dependency (i.e., they feel they would be hurt by the loss of the relationship) on their husbands (Kalmuss & Straus, 1990).

The Microsystem

Spouse-abusing couples report very discordant marital interaction. They are characterized by high levels of conflict, poor communication, marital dissatisfaction, inequality, and violence toward the children (D. Coleman & Straus, 1990; Hotaling & Sugarman, 1986; Margolin, John, & O'Brien, 1989). Abusive husbands may be controlling and extremely jealous, monitoring where and with whom their wives interact (Frieze & Browne, 1989). These husbands fear abandonment by their wives and may react with anger at any attempt to create emotional distance (Dutton, 1988).

In marital communication, abusive husbands display greater levels of negative interaction, high levels of defensiveness and hostility, and a pattern of attempted withdrawal from conflict (Margolin, John, & Gleberman, 1988). They are characterized by more nonconstructive approaches to conflict (including verbal attack, anger, and withdrawal) and fewer constructive approaches (such as negotiation and initiating a problem-solving discussion). Rather than letting minor arguments drop without a resolution, abusive couples may strive to reach resolution of all disagreements (Lloyd, 1990). Overall, marital interaction in the abusive marriage is characterized as enmeshed, nonspontaneous, volatile, and unpredictable (Lloyd, 1988; Margolin et al., 1989).

Stets (1988) conceptualizes physical abuse in marriage as a tactic of control. The wife's refusal to comply with her husband's demands is often perceived by the husband as a challenge to his right to control her actions. Such a challenge is likely to be met with a show of physical force, since the consequences to him for using violence are minimal. Because she is unable to fight back effectively, his wife is likely to submit to his will, may even forgive his abuse, or take the blame upon herself.

The Exosystem

Two exosystem factors have consistently been linked to the occurrence of abuse in marriage. First, unemployment and low income may contribute to family stress, which heightens the possibility of abuse in marriage, especially in marriages where dysfunctional interaction patterns already exist (Hotaling & Sugarman, 1986). In addition, the economic dependence of an abused wife upon her husband may make leaving the abusive situation nearly impossible (Kalmuss & Straus, 1990).

Second, these couples are isolated from support systems (relatives, friends, community organizations), which further exacerbates the impact of stress and hinders family members from seeking help (Dutton, 1988). Communities play a key role through their response to abuse; in some cases, local custom may serve to keep the abused wife in her marriage. Law enforcement officials may hesitate to intervene or prosecute cases of domestic violence, and other service providers may actively discourage an abused wife from seeking outside help. This lack of intervention can have serious consequences, resulting in further severe abuse or murder (Geffner & Pagelow, 1990).

The Macrosystem

Abuse is so prevalent in marriage that Straus (1977) coined the phrase, "the marriage license is a hitting license." Why is it that physical and sexual abuse in marriage are so much more acceptable than the same actions directed at a stranger? In addition to being legitimized by the norms of family privacy and the permissibility of violence against loved ones, spouse abuse is affected by our fundamental notions about men and women in marriage (Breines & Gordon, 1983). The tradition of patriarchal control of marital decisions and resources gives the man the right to use the ultimate resource (violence/coercion) to enact that control. In a society that places overriding emphasis on the importance of marriage to women's self-identity, the notion that "any man is better than no man" serves to constrain women to remain in an abusive situation (Lloyd, 1991). The problem of spouse abuse is further exacerbated by the fact that intervention is less likely in cases where the victim is an adult (and therefore able to help herself) versus a child (and therefore helpless).

Implications of Abuse in Marriage for the Life Course

The most immediate impact of spouse abuse is fear, followed by helplessness, confusion, isolation, and humiliation (Geffner & Pagelow, 1990). Because the victimization is repeated, and since there is a close relationship between abuser and victim, the abused wife may respond much like a hostage or torture victim, eventually identifying with and becoming bonded to the abuser (Dutton, 1988). As time progresses, abused wives may show high levels of anxiety, depression, stress-induced illness, and suicide attempts, as well as symptoms of posttraumatic stress disorder (Geffner & Pagelow, 1990).

The life course implications of abuse in marriage touch the children who witness the abuse as well. As previously noted, some children who witness marital abuse will repeat the pattern in their own marriages (Rosenbaum & Maiuro, 1990). However, the impact of witnessing violence extends well beyond intergenerational transmission. Children who have witnessed the abuse of their mothers display more behavior problems, particularly aggression, immaturity, and hyperactivity, poor social skills with peers, and difficulty coping with negative emotions (Jouriles, Murphy, & O'Leary, 1989). Overall, the evidence is mounting that growing up in an abusive, discordant atmosphere has serious implications for future interpersonal functioning.

Abuse of the Elderly

Mistreatment of the elderly can be classified into two basic types: neglect and abuse. *Passive neglect* is defined as the unintentional failure to provide assistance for the elder; for example, isolation or not providing health services. *Active neglect* is the intentional failure to provide adequate care and services; for example, withholding food or medication, failing to provide personal care, or using physical restraints or excessive medication (Douglass, 1988; Hickey & Douglass, 1981). Physical abuse entails acts such as slaps, burns, scratches, whippings, and beatings (Kimsey, Tarbox, & Bragg, 1981; Pillemer & Finkelhor, 1988). While usually occurring less frequently than other types of abuse or neglect, the consequences of physical abuse are obviously more severe and more easily detected (Steinmetz & Amsden, 1983).

Estimates of the incidence of elder abuse that are based on representative community surveys find that from 3.2% to 4% of elderly individuals in this country are severely abused or neglected by family members annually (M. Block & Sinnott, 1979; Pillemer & Finkelhor, 1988). Other estimates of the rate of abuse, which are based on nonrepresentative surveys of professionals and care providers, are much higher. For example, Kosberg (1983) indicates that the lifetime prevalence rate of elder abuse by family members is 25%. Unfortunately, only one sixth of these cases come to the attention of the authorities (Goldstein, 1989).

The Ontogenetic Level

Many studies have identified characteristics of both abusers and victims that contribute to the abuse of the elderly. Some researchers emphasize that the perpetrator of elder abuse is typically a female adult child (Quinn & Tomita, 1986; Steinmetz, 1981), reflecting the fact that the overwhelming majority of caregivers of the elderly are female in the first place (Brubaker, 1990b). However, Pillemer and Finkelhor (1988), using a random survey of adults, have found that abusers are more likely to be spouses than adult children. Such spouse abuse among the elderly may be a continuation of abuse that has occurred throughout the duration of the marriage, or it may be of recent origin, arising from increasing dependence of the victim and caregiving demands.

Personal characteristics of abusers may include psychiatric problems or mental illness, alcohol and drug use, witnessing violence in one's family of origin, a lack of understanding of adult development and aging, and a lack of caregiving skills (Lau & Kosberg, 1979; Pillemer & Suitor, 1988; Rathbone-McCuan, 1980). The abuser of an elderly family member may be under a considerable amount of mental, emotional, and/or financial stress as the result of caregiving demands that inhibit the ability to provide adequate care (Hickey & Douglass, 1981; Steinmetz & Amsden, 1983). The financial responsibilities and needs of two generations as well as the strain on the value systems (i.e., should caregivers place their priorities with the elder or with children who may still need their support) create a potential crisis situation (Steinmetz, 1983).

Women over 75 years of age who reside with relatives are the most likely victims of elder abuse. However, some research indicates that males are at twice the risk for abuse, a risk that is masked by the comparatively small numbers of elderly males. Since elderly males have a greater tendency to remarry or live with family, they may be at greater risk through their increased dependence on spouses and family members for care (Douglass, 1988; Pillemer & Finkelhor, 1988). The vulnerable elderly (those with advanced age, frailty, chronic disease, and physical or mental impairment) are likely to be abused or neglected. Thus the greatest risk lies with those least capable of independent living (Lau & Kosberg, 1979; Steinmetz, 1983).

As a final note, the issue of dependency is not nearly as clear cut as it initially appears. Although many studies emphasize the elder's dependency on the abuser (Rathbone-McCuan, 1980; Steinmetz & Amsden, 1983), at least one investigation has found that abusers were likely to be dependent on the elder in a variety of areas, particularly financially (Pillemer, 1985). As with other forms of family abuse, abuse of the elderly may reflect a dynamic of mutual dependency and enmeshed relationships.

The Microsystem

The family dynamics of elder abuse, more so than any other type of family abuse, are affected by the long history of interaction between abuser and victim. Steinmetz (1983) purports that when the elder becomes dependent on the adult child, dramatic changes in relationships take place. Roles are reversed, thereby altering the complex, generationally based set of responsibilities, obligations, and rights. These changes may bring relationship issues such as unresolved conflicts out into the open. If parent and child have conflicts from the past that have not been settled, then there is a greater potential for abuse to occur (J. Henton, Cate, & Emery, 1984).

Power conflicts between the elder and family members may also contribute to the occurrence of abuse (J. Henton et al., 1984; Pillemer & Suitor, 1988). The elderly family member may be unwilling to relinquish power and control over other family members, thereby creating scenes, throwing temper tantrums, or becoming abusive themselves. For caregivers who are faced with the increasing stresses of caregiving or spiraling noncompliance on the part of the elder, the use of violence may be a method of last resort in order to maintain control (Quinn & Tomita, 1986). Caregivers may also respond by withholding food, use of physical restraints, or excessive medication, to make the elder more manageable (Hickey & Douglass, 1981).

Finally, since elderly individuals usually have money and own material goods and property, they are in a unique situation (as compared to other types of family abuse) for potential exploitation. Elders may suffer the illegal or unethical exploitation of their assets, and they may be denied the right to read their own mail, go where they wish, remain in their own homes, or conduct their own affairs (Douglass, 1988; Quinn & Tomita, 1986).

The Exosystem

It is apparent that both the elder and the caregiver have or perceive few social and economic resources available to them to ease the stress of familial care of the elderly. Douglass and Hickey (1983) identify "at risk" elderly as less conscious of alternative living arrangements or means of support than others their own age. J. Henton et al. (1984) discuss the importance of considering issues such as financial and physical resources, and length of care before assuming the care for an elderly family member. Virtually all research emphasizes the need for the development of support systems for both the abused elder and the caregiver in terms of assessment of abuse, counseling, prevention, intervention, and social policy (Hogan, 1990; Pillemer & Suitor, 1988).

Structural changes in the family during the 20th century may also have contributed to the abuse of the elderly. Historically, the trend has been toward smaller families, which leaves fewer potential family caregivers for the elderly population. In addition, the increase in divorce and subsequent remarriage has significantly blurred the lines of obligation to elder family members. The responsibility for an elderly parent under conditions of few alternative caregivers, low resources, and blurred responsibility may precipitate the use of abuse (J. Henton et al., 1984).

The Macrosystem

Several sociocultural attitudes have been identified as influencing the probability of elder abuse. *Ageism* is a negative attitude toward the elderly that portrays elders as senile, lonely, unproductive, and ill. Ageism contributes to elder abuse by devaluing the elderly, leaving the impression that they deserve the abuse (J. Henton et al., 1984). Since the majority of elder abuse victims are female, sexism is another important issue to address. The fact that women have little power and are encouraged to maintain passive roles allows them to internalize negative perceptions of females and see themselves as useless (Quinn & Tomita, 1986). As a result, they become targets for abuse.

Implications of Elder Abuse for the Life Course

Abuse and neglect of the elderly may result in a failure to thrive syndrome that is characterized by malnutrition, dehydration, abnormal blood chemistry values, and pressure sores (Quinn & Tomita, 1986). Data suggest that abuse causes loss of dignity, lowered feelings of self-worth, and regression into senility (Hickey & Douglass, 1981; Kimsey et al., 1981).

In general, the pattern of abuse can be expected to continue unless there is intervention. Unlike abused children who eventually grow up and leave their abusive environments, the abused elderly tend to remain in this situation. Their dependency can only increase, creating more stress for the abuser and victim and reducing the alternatives for care. Many times the abuser is the only thing standing between the elder and a nursing home, an alternative so distasteful that the elderly individual perceives the abuse to be the lesser of two evils (Quinn & Tomita, 1986).

Frequently, decisions to take in an elderly relative are made under conditions of haste and great stress. Families may not have all the facts they need to make effective decisions. For example, the elderly may not continue to qualify for financial assistance and benefits after moving in with the family, placing additional strain on their resources (J. Henton et al., 1984; Steinmetz, 1983). Therefore, the need to make a informed decision to care for elderly members is essential, as the consequences of familial care for the elderly can be overwhelming.

Implications for Intervention

Physical and sexual abuse of family members are serious problems that have far reaching consequences. Their impact extends to all aspects of interpersonal functioning, affecting both current and future relationships between parent and child, boyfriend and girlfriend, husband and wife, and adult child and aging parent. Programs need to be developed on three levels: primary (prevention of negative relationship interaction, to be targeted toward all individuals), secondary (interventions with target high-risk groups), and tertiary (treatment for individuals already in abusive relationships) (Lloyd, 1991).

Primary intervention encompasses education and skills training. At the core of primary prevention is the notion that education can counteract the negative influences that may produce the dysfunctional behavior in the first place (Newman & Lutzker, 1990). Thus primary intervention into the problem of family abuse is essentially family life education—the provision of family members with the requisite skills of interaction that are necessary for effective familial and interpersonal relationships. This education must occur on multiple levels, and might include education of parents in child management techniques, conflict management skills for courting and married couples, sexual communication skills for adolescents, and stress management skills for all family members. Ultimately, under an ecological framework, primary intervention would also include education for the community at large on the importance of community support, as well as the dangers of failing to challenge the current belief systems that inadvertently support family abuse. In addition, effective prevention of family abuse must include strategies for changing the nature of male-female relationships, from a pattern of patriarchy to one of equality (Lloyd, 1991).

Secondary intervention would target education/counseling for high-risk groups. A group considered to be "high risk" for family abuse includes those who have witnessed or experienced physical and/or sexual abuse as a child (and thus who are "at risk" for repetition of the pattern of dysfunction). In addition, families currently experiencing high levels of financial stress, and families who are isolated from potent support systems could be targeted for services. One way of accessing such high-risk groups is through the training of "gatekeepers" or natural helpers (friends, neighbors, postal workers, teachers, etc.) to recognize signs of potentially abusive situations (Hooyman, 1983).

Tertiary intervention focuses on working with individuals currently involved in relationships characterized by physical or sexual abuse. After the identification of such individuals, many programs and services may be appropriate and necessary. Domestic violence shelters, rape crisis hot-lines and programs, child protective services, and safe homes for the abused elderly are all examples of crisis intervention services that have been developed for victims of family abuse. It is important to note that intervention must be provided for both victims and abusers alike if the abuse is to be halted and psychological consequences minimized (B. Emery et al., 1988).

Ultimately, one of the key answers to breaking the pattern of abuse that plagues so many families is the presence of alternate support relationships. For the child or adult involved in the abusive situation, the support received from a significant other can make all the difference (Egeland et al., 1988). Our willingness to reach out to those who are at risk of abuse, as well as those currently experiencing abuse, is at once elegantly simple and frighteningly complex in a society that values family privacy and individual achievement over community support.

9

Resiliency in Families

The Role of Family Schema and Appraisal in
Family Adaptation to Crises

HAMILTON I. McCUBBIN
MARILYN A. McCUBBIN
ANNE I. THOMPSON

With the wealth of observations and data collected longitudinally on American families involved in the vicissitudes of war (H. McCubbin, Dahl, & Hunter, 1975, 1976; H. McCubbin, Dahl, Metres, Hunter, & Plag, 1974), we discovered and explored resiliency in families with an eye toward identifying those family properties and processes that promoted family endurance, coping, and survival.

These seemingly incompatible topics of resiliency and war's cata-strophic impact on families bring to mind the foundation and roots of family stress theory, which has evolved over the past four decades with major spurts of theory building emerging in the context of war-induced family research. World War II served as the key stimulus for Reuben Hill's (1949) ABCX Family Crisis Model. Vietnam and its impact on families stimulated the development of the Double ABCX Model of Adjustment and Adaptation (H. McCubbin & Patterson, 1983) and the Resiliency Model of Family Stress, Adjustment, and Adaptation (M.

AUTHORS' NOTE: This chapter was originally presented as the Diane Huber Lecture as part of the Family and Child Studies Lecture Series, Miami University, Oxford, OH.

153

McCubbin & McCubbin, 1991, 1992). In all of these theory building efforts family appraisal emerged as being of central importance to the processes of family adjustment in the face of a stressor (Burr, 1973; Hill, 1949), and family adaptation in the face of a crisis situation (H. McCubbin & Patterson, 1983; M. McCubbin & McCubbin, 1991, 1992). In the situation of family crises, where the family's established patterns of family functioning are challenged and new or instituted patterns are called for to achieve a satisfactory level of family adaptation, the family's schema as presented in Figure 9.1, the third or global level of appraisal gains unique importance. In this chapter we will expand upon our understanding of family schema, establish propositions of the relationship between family schema and family functioning, and by drawing from case study observations from the families under the stress of war describe the complex interface and interaction between family schema and functioning. Finally, we will apply the construction of family appraisal to the study of ethnic families and their functioning as an additional examination of the efficacy of family schema in family stress theory.

Family Appraisal Schema and Its Components

In this chapter we are stimulated to reexamine the family's ability to appraise and frame a major catastrophe—war and its extreme consequences of loss and death—into a shared sense of purpose and opportunity that in turn serves as a solid foundation, a compass and road map, if you will, for changes in family system functioning, coping, and adaptation. This appraisal component of resiliency in families, which we labeled *family schema,* encompasses the family's shared values, goals, priorities, expectations, and worldview (M. McCubbin & McCubbin, 1992). In the face of a crisis, which we define as a situation demanding changes in the family's established patterns of functioning (Hanson & Johnson, 1979; H. McCubbin & McCubbin, 1988; H. McCubbin, Thompson, Pirner, & McCubbin, 1988) the family unit is called upon to appraise its past and its future in shaping the new or instituted patterns of functioning as well as the specific coping behaviors and strategies that they will employ to manage the crisis situation. We believe that families hold a set of beliefs, values, goals, priorities, and expectations—which we call a family schema—about themselves in relationship to each other, and about their family in relationship to the community and the social system beyond its boundaries.

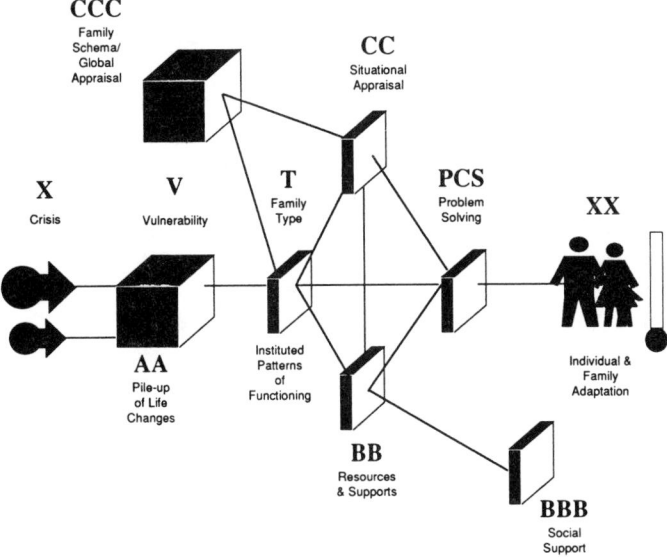

Figure 9.1. Outline of the Resiliency Model of Family Stress, Adjustment, and Adaptation Focus on Family Schema

Our conceptualization about this global level of family appraisal has been shaped by the insightful work of David Reiss and his colleagues (Reiss, 1981; Reiss & Oliveri, 1980), who have emphasized the importance of family paradigms in the stress process, and by other theorists concerned primarily about individual responses to stress, who have emphasized the central importance of global orientations, as in the concept of coherence (Antonovsky, 1979), individual hardiness (Kobasa, Maddi, & Kahn, 1982), family hardiness (M. McCubbin, 1990) and resiliency (H. McCubbin & McCubbin, 1988). The hierarchical ordering of levels (stressor specific, situational, and global) of appraisal in the context of the family system was conceptualized, discussed, and initially tested through a LISREL analysis (Lavee, McCubbin, & Patterson, 1985) in the study of military families faced with the threat of war. Clearly, from our perspective a third pervasive level of family appraisal that we refer to as family schema is involved in the process of family adaptation.

A family schema is conceptualized as consisting of several important dimensions, shared values, and goals, a sense of family collectivity, identity, and mutual expectations. Within the overriding framework of values, goals, and expectations family schema encompasses important components of family unity and commitment that are critical to family adaptation. In Table 9.1 we outline a range of possibilities of the underlying components of family schema, realizing that the elements may vary from family to family and be prioritized differently for families from different cultures and of different races, particularly in response to family crises.

Families who reveal their schema tend to emphasize their investment in themselves, their values and goals, their investment in the family's collective "we" rather than "I," their sense of shared influence, trust in others, as well as their optimistic view of life situations complemented by a relativistic view of life circumstances and willingness to accept optimal rather than perfect solutions to all their demands (M. McCubbin & McCubbin, 1992).

The family schema, unlike other constructs of the resiliency model (e.g., vulnerability, pile-up, resources) is relatively stable for the most part because it is used as a point of reference, a guide or standard, against which situational and stressor level appraisals are compared and shaped. As already noted (M. McCubbin & McCubbin, 1991, 1992), we believe that the family schema is also more enduring than situational appraisals (Level 2) and stressor appraisals (Level 1) because it encompasses the family's shared values, goals, and internal sense of identity and expectations.

Under drastic conditions, the family schema can be reshaped and remolded in response to modifications the family makes in their established patterns of functioning to cope with a crisis situation. Generally, the family schema is the family systems' road map that serves to guide the family's definition of a stressor, shape the family's appraisal of the stressful situation, and formulate the family's paradigm for coping with a crisis situation. It is a compass that sets the agreed upon course or direction for the family in an effort to achieve shared family goals, ensure adherence to shared family values, and meet shared family expectations, particularly while managing family system changes in a crisis situation.

Family schema incorporates the family's shared beliefs, standards, and priorities, which are also critical to guide the family's efforts in changing its patterns of functioning while preserving the family's integrity, identity, and esteem in the process.

Table 9.1. Possible Basic Underlying Components of Family Schema

Shared Family Values
Education
Peace
Spiritual beliefs
Security and stability
Family integrity and unity
Physical and emotional health
Independence and autonomy
Work and employment
Respect for and care of ill members
Respect for and care of elder members
Respect for government and laws
Respect for persons of different races

Shared Family Goals
Education for all members
Financial security
Members in good social standing
Home or family dwelling
Promotion of health for all members
Self-sufficiency of members

Shared Family Expectations
Harmony in the family
Shared power and decision making
Resolution of conflicts
Having a network of socially supportive relationships
Mutual support of family members
Mutual respect of family members
Promotion of independence of family members
Commitment to family unity
Relativism in decision making
Distribution of family tasks and responsibilities
Flexibility in rules and expectations
Open communication

In the process of changing its established patterns of functioning, (i.e., getting a second job, spouse employed, change in routines, etc.) the family may also add to or modify its values, goals, or expectations, or it may alter the relative weight it attaches to these values, goals, and expectations. In so doing, the family unit legitimates and gives credence and meaning to the changes in the family's patterns of functioning and behavior. Out of this family effort emerges the underlying family process of rendering legitimacy and congruency between the family's schema and its newly instituted patterns of functioning, as well as the coping strategies and behaviors it may employ to manage a stressor or crisis situation. This congruency between the family's schema and family functioning is important for determining the efficacy of the family's overall efforts to adapt to a crisis situation.

A case example of family adaptation to the vicissitudes of a war-induced crisis will bring to light the dynamic interplay between family schema and family functioning and at the same time reveal the importance of orchestrating both changes in the family schema and functioning in an effort to achieve legitimacy and congruency as integral processes in achieving a satisfactory level of family adaptation.

Conflict in the Persian Gulf involved military aircraft to conduct bombing sorties on specific enemy targets. Precision bombing involves placing the pilot, navigator, and aircraft at risk with every sortie. It was no different for sorties conducted in the Vietnam War. On January 12, 1968, on a bombing run in an A6 Intruder, Lt. Steve Marsek, a U.S. Naval Academy graduate, and the navigator went down with their aircraft after being hit by antiaircraft gunfire. The pilot, who ejected safely and was recovered by a rescue helicopter, reported that Lt. Marsek remained with the aircraft that plunged straight into the ground after he, the pilot, ejected. In his estimation it was highly improbable that Lt. Marsek survived. Military policy called for the recovery of a body to confirm death, thus the Department of Defense officially listed Lt. Marsek as "missing in action," a classification that remained unchanged for 5 years, leaving the Marsek family in limbo. This devout Catholic family included Mrs. Marsek, 28 years of age, and a 5-year-old son, Jim, who idolized his father and remained convinced that his father, Lt. Marsek, would come home.

With the facts laid out before her, followed by her husband's pilot and friend's visit to the Marsek home on a farm in Wisconsin, Mrs. Marsek concluded that the prospect of her husband returning was nil. For two years following the crash, Mrs. Marsek sought out friends and her husband's colleagues, persons who could give meaning and insight to her loss and guide her future plans. They agreed that her husband had died in the crash; even the military agreed with this interpretation.

Mrs. Marsek felt it was time for the family to move on. Now age 32, she felt it was important to move on with her life, possibly remarry and thus establish a new family; courses of action that she felt her husband would have encouraged. Her son Jim, now age 9, objected to her dating, while reiterating time and time again that his "father was coming home." Her efforts to establish new family patterns of functioning that included plans for building a new home, becoming a farmer in her own right, and dating were met with considerable resistance from her mother and sisters as well. Her efforts to explain the facts to her son were also refuted, ending in arguments and sadness for both. Her requests to the military to change her husband's status to "killed in action" brought angry reactions from her son and friends in the community who, without knowing the facts, labeled her as being selfish. The crowning blow of resistance came from her parish priest who confronted her with reminders of the grievous sin of marrying or carrying on a relationship without the official classification of death.

The Marsek family schema—involving values of deep religious beliefs, family integrity and unity, and financial security, as well as shared family expectations of open communication, harmony in the family, shared power and decision making, mutual support of family members, and flexibility in rules and expectations—was being challenged. In response and rather than staging a confrontation with the family's shared values and expectations through forcing changes in the family's functioning, Mrs. Marsek chose to give priority to the importance of family harmony and stability while working with the military to let the facts influence a change in her husband's status.

Three years had passed when the Department of the Navy confirmed her husband's death, thus removing the Catholic Church's pressure on Mrs. Marsek and the threat of excommunication. The possible conflict with the family's shared religious beliefs was removed. But Jim still resisted any changes in the family patterns; he demanded time with mother, family outings, time with extended family, and allowing only casual dating relationships. Mrs. Marsek's efforts at dating still brought about open conflict with and resistance from her now 10-year-old son.

The Marsek family clash between the shared schema and family functioning changed overnight. On a trip to the Colorado Rockies at a gathering of families who shared the common experience of having a member missing or a prisoner of war, Jim was the catalyst for changes in the family system. He changed his appraisal of the situation. As a result of prior meetings due to the Marsek family's involvement in a longitudinal study, the senior author and Jim became good friends. While on a walk in the mountains, Jim called my (the senior author's) attention to a dead tree standing tall with limbs without leaves. In pointing to the tree he quietly explained that "This is my dad; he is dead. He died in Vietnam." Then turning my attention to a little healthy and growing sapling at the base of the same tree, he noted that "this is me. My dad died so that I could grow up to be big and strong." The sun shone through the dead limbs above and upon the little sapling, giving the impression that it was being nourished in a special way. Jim appeared relieved with this revelation and ran to his mother who was walking ahead. He restated his observations and feelings with greater intensity and excitement that his father was gone, while he embraced his mother with a big hug and kiss.

Follow-up interviews six months later revealed substantial changes in the family's patterns of functioning. Mrs. Marsek dated openly and regularly with Jim offering affirmations and expressed interest in the prospect of adding a new adult member. The family built a new home on the same farm, but they now lived independently of Mrs. Marsek's mother with whom they had lived during the past five years. They purchased additional cattle with Jim playing a major independent role as a farmer. Mrs. Marsek had chosen to encourage her son's involvement in the church but personally remained at a distance. The crisis situation that focused on a missing father and his accounting has been reappraised and given new meaning. While the family struggled with the sense of personal loss and grief, they also struggled to lay the foundation for a new life without him and his military financial allotment, which gave them financial security. Mrs. Marsek was now employed and working on her master's degree while they managed a farm. The family changed their values and expectations and created new patterns of functioning that in turn gave meaning to their new life and future. This meaning, which included hope, autonomy, room for a stepfather and a new family, gave the family unit a sense of order and coherence. These changes in family functioning appeared to be congruent with the family's appraisal of the situation. There appeared to be a congruency between the family's schema and newly instituted patterns of family functioning.

We have only begun to define, operationalize and assess complex interaction between the family's schema and the family's patterns of functioning and how together they shape the course of family adaptation to crisis situations. A family's schema appears to evolve over time as a result of the efforts of family members to develop shared values, goals, and expectations unique to the family unit, which in turn is reinforced and maintained by the family's establishment of predictable patterns of family functioning. The relationship between family schema and family functioning may be summarized in five general propositions, stated below and depicted in Figure 9.2.

Proposition 1: A family's schema shapes and is in turn shaped by the family's established and changing patterns of functioning.

Proposition 2: A family's schema, while characterized as being relatively stable and resistant to change, is most likely to be modified in direct response to extreme family crisis situations that predictably involves drastic modification in the family's established patterns of functioning to achieve a satisfactory level of adaptation.

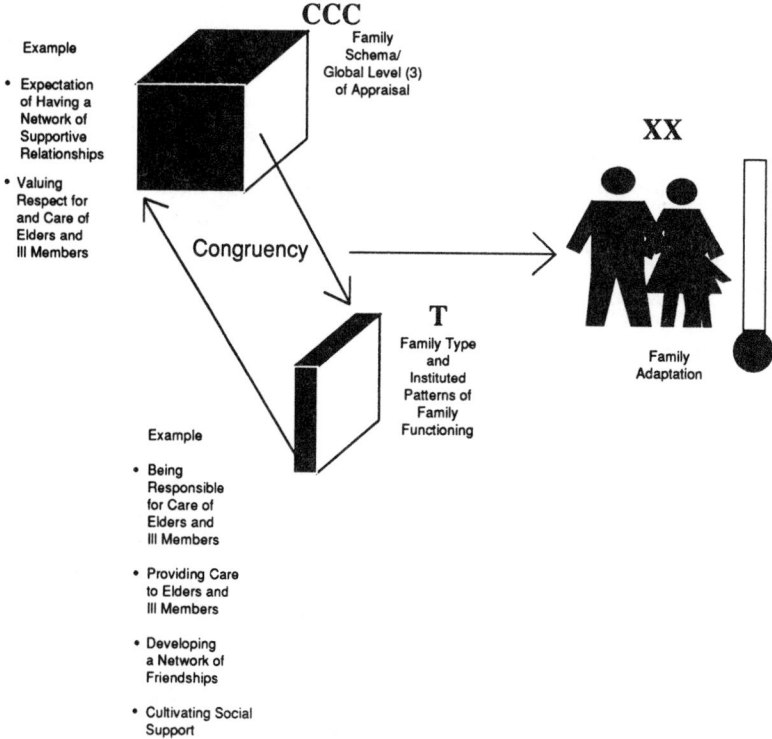

Figure 9.2. Interaction Between Family Schema and the Family's Instituted Pattern of Functioning in Shaping Family Adaptation

Proposition 3: A family's schema consisting of shared values, goals, and expectations shapes the family's appraisal of the crisis situation as well as the family's appraisal of a stressor and its hardships.

Proposition 4: A family's schema consisting of shared values, goals, and expectations shapes the coping behavior and strategies families employ in the management of stressors, their hardships, as well as family crises.

Proposition 5: In response to crisis situations involving changes in the family's schema and patterns of functioning, the family unit will strive to give meaning to the changes that, in time, renders legitimacy to changes, and promotes a sense of coherence in the family unit.

Further Examination of Family Schema: Focus on Ethnic Families

The efficacy of any theory building efforts is determined by the degree to which we are able to test empirically the assumptions and specific hypotheses that may be derived from general propositions. Family stress theory, which has tended to emerge inductively from direct observations of families under stress, lends itself to empirical testing. To carry our examination of family schema a small step further and at the same time attempt to move from the unique trauma of families involved in war, we turn our attention to the study of ethnic families, their stressors, appraisal, and coping. The study of ethnic families in America is not only needed to guide our interventions in support of these families, but the ethnic populations provide family scholars with a unique opportunity to explore and determine some of the underlying components of family schema.

Ethnicity and culture play a critical role in the shaping of a family's world view or schema—its values, goals, and expectations (Cheatham & Stewart, 1990; Handy & Pukui, 1978; Mindel, Habenstein, & Wright, 1988; Spickard, 1990; Takaki, 1989). With this basic observation in mind, it seemed reasonable to argue that ethnic families would be viable populations for the study of family schemata. Anthropological and sociological studies point to the importance of family expectations such as believing in the importance of a strong network of supportive relationships in the community and also sharing the family value of being responsible for caring for their own members who may be elders or seriously ill. These expectations and values appear to be of greatest importance to ethnic families. If we can empirically confirm the relative importance of such expectations and values to ethnic families, particularly in contrast to Caucasian families, and test their unique importance in explaining family functioning and adaptation we can begin to establish the relative importance of these values in family schema. Two hypotheses may be advanced here to demonstrate the value of two independent but complementary lines of reasoning. The first line of research is based on the observation that ethnic families have traditionally emphasized and valued social networks and social support as vital to their coping and adaptation (Handy & Pukui, 1978; Mindel, Habenstein, & Wright, 1988; Takaki, 1989). We may then hypothesize that:

H1: In contrast to Caucasian families, ethnic families represented by subsamples of Hawaiian, Asian (Japanese and Chinese), and mixed race (Filipino and

Korean) families, will reveal a significantly greater expectation and valuing of social network support from the community in explaining a significant and unique percentage of the variance in the criterion of family adaptation.

Following a second line of reasoning we may argue that while ethnic families have adopted the traditional family value of caring for their elders and the ill, in the context of contemporary society often demanding dual wage earners to achieve economic stability, there exists a greater probability of an incongruity between the family's schema embracing this value and the family's effort to adapt. In fact we expect this incongruity to reveal itself as a powerful factor in explaining family maladaptation. Thus a second hypothesis may be offered:

H2: In contrast to Caucasian families, ethnic families represented by subsamples of Hawaiian, Asian (Japanese and Chinese), and mixed race (Filipino and Korean) families, will reveal a significantly stronger emphasis on and valuing of providing care to family members (children, the elders, and the seriously or chronically ill) and this valuing of family care responsibilities will explain a significant percentage of the variance in indices of family system maladaptation.

Methodology

Using a random digit dialing process, the research team at the University of Wisconsin-Madison contacted 389 families on the island of Oahu in the Hawaiian Islands in an effort to understand what pressures impact on family life in Hawaii and what strengths and capabilities Caucasian, Asian, Hawaiian/part-Hawaiian, and other mixed race families have to manage stress and change. Some 54% of those contacted (210 families) agreed to participate in the telephone survey, which took from 10 to 60 minutes to complete. Guided by the resiliency model (M. McCubbin & McCubbin, 1992), the structured interviews focused upon (a) the pressures these families faced, (b) the strengths they have to cope with stress, (c) the family's problem-solving and communication style, (d) the family's coping strategy, and (e) the family's overall well-being and satisfaction. In this report of the survey, the results are limited to 200 families who met the basic criteria of (a) being a family unit and (b) having a respondent who played a leadership role in the family.

Survey Interview Instruments

Given the special demands of conducting an in-depth survey by phone and focusing upon sensitive and personal information, instruments were selected and pretested for final inclusion in the study. The instruments met two basic criteria: (a) the critical instruments had evidence of established reliabilities and validities; and (b) they could be administered with relative ease by phone. Two special instruments were created to meet the needs and goals of the study and to fill gaps in the existing battery of instruments.

Family adaptation (XX). The family APGAR (Smilkstein, 1978) index of family well-being was introduced as a utilitarian screening device and was based on the premise that a family member's appraisal of family functioning could be assessed by a member's report of satisfaction with five parameters of family function: adaptation, partnership, growth, affection, and resolve. This instrument has been validated (.80) with the Pless Satterwhite Family Function Index (Pless & Satterwhite, 1973) as well as with (.64) estimates of family function made by psychotherapists. The APGAR index of internal consistency is .80 and a test-retest reliability of .83. APGAR measures the use of resources for problem solving (adaptation, sharing of nurturing and decision making, partnership), physical and emotional maturation achieved through mutual support (growth), caring and loving relationship (affection), and the devotion of time to other members. Three additional items were added to the APGAR asking for the respondent's general appraisal of satisfaction with the quality of the relationship with his or her spouse, with the child(ren) and with the affection he or she received. The internal consistency for this variation of the APGAR was .73.

Family maladaptation (XX). The Family Maladaptation Index (previously referred to as the Family Distress Index) (H. McCubbin & Thompson, 1990) was created for this study. It is a checklist of pressures and stressors that families face, consisting of violence in the home, alcohol/drug use, financial/money problems, and confrontation with racism/discrimination, as well as divorce/separation. Given the multidimensional nature of this index of distress we accepted an alpha coefficient measure of .54.

Pile-up vulnerability: Family care responsibilities (V). Another measure was created for this study to assess what we refer to as "pile-up", that is the accumulation of additional pressures. This index measures the degree to which additional burdens are placed upon the family unit as a result of having to find quality child care, caring for an older family member, and/or caring for a seriously ill or chronically ill member. The alpha reliability for this index is .69.

Family appraisal (CC). The measure of Family Coherence (H. McCubbin, Larsen, & Olson, 1987) that consists of four items selected to record the degree to which families call upon their appraisal skills to manage stressful life events, strains, and changes. This index includes the acceptance of stressful events, accepting difficulties, a positive appraisal of a problem, and having faith in God. The psychometric properties of the Family Coherence Index include a reliability (internal reliability) index of .71 and a validity coefficient (correlation with the original Family Crisis Oriented Personal Evaluation Scales) of .80.

Family resources (BB). The Family Hardiness Index (H. McCubbin, McCubbin, & Thompson, 1987) was developed to measure the characteristic of *hardiness* as a stress resistance and adaptation resource in families, which would function as a buffer or mediating factor in mitigating the effects of stressors and demands and as a facilitation of family adjustment and adaptation over time. Family Hardiness specifically refers to the internal strengths and durability of the family unit and is characterized by a sense of control over the outcomes of life events and hardships, a view of change as beneficial and growth producing, and an active rather than passive orientation in adjusting to and managing stressful situations. The Family Hardiness Index is a 20-item instrument consisting of four subscales (Co-Oriented Commitment, Confidence, Challenge, and Control) that calls for the respondent to assess the degree to which (False, Mostly False, Mostly True, True) each statement describes their current family situation. The co-oriented commitment subscale measures the family's sense of internal strengths, dependability, and ability to work together. The confidence subscale measures the family's sense of being able to plan ahead, being appreciated for efforts, their ability to endure hardships and experience life with interest and meaningfulness. The Challenge subscale measures the family's efforts to be innovative, active, and to experience new things and to learn. The Control subscale measures the family's sense of being in control of family life rather than being shaped by outside events and circumstances. The psychometric properties of the Family Hardiness Index include a reliability (internal reliability) of .82 and validity coefficients ranging from .15 to .23 with criterion indices of cohesiveness, flexibility, and stability (M. McCubbin, McCubbin, & Thompson, 1987).

Community support (BB). A Community Services Index was created to assess the degree to which families utilize community services. This index was part of the coping measure and encompasses the degree to which the family coped with family problems by (a) seeking information from the family doctor, (b) seeking professional counseling, (c) seeking assistance from community agencies and programs, and (d) seeking help from other families. The internal consistency of the Community Services Index is .73.

Social support (BBB). The Social Support Index (H. McCubbin, Patterson, & Glynn, 1987) was adapted from a longer instrument of the same name. This abbreviated tool consists of three items and focuses upon the degree to which the family is satisfied with the affection they receive (emotional support), recognition and affirmation (esteem support), and their relationship with relatives (network support). The alpha reliability for this instrument is .71.

Family problem solving (PSC). The Family Problem Solving Communication Index (M. McCubbin, McCubbin, & Thompson, 1988) was developed specifically for family stress research, based on the previous experience of the research team in dealing with families under extreme stress. The questionnaire is used to assess the reactions of the family in struggling with problems and conflicts. The inventory includes two subscales, Incendiary Communication and Affirming Communication. Incendiary communication is that type of communication that is inflammatory and makes a situation worse rather than better, while the affirming communication style is more supportive and has a calming influence. The overall alpha reliabilities for these scales are .85 and .89, respectively. Validities for the Incendiary Communication style have been established for both indices (H. McCubbin & Thompson, 1989).

In addition, basic demographic information was obtained that focused on age, marital status, income, level of employment, and education for both the respondent and his or her spouse, as well as ethnicity of the respondent and spouse as well as the family ethnicity.

Overview of Families

The majority of respondents (86%) were either married, remarried, or cohabiting, while only 14% were divorced, separated, or widowed. The respondents had lived in the islands an average of 29 years. The number of children in the families ranged from zero to nine. The mean number of children in the families across all ethnic groups was 2. The ages of the respondents ranged from 20 to 79 years, while the mean age across all ethnic groups was 43.8 years. The annual combined family income for these families as reported by the respondents was divided into low income ($20,000 or less), medium income ($20,001 to $50,000) and high income (more than $50,001). About one fifth (21.3%) fell in the low-income group, while one half (50.5%) were in the medium- income group, and almost one third (28.2%) were in the high-income group. More than two thirds (68.8%) of the respondents indicated that they were employed full time outside the home while an additional 8.5% were employed part time either outside or inside the home. More than one fifth (22.6%) of the respondents indicated that they were not employed for pay. This group included housewives, retired people, and those who were unemployed. Almost three quarters of the spouses of the respondents (73.7%) were employed full time outside the home, while a very small percentage (5.7%) were employed part time either outside or inside the home. About one fifth (20.6%) were not employed for pay. Forty percent of the respondents indicated that they had at least one college degree while another one fourth had some college or vocational training after high school. More than one third (35%) indicated that they were a high school graduate or less. Respondents' spouses highest level of education was somewhat similar to that of the respondents. More than one third (38.6%) had a college or graduate degree, while 21% had some college or vocational education. Forty percent had a high school education or less.

Each of the families interviewed was asked to indicate where they would place their family if they could only put the family into a single ethnic category that they most strongly identified with. They were classified in four groups, Caucasian, Asian, Hawaiian and part Hawaiian, and mixed race (Filipino predominantly). The following results are based on this self-identification of family ethnicity.

Caucasian Families

The respondents ($N = 78$) indicated that their family ethnicity was Caucasian. The mean age of these respondents was 42.2 years and more than half (59.7%) of the Caucasian respondents were female. The vast majority (88.5%) were married, remarried, or cohabiting while only 11.5% were divorced, separated, or widowed. The number of children in the family ranged from zero to nine, while the average was two children. These families had lived in the Islands an average of 15.7

years. Less than one fifth of the Caucasian families (17.6%) indicated that they fell in the low-income group ($20,000 or less), while almost half (47.3%) were in the $20,001-$50,000 group. More than one third (35.1%) of these families indicated that their annual combined family income was in excess of $50,001. Almost three fourths (73.1%) of the respondents indicated that they were employed full time, while an additional 9% were employed part time outside the home. The remaining 18% were not employed for pay. More than three fourths (76.1%) of the spouses of the respondents were employed full time outside the home while 7% were employed part time either in or out of the home. Nearly 17% (16.9%) of the spouses were not employed for pay. A large percentage (47.4%) of the Caucasian respondents were college graduates or had a graduate degree. Another quarter of the respondents (25.7%) had some college or vocational training following high school and an additional quarter (26.9%) had completed only high school or less. Among the spouses nearly half (49.3%) had a college or advanced degree while about one-fifth (21.2%) had some education following high school, and nearly one-third (29.6%) had completed high school or less.

Hawaiian Families

The families included in this group ($N = 37$) were those who indicated that they viewed their family as Hawaiian or at least part Hawaiian in contrast to any other ethnic background. They ranged in age from 23 to 77 years with an average age of 44 years. An extremely large percentage (81.1%) of the respondents in this group were female, while only 18.9% were male. The number of children in the Hawaiian families ranged from zero to 10 with the average number slightly more than 3. More than three fourths of this group (78.4%) were married, remarried, or cohabiting while about one fifth (21.6%) were divorced, separated, or widowed. The average length of residence in the Islands for this group was 42.9 years. More than one third (36.1%) of these families indicated that their income was less than $20,000 per year. An additional 52.8% indicated that they were in the medium income group ($20,001-$50,000), while a very small percentage (11.1%) were in the high income group with an income in excess of $50,001. Only slightly more than half (52.8%) of the respondents were employed full time outside the home, while another 13.9% were employed part time outside the home. One third (33.3%) were not employed for pay. Among the spouses of the

Hawaiian respondents, nearly two-thirds (63.3%) were employed full time outside the home and none of them were employed part time. More than one-third (36.7%) were not employed, that is, they were unemployed, retired, or full-time housewives. Only about one-fourth (24.3%) of this group had completed at least one college degree while an additional 18.9% had some college or vocational training after high school. More than half (56.7%) of the Hawaiian respondents had a high school education or less. Among the spouses, slightly more than one-fifth (13.3%) had a college or graduate degree and about one-fourth (23.4%) had some post high school education or training. Almost two thirds (63.3%) of the spouses had a high school diploma or less.

Asian Families

Those respondents (N = 49) who indicated that they were either Japanese or Chinese were included in the Asian family group. Of the Asian respondents, about two-thirds (63.3%) were female and about one-third (36.7%) male, ranging in age from 22 to 75 with an average age of 46.4 years. More than four-fifths (85.7%) were either married, remarried, or cohabiting while the remaining respondents (14.3%) were divorced, separated, or widowed. The number of children in the families ranged from zero to six, with the average number of children being two. These families had lived in the Islands an average of 41.4 years. Among the Asian families the largest number of families (51%) indicated that their combined annual income was in the $20,001-$50,000 range, which put them in the medium-income category. A very small percentage (12.8%) were in the low-income category, while about one-third (36.2%) earned in excess of $50,000. Nearly 70% (69.4%) of the Asian respondents indicated that they were employed full time outside the home, and an additional 8.1% indicated that they were employed part time. About one-fourth (22.4%) were not employed. More than three quarters (76.7%) of the spouses of the Asian respondents were employed full time outside the home while an additional 7% were employed part time. Only 16.3% of the spouses were not employed for pay. More than half (51%) of the respondents indicated that they had completed at least one college degree and an additional 22% indicated that they had some training, either college or vocational, following high school. Slightly more than one-quarter (26.5%) had completed high school or less. More than one-third (34.9%) of the spouses of the Asian respondents had completed high school or less while about one-fourth had some training following high school. About two-fifths (41.9%) had one or more college degrees.

Mixed Race Families

This group ($N = 36$) consisted predominantly of Filipino and Korean families with a few Portuguese families, and included those families who did not see themselves as being more identified with one ethnic background than another. While we had reservations about grouping these families as "mixed" even though they saw themselves as such, both demographically and their overall responses revealed that they were different in many respects. The information indicates that they are quite mixed; by clustering in the low-income group they are similar to the Hawaiians, which makes them distinct from the Asians' and Caucasians' families; being predominantly married and employed they are similar to the Asians and distinct from the Hawaiians; on the other hand they are similar to the Hawaiians on educational attainment at the high school or less level as distinct from the Asian and Caucasian families. Half the respondents in this group were male and half were female. The mean age in this group was 43.5 years and the respondents, who ranged in age from 25 to 78, had lived in the Islands for an average of 28 years. These families had zero to eight children in the family with an average of nearly three children. More than half (54%) of the mixed race group had a combined annual income of $20,001-$50,000, which placed them in the medium-income group. About one-fourth (25.7%) were in the low-income group and one-fifth (20%) were in the high-income group, that is, with an income in excess of $50,001 per year. Three quarters (75%) of the respondents in this group were employed full time outside the home while an additional 2.8% were employed part time. More than one-fifth (22.2%) were not employed for pay. Among the spouses in the mixed race group, almost three-fourths (74.2%) were employed full time outside the home and another 6.5% were employed part time. Nearly one fifth of the spouses (19.4%) were not employed for pay. Only one quarter of the respondents (25%) indicated that they had at least one college degree, while one-third had some training after high school. More than two-fifths (41.7%) had completed high school or less. More than one third (34.4%) of the spouses of the mixed race respondents had completed at least one college degree and 15.6% had some training following high school. However, half (50%) had a high school education or less.

Results

What critical factors—vulnerability, resources, appraisal, problem solving, or coping—fosters the family's achievement of an optimal level of family adaptation appears to vary to a major degree by the ethnic background of the family unit.

In the case of Caucasian families, adaptation is explained by three factors: (a) the number of children in the family unit ($\beta = -.51$, $F = 18.69$, $p = .001$); (b) family hardiness, particularly the family's commitment to the well-being of the unit ($\beta = .63$, $F = 43.76$, $p = .001$); and by (c) the family's level of social support ($\beta = .40$, $F = 46.32$, $p = .001$). With 73% of the variance of the criterion of family adaptation explained by these three factors, the findings take on added importance. In summary, in the case of Caucasian families adaptation is explained by two critical factors of social support and the family's commitment to itself, referred to here as family hardiness. The number of children in the family unit, however, had a negative association with adaptation; the greater the number children the lower the level of family adaptation in Caucasian families.

Family adaptation in the case of Hawaiian families is explained by a unique set of factors. Specifically, family adaptation appears to be associated with (a) a combined family income of $20,000 to $50,000 per year ($\beta = .37$, $F = 4.03$, $p = .06$); (b) the social support they receive ($\beta = .69$, $F = 14.61$, $p = .0001$); and by (c) family hardiness, particularly the family's sense of challenge in their lives ($\beta = .31$, $F = 13.61$, $p = .0001$). In summary, adaptation in Hawaiian families is strongly associated (with 64% of the variance explained) with having a middle-range income, being part of a network of socially supportive relationships, and by a strong sense of family hardiness.

In contrast, adaptation in Asian families is associated with a smaller cluster of independent factors. Specifically, family adaptation is associated with (a) the strength of the social support Asian families receive ($\beta = .80$, $F = 65.07$, $p = .0001$); and (b) by the family's internal strengths of family hardiness characterized by its strong emphasis on commitment to the well-being of the family unit ($\beta = .19$, $F = 36.87$, $p = .0001$). In summary, in the case of Asian families, family adaptation is positively and strongly associated (68% of the variance explained) with the strengths of the family's network of socially supportive relationships and by the family's internal strengths of hardiness with its emphasis on a strong commitment.

The critical explanatory factors in the case of family adaptation for families of mixed races are unique in many respects. Family adaptation is positively associated with (a) the family's level of socially supportive relationships ($\beta = .82$, $F = 57.31$, $p = .0001$); and (b) the family's emphasis upon affirming communication in its problem-solving efforts. The family's use of community services in its effort to cope with family hardships appears to be important but inversely related to family adaptation ($\beta = -.17$, $F = 31.84$, $p = .0001$). In summary, in the case of families of mixed races, family adaptation is strongly associated (79% of the variance explained by the three factors) with the family's network of socially supportive relationships, by the family's emphasis on problem solving through affirming communication, and by not being involved in community services supportive of these families.

Of particular importance to our study of family schemata is the role of social support as a critical explanatory variable in understanding family adaptation. As hypothesized (H1), *social support,* defined as satisfaction received from emotional, esteem, and network support, emerges as being of paramount importance to all families, quite irrespective of ethnicity. Confirmatory of our original hypothesis, when contrasted with social support in Caucasian families, those families of ethnic origins—Hawaiian, Asian, and mixed race—appear to demonstrate a stronger dependence upon and valuing of social support. As presented in Figure 9.3, in contrast to Caucasian families (11%), social support appears to have greater explanatory power of family adaptation in Hawaiian families (41%), Asian families (64%), and families of mixed races (67%).

Our examination of the critical explanatory factors associated with family maladaptation defined in terms of family difficulties encompassing such issues as physical and/or psychological violence, alcohol/substance abuse, economic problems, and racism, as well as divorces and/or separation—also reveals the relative importance of family ethnicity. In the case of Caucasian families only one factor emerged as being of some importance. While explaining only 12% of the variance of the criterion of family maladaptation, affirming family problem-solving communication ($\beta = -.35$, $F = 9.45$, $p = .003$) appeared to be an important buffer. The greater the affirming communication in the family environment, the lower the degree of family maladaptation in Caucasian families.

In contrast, family maladaptation in Hawaiian families can be explained by four important factors, two of which appear to be exacerbators of or contributors to family maladaptation; the remaining two appear to act

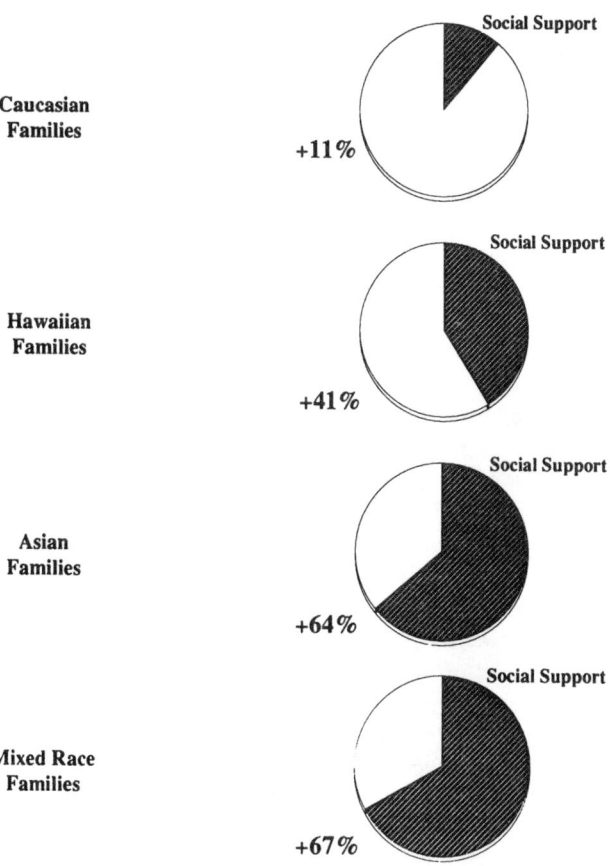

Figure 9.3. Comparative Analysis of Ethnic Families on the Amount of Variance in Family Adaptation Explained by Social Support

as buffers against distress. Specifically, (a) the number of children in the home ($\beta = -.30$, $F = 2.94$, $p = .09$) and family hardiness ($\beta = -.28$, $F = 7.48$, $p = .0001$) and the family's emphasis on commitment to the well-being of the family unit are inversely related to family maladaptation; having more than one child and a deep commitment to the family appears to serve as buffers or mediators against family maladaptation. In contrast, (b) the family's emphasis on an incendiary style of problem-solving communication ($\beta = .33$, $F = 8.29$, $p = .0001$) and (c) the family's burden of family care responsibilities—which includes caring for the elders and the seriously or chronically ill—both appear to exacerbate or contribute to the family's maladaptive responses. By emphasizing an incendiary or inflammatory style of problem-solving communication and taking on family care responsibilities, Hawaiian families appear to increase their chances of developing or maintaining maladaptive functioning in the family. When we consider that these factors explain a notable 57% of the variance of the criterion of family adaptation, the findings take on added importance.

In the context of Asian families, the explanatory variables of family maladaptation appear to be different from their Caucasian or Hawaiian counterparts. Family maladaptation is explained by (a) adult respondents who have a high school education or less ($\beta = -.29$, $F = 3.67$, $p = .06$); by (b) a combined family annual income in the range of \$20,000 to \$50,000 ($\beta = .25$, $F = 3.40$, $p = .04$); and by (c) family care responsibilities for the elderly and seriously or chronically ill ($\beta = .44$, $F = 5.74$, $p = .002$). Surprisingly, having a high school education or less appears to serve as a buffer and mediator against family maladaptation. In contrast, being in the middle-income group and having family care responsibilities appear to serve as exacerbators of family maladaptation, at least in Asian families. With nearly a third (31%) of the variance in the criterion of family maladaptation explained by these three factors, it is reasonable to give weight to these findings.

An examination of the results from our analysis of maladaptation in families of mixed races again reveals a different cluster of explanatory variables. Specifically, mixed race families appear to have a greater number of buffers or mediators including (a) the age of the adult family representative ($\beta = -.27$, $F = 6.09$, $p = .006$); (b) the family's emphasis upon an affirming style of problem-solving communication ($\beta = -.33$, $F = 11.66$, $p = .0001$); and (c) family coherence ($\beta = -.29$, $F = 11.65$, $p = .0001$) with its emphasis on confidence, trust, positive appraisal, and faith in God. In contrast, family maladaptation in mixed race families appears to be exacerbated by (d) the adult respondent having a high school education or less ($\beta = .46$, $F = 8.69$, $p = .006$); and (e) the family's burden of family care responsibilities ($\beta = .50$, $F = 10.61$, $p = .0001$), including the care of the elders and the serious or chronically ill. Given the explanatory power of these five factors (68% of the variance explained) the findings merit consideration.

Of particular importance to our study of family schemata is the role of family care responsibilities as a critical explanatory variable in understanding family maladaptation. As hypothesized, family care responsibilities, defined as having a shared sense of responsibility to care for family elders and the seriously or chronically ill, is a powerful explanatory factor in understanding family maladaptation, particularly in ethnic families. Confirmatory of our original hypothesis (H2), when contrasted with the level of emphasis of family care responsibilities in Caucasian families, those families of ethnic origins—Hawaiian, Asian, and mixed race—appear to indicate a stronger emphasis on providing care to family members and this emphasis explains a significant percentage of the variance of the criterion of family maladaptation. As presented in Figure 9.4, in contrast to Caucasian families (0%), family care responsibilities appears to have greater explanatory power of family maladaptation in Hawaiian families (9%), Asian families (17%), and families of mixed races (23%). Family care, an important value and part of the family schema in ethnic families, appears to be incongruent with the family's efforts to adapt, and, in fact, may be an important factor in the family's maladaptive responses.

Summary and Conclusions

Our efforts to conceptualize and understand family adaptation to crisis situations has placed the construct of family schema, a global level of family appraisal consisting of shared values, goals, and expectations at center stage. By drawing from observations of family efforts at adaptation in the face of the hardships of a past war in Vietnam, and stimulated by the presence of the recent war in the Persian Gulf, we attempted to define and refine the construct of family schema, formulate propositions to stimulate future research, and through a case study strategy demonstrate the face validity of family schema in shaping family patterns of functioning and adaptation. We have underscored the complex but meaningful interaction between the family's established patterns of functioning and family schema, each influencing one another in a process designed to foster family adaptation and coherence in functioning.

Believing that these constructs of family schema may have broader applications for studying and understanding family functioning and adaptation we turned our attention to the study of ethnic families with an eye toward testing the influence of family values and expectations on family adaptation. By hypothesizing and testing the explanatory power of social support, a shared family value, we demonstrated that

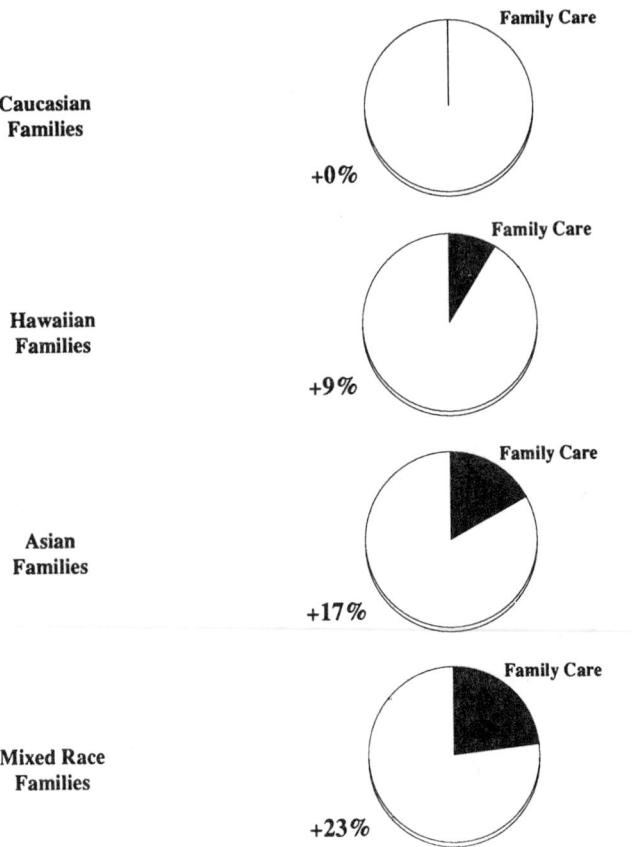

Figure 9.4. Comparative Analysis of Ethnic Families on the Amount of Variance in Family Maladaptation Explained by Family Care Responsibilities

selected family values may be "valued" differently in families of different ethnic backgrounds and that the strength of the positive association between the family value of social support and the criterion of family adaptation will also vary by ethnicity. The importance of family schema, and particularly shared values, in explaining family adaptation appears to be affirmed in this investigation.

In turning our attention to the study of family schema, particularly family expectations as a part of family schema, as a factor in understanding family maladaptation we revealed yet another role for appraisal in shaping family functioning. The expectation of families of assuming responsibility for the care of elders and the chronically or seriously ill was chosen for careful examination. Recognizing that this shared expectation to care for the elders is commonly underscored in the literature on ethnic families, and realizing that families today struggle to make ends meet through dual wage earners, thus leaving the family vulnerable to the impact of additional burdens, we assumed that families would be struggling with this incongruity between schema (including family care responsibilities) and established patterns of functioning. Consequently, we could examine the relationship between this family expectation to care for their elders and the ill and the criterion of family maladaptation, which we hypothesized to be the most reasonable relationship (rather than adaptation) considering the likelihood of a "rub" between family schema and its shared values and family patterns of functioning. The study confirmed this hypothesis and at the same time shed light upon the degree to which family care is accepted as an expectation in ethnic families. We also learned that family care as an expectation also varies in its importance across ethnic groups.

The study of family schema is predictably complex, for by pursuing such a line of scientific inquiry we are probing deeper into the soul of the family, its values, goals, and expectations. We must be cautious not to approach this subject of family schema with a premature demand for empiricism and experimental manipulation before we have had a chance to map out and understand the interplay between a global level of appraisal and family adaptation. By examining the application of the construct of family schema to our understanding of family adaptation in ethnic families, we have made one small confirmation as to the extreme importance of family appraisal in shaping family functioning, adjustment, and adaptation.

PART 3

Family Interventions

10

Life-Span Family Life Education

CHARLES B. HENNON
MARGARET ARCUS

According to Kerckhoff (1964), family life education arose around the turn of the century in response to social and cultural "upheavals" that were perceived to have a negative impact on individuals and families. These changes (e.g., industrialization and urbanization, the changing roles of women, changes in social institutions and in occupational and economic behaviors) resulted in an apparent loss of social control, and in particular, parents and other adults "seemed unable . . . to obtain the same socialized behavior from children as had previously been possible" (Kerckhoff, 1964, p. 881). Because of this concern, early attention in family life education was directed toward parents and parent education. Such programs were seen as one way to improve family living and thus to reduce family-related social problems.

Since those early beginnings, however, there has been some movement toward a life-span focus in family life education. This development has been based on the assumption that people of all ages need to learn about the many aspects of family life and on the belief that there are opportunities for family life education at each developmental phase (e.g., Avery & Lee, 1964; Hey & Neubeck, 1990; National Council on Family Relations, 1970). Over time, both the content focus of family life education and the audience to whom it is directed have expanded (Darling, 1987).

AUTHORS' NOTE: This document is No. 14-91 of the Family and Child Studies Center manuscript series, Miami University, Oxford, OH, 45056.

The purpose of this chapter is to examine family life education from a life-span perspective. A brief overview of this perspective will be provided and the current life-span status of family life programs will be discussed, organized by three broad age categories. Two models, empowerment and medical, for life-span family life education will be reviewed. The chapter will then focus upon building integrated life-span family life education programs. Attention will be given to assessing needs, grounding family life education in theory and research, evaluating programs, linking with therapy, and reaching the public. Potential limitations of life-span family life education will also be noted.

A Perspective on Life-Span Family Life Education

Family life education is a field of study and practice whose major purpose is to help strengthen and enrich family living (Arcus, Moss, & Schvaneveldt, in press). Its focus is preventive rather than therapeutic, and its objectives include helping individuals and families (a) to gain knowledge about concepts and principles that are relevant to family living, (b) to explore personal attitudes and values and to understand and accept the values of others, and (c) to develop interpersonal skills that contribute to personal and to family well-being. Through programs in family life education, individuals and families are assisted to develop their potentials both as present and as future family members and to meet their needs for family living over the life course.

Family life education is a broad area of study, encompassing many different topic areas (Darling, 1987). While several different "lists of topics" have been developed over the years (e.g., National Commission on Family Life Education, 1968), the most current conceptualization of the content of family life education is presented in the Framework for Life-Span Family Life Education (Arcus, 1987). This framework identifies, as the key content of the field, seven major topic areas (human development and sexuality, interpersonal relationships, family interaction, family resource management, parenthood, ethics, and family and society) and three interpersonal processes (communication, decision making, problem solving). This framework goes beyond a mere listing of areas, however, and specifies some of the important knowledge, attitudes, and skills relevant to each area. The interpersonal relationships area, for example, includes knowledge such as factors influencing mate selection, attitudes such as respecting self and others, and skills such as initiating, maintaining, and ending relationships.

Although the content areas listed in the framework can be seen as distinct areas of study and are sometimes the focus of specialized areas of practice within the field, it is generally believed in family life education that meeting the educational needs of individuals and families requires integration across the content areas. When educating about the development of sexual relationships, for example, one would not only include content specified in the areas of human development and sexuality and interpersonal relationships plus the processes of communication, decision making, and problem solving, but would also incorporate appropriate content from other areas such as ethics (i.e., respect for persons, nonexploitative behaviors, social responsibility) and family interaction (i.e., effects of the family on the self-concepts of its members, life-style choices).

In order to reflect the underlying assumption that family life education is relevant to individuals of all ages, the Framework for Life-Span Family Life Education is organized according to broad age categories. These broad categories (children, adolescents, adults) were used rather than specific age ranges (6-12, 13-19, 20-29, etc.) since it was believed that development related to these topic areas is not tied to such specific ages (National Council on Family Relations, 1984). The framework is intended to demonstrate that each topic may be addressed at each age level by varying the focus and/or the complexity of the content. In the area of ethics, for example, education for children would focus on taking responsibility for actions, while in adolescence, education would broaden to include developing a personal ethical code. Further expansion in this content occurs at the adult level, with attention to assisting in the formation of ethical concepts and behavior in others.

This life-span perspective in family life education appears to be based on two interrelated assumptions. The first of these is that family life education is relevant to individuals of all ages and to all families, whatever their stage of the family life span and whatever their special circumstances. The impetus for some programs may be related to various normative developments for individuals and families, such as getting married, becoming a parent, or retiring from a job. These developments may be age-related (attaining puberty), event-related (loss of a family member), or a combination of age and event (first marriage during young adulthood). Other programs may be nonnormative, that is, related to the special needs and transitions affecting some but not all individuals and family members (e.g., parenting children with special needs, getting divorced, facing unemployment or under-employment). The response of family life educators to both normative and nonnormative events and transitions has resulted in the develop-ment of a number of specialty areas within family life education, with some specialties well established (parent education, sex education, marriage preparation) and others emerging (parent education for ado-lescent parents, sexual abuse education and prevention, marriage the second time around).

The second assumption underlying the life-span perspective is that programs in family life education should be based on meeting the educational needs of individuals and families that are generated by these normative and nonnormative developments (National Commis-sion on Family Life Education, 1968). These needs may be identified in several ways. Some needs, for example, may be *felt needs* (i.e., those needs expressed by individuals and families themselves, such as "I need to be more assertive in my relationships" or "We need help in dealing with a family problem"). These kinds of needs are commonly reflected in family life programs through program objectives, rationales, and activities.

Needs may also refer to *developmental needs*. These needs are com-mon to most individuals and families, and refer to such things as dealing with one's changing sexuality at puberty or preparing for retirement. These needs are generally identified through reference to the empirical literature in the field and to the collective wisdom and experience of family life educators. Many documents in family life education, such as the Framework for Life-Span Family Life Education referred to above, are based on developmental needs.

In many cases, there is an overlap between these two kinds of needs. The educational needs of new parents, for example, may be both a felt need expressed by the parents themselves and a developmental need emerging from their new roles and responsibilities. The match between felt needs and developmental needs cannot always be assumed, how-ever. Although marriage educators may believe that preparation for marriage is a developmental need, at least some participants in prepa-ration for marriage programs claim that they do not need it (that is, it is not a felt need) (Fournier, 1980).

There is another kind of need that deserves attention in family life education, and that might best be called *societal needs*. These are needs that emerge from both current and anticipated social, economic, and political conditions, and that impinge in important ways on the lives of all individuals and families. Examples of these needs include the need to combat prejudice and to manage the finite resources of the world with greater care and greater attention to social justice. If family life education is to attain its goal of meeting the needs of all individuals and families, then family life education must also address these societal needs. Later in this chapter, the different types of needs and needs identification will be covered in more detail.

Age Groups and Family Life Education

It is not possible in this chapter to provide a systematic review of family life programs across the life span. Rather, the broad age categories and the topics of the Framework for Life-Span Family Life Education (Arcus, 1987) will be used to identify some of the major directions, issues, and limitations in the practice of family life education.

Family Life Education for Children

As suggested in the framework, there are many basic family life concepts, skills, and attitudes to be learned during childhood—developing self-esteem, dealing with emotions, making friends and being a friend, learning about family roles and responsibilities, helping with family tasks, recognizing and appreciating the similarities and differences in families, learning to make choices, and learning to manage time and money. While these kinds of learnings are also the focus of much family socialization, they receive formal attention in family life education programs for a variety of reasons. Some families may be unable or unwilling to educate their children about these concepts, while in others, their efforts may be unsuccessful or may not happen at the right time.

For the most part, formal programs in family life education for children are found in the elementary school. (While there may be activities and learnings around family topics in day-care centers and nursery schools, it is doubtful whether these are appropriately called family life education.) Numerous curriculum and teaching units are available on family life topics. In general, however, these documents are indicators of what can or should be done rather than what is being done, since little information (evaluative or otherwise) is available on family life education in elementary schools.

Family life education for this age group tends to be organized around individual development rather than family development; that is, students are taught the same kinds of things because of their similar developmental levels regardless of whether they are the first child in an expanding family unit or the last child in a family that has begun to launch its older children. In many ways, this kind of "common needs" approach makes sense because many of the needs and interests of children at this stage are similar. It is possible, however, that this approach may ignore some important needs of children that may be related to the structure, developmental stage, or other characteristics of their own family.

As suggested in the Framework for Life-Span Family Life Education (Arcus, 1987), a broad range of topics can appropriately be included in elementary school family life education (e.g., the growth and development of people of all ages, interpersonal and family relationships, becoming good members of society). To some extent, such topics are based on the expressed concerns and interests of young children and are related to their present family and interpersonal roles and experiences. However, it is also possible that much of what is taught at this age is based upon what adults want and think children should know—being good family members, sharing, taking responsibility, understanding consequences. Thus family life education at this stage appears to be influenced more by developmental and societal needs than by felt needs.

Not all family life education topics are typically included in elementary family life education, and sexuality education tends to be the most troublesome. In recent years, with increasing attention to the problem of child sexual abuse and its prevention, schools have begun to offer programs designed specifically to educate children about sexual abuse. One of the most common paradigms for this education is "safety education" (e.g., Health and Welfare Canada, 1989), an approach that views sexual abuse as a danger from which one must learn to protect oneself and that tends to place the onus for protection on the potential victim. While these programs provide information for children and a forum for discussion, most do little to help children acquire and practice the behavioral skills necessary for self-protection. Scales (1986) has noted that education to prevent the social problem of child sexual abuse differs from typical educational approaches to the social problem of teenage pregnancy, in that education concerning sexual abuse makes clear efforts to reach children at a young age without pulling any punches and with few cheap jabs or double messages.

A second paradigm, "the sexuality approach," is less common, but when sex abuse education does follow this paradigm, it includes not only the behavioral skills necessary for self-protection, but also an emphasis on building self-esteem set in a context of sexuality as a healthy, normal, and positive aspect of one's life experience. Although this latter approach is less common, there is some evidence that particular attention to the development of self-esteem is an important mediating variable in child sexual abuse, helping to protect the child or to lessen the impact of the abuse (e.g., Health and Welfare Canada, 1989).

Although most family life education for children is found in the elementary schools, it may occur in other settings as well. One example might be the Family Cluster model of family enrichment. "A Family Cluster is a group of four or five complete family units which contract to meet together periodically over an extended period of time for shared educational experiences related to their living in relationship within their families" (Sawin, 1979, p. 164). Among other things, a cluster can provide mutual support, skills training, and the opportunity to celebrate life. Through Family Clusters, it is expected that children will gain affirmation and will have the opportunity to observe both their parents and other adults as they address issues of relationships and of living in families. The extent to which the educational experiences in Family Clusters are related to the needs of children (rather than to those of the adults) is unclear.

Family Life Education for Adolescents

Adolescence is often seen as a critical time for education about family life. Most adolescents would appear to be interested in the family life topics identified in the Framework for Life-Span Family Life Education (e.g., understanding oneself and others, forming and maintaining relationships, making decisions about sexuality), and at least some adults see it as an opportunity for ensuring some anticipatory socialization for the adolescent's future roles in marriage and parenthood. Because the school setting provides a "captive audience," most family life education for adolescents is found in the schools, organized and presented more formally than at the elementary level.

There have been numerous surveys of these school programs over the years (e.g., Baker & Darcy, 1970; R. Mason, 1977; Sheek, 1984; The Vanier Institute of the Family, 1971), and from these, a composite profile of family life education for adolescents may be inferred. Typically, family life education is offered by departments of home economics, guidance/counseling, social studies, or health/physical education, either as a separate course or as a unit within a course. Courses in family life education are at least one semester in length, and may include either a broad range of family life topics (as suggested in the Framework for Life-Span Family Life Education), or may emphasize one particular area such as sexuality or parenting. A more common approach, however, is to offer a unit within another course. Because these units are of relatively short duration (a few hours to a few weeks), these efforts at family life education may be limited in either breadth or depth (or both).

In most cases, this family life education is elective, although there has been a recent move toward a mandated experience in some states, typically a short unit on sex education. Most family life education is open to both boys and girls, but appears to be elected more often by girls. This suggests that although there may be many family life education opportunities available for adolescents, these experiences may be limited not only in scope but also in the number of students who take advantage of them.

Concerns about the quality of family life education in the schools have also been expressed by Rodman (1970). He reviewed family life education textbooks and found that authors tended to ignore the findings of social science and to emphasize oversimplified and contrived family stories. He suggested that family life education would most effectively accomplish its goals of self-understanding and own-family understanding if family life educators were to incorporate more academic-intellectual material designed to increase the adolescent's understanding of families in general. It is unclear to what extent this may have happened since Rodman's review.

Because family life education is viewed as preventive rather than therapeutic, this has led some to believe in the "promise" of family life education. That is, to believe that if we educate young people about family life educational concepts, issues, or problems, we will then be able to reduce certain kinds of social problems. In the area of sexuality, for example, Jorgensen (1981) notes the argument made by some educators that family life education and/or sexuality education will help to reduce the adolescent pregnancy rate by providing the knowledge and motivation needed to help young people make intelligent decisions about their sexual behavior and use of contraception. He suggests that this is a promise that cannot be kept, first, because the problem is so complex with many antecedents unrelated to, and unaffected by, the educational system, and second, because of the difficulty of establishing any kind of cause-effect relationship between such education and any change in behavior. DeLissovoy (1978) raises a similar issue with respect to parent education for adolescents and states that "caution and constraint [should] be exercised in the promotion of high school 'parent education' courses as a promise of more functional, more effective parenting" (p. 316). While he does not question the goals of parent education programs, he suggests that the target audience is inappropriate for developmental reasons and thus "little in the way of effect in the quality of parenting will be forthcoming from these efforts" (p. 316).

The views expressed by Rodman, Jorgensen, and DeLissovoy raise important questions for family life education for adolescents: (a) What are the most appropriate goals and content for this age group, given the developmental levels of most adolescent?; (b) How best can these goals be attained within the context of schools and schooling?; and (c) Can school-based family life education be expected to resolve significant social problems, when as Scales (1986) suggests, we are unwilling to be as direct and open in adolescent sexuality education as we are in child sexual abuse education? Clearly, answers to these and other questions are important if programs in family life education for this age group are to be both meaningful and effective.

Although most family life education for this age group is offered within the school system, Scales and Kirby (1981) have examined exemplary sex education programs offered by nonschool organizations. They found that these programs had greater freedom and flexibility than school programs because they were not constrained by legal requirements or influenced by the nature of classroom instruction. They also did not have to be "acceptable to all," since they tended to attract participants with shared values. Out-of-school programs were more likely than school programs to involve the adolescents in program development. This involvement helped to stimulate interest in the programs and to ensure that they met the needs of their participants.

Family Life Education for Adults

The period of adulthood is also a key time for family life education, and this is reflected in the Framework for Life-Span Family Life Education. Not only are adults concerned with their own needs for family living, but most will bear some responsibility for the family life socialization of the next generation. Family life education for adults is related more to adult family life experiences than it is to age per se, that is, getting married or becoming parents is more likely to serve as the focal point for the educational experience than is the age at which the experience occurs. At the same time, there are some commonalities across the adult years that may influence the development of family life education. For example, most people marry for the first time during early adulthood, therefore marriage preparation programs are typically designed for and directed toward young adults.

There is a substantial body of literature concerning family life education for adults. That literature cannot be reviewed systematically here, but some of the major areas of adult family life education will be identified and briefly discussed. Brief reference will be made to other areas that are emerging or that are in need of attention.

Two areas of specialization in adult family life education are well-established and commonly available: marriage preparation and parent education. Both areas have emerged because of inherent limitations in the family of orientation as an agent of socialization for marriage and parenthood (Hill & Aldous, 1969). The general purpose of marriage preparation is to help prospective mates to gain knowledge about and discuss the critical tasks and issues in marriage, to acquire behavioral skills and problem-solving strategies that might enhance the marital relationships, and to evaluate one's own relationship (Bagarozzi & Rauen, 1981). It is believed that such education is needed to combat the romanticism of many premarital couples and to help them to examine the unrealistic expectations and untested assumptions that they may hold. Many different models and approaches to marriage preparation have been developed and some have been modified for use with different audiences. In recent years, special attention has been given to providing marriage preparation for couples who are marrying for the second time and for those marrying during the later years.

The purpose of parent education programs is to enhance or improve parental role performance (e.g., Harmin & Brim, 1980). In general, this includes gaining a better understanding of children and how they develop, understanding oneself in relation to one's children, and acquiring a repertoire of skills and strategies to use in fulfilling the parental role. While there is no universal method or approach in parent education, the most typical approach uses small group discussion and interaction. Some programs (e.g., Gordon, 1970) follow a specific curriculum, while in others, parents are involved in the selection of content and experiences. There is some evidence that parent education is more likely for middle to upper socioeconomic class parents, that it tends to emphasize the parenting of young children, and that mothers are more likely than fathers to be involved in parent education (Croake & Glover, 1977). Recent trends include programs designed specifically for stepparents and for adolescent parents.

Although a more recent development than either marriage preparation or parent education, programs in marriage and family enrichment have also become well established (e.g., Hof & Miller, 1980; L'Abate & Weinstein, 1987). These programs are based on a belief that couples and families have strengths and resources that can be utilized as the basis of experiences to enhance growth and development within the relationship. As with most adult family life education, there are a variety of approaches to enrichment. Hof and Miller (1980), for example, have identified three approaches to marriage enrichment: intensive weekend retreats, weekly marital growth groups, and structured programs such as couples communication programs. In spite of this diversity in approach, some of the common features of marriage enrichment include: (a) a process that is dynamic, experiential, educational, and preventive; (b) a focus on both relational and individual growth; and (c) a perspective that sees the enrichment experience as a beginning, not an end. According to Hof and Miller, one of the challenges in enrichment education is to match the diverse kinds of programs with the specific needs and abilities of the participants and to recognize that not everyone may benefit from an enrichment experience. However, Guerney and Maxson (1990, p. 1128) note in their review of marital and family enrichment research that, "after receiving enrichment, the average participant was better off than 67% of nonparticipants." These authors also note that distressed participants have a higher Effect Score (in meta-analysis, a standardized measure calculated for each outcome measure, the magnitude of which reflects degree of treatment gains compared to control or alternate-treatment groups) than do nondistressed participants in the meta-analysis conducted by Giblin, Sprenkle, and Sheehan (1985). This same meta-analysis indicates that highly structured programs are better than less structured programs. Guerney1 and Maxson (1990) suggest, based on their review of the literature, that no more research needs to be devoted to the basic question of whether enrichment programs work; it is clear that such programs do work, even though they may not always be without negative effects. There appears to be some basis for optimism concerning the impact of enrichment.

One of the normative transitions for individuals of all ages is that of dealing with the loss of loved ones. This transition is particularly important for adults since they must not only deal with their own reactions but may also need to help younger family members with the same transition. Much of the literature on "death education" is not relevant to adults, as it deals primarily with issues related to this topic in elementary, secondary, and tertiary education (e.g., Ulin, 1977); nevertheless, there are several programs that have been developed primarily for adults. One example is the Grief Workshop developed by Wood (1987). This workshop combines both educational experiences and the development of a support system in order to help adults deal with loss and grief. A seminar experience provides the opportunity to gain information, to interact with others who are facing the same experience, and to form support networks. This Grief Workshop is typically organized during holiday periods, a time that is especially difficult for those who have lost loved ones. The Widow-to-Widow program developed by Silverman (1976) emphasizes the provision of support services to the newly widowed by someone who has already faced that experience.

Other adult needs and transitions that have received some attention include such areas as special programs designed for adults who are coping with divorce or programs for parents who wish to take a more active role in the sex education of their children. (There is little, however, for adults who wish sex education for themselves, rather than for their parental role.) Some of the emerging program areas include stress management and coping for rural families, and special programs for adults involved in caring and caregiving for their aging parents. Some of these latter programs indicate the creativity of those involved in adult family life education. As new needs emerge, family life educators attempt to respond to these needs for information and support.

The Framework for Life-Span Family Life Education (Arcus, 1987) is useful for helping educators identify key knowledge, attitudes, and skills for the matrix formed by seven major family life topic areas and three interpersonal processes across the life span. This framework is based upon meeting educational needs (felt, developmental, and societal) of individuals and families that are generated by normative and nonnormative life-span development. In this chapter, the framework has been used to identify some of the major directions, issues, and limitations in the practice of family life education for children, adolescents, and adults.

This chapter will now build upon these ideas by directing the reader's attention to some fundamental issues involved in providing life-span family life education, specifically to helping models used and how the profession can be strengthened by the creation of "integrated" family life programs. This means that the various components of the program are carefully articulated throughout: from original conception and needs analysis; through setting goals and objectives; identification of the empirical and theoretical bases for the knowledge, attitudes, and skills to be taught; incorporating the relevant pedagogy and delivery system; implementing the program; conducting the evaluation; and on to program refinement and enhancement.

Helping Models

There are several helping models used to frame life-span family life education. It is believed that the model that the educator finds most agreeable will thus act as a paradigm that shapes many aspects of an intervention, especially the educator's view of the necessity of programs and how needs will be identified (including values used to prioritize and assess these needs), and the approach taken in conceptualizing and developing an educational program addressing these needs. While discussing helping models, this chapter will also note implications for the family life education profession.

Brickman and colleagues (1982) identify a typology of helping models that can guide the development of family life education across the life span. These models vary concerning who is responsible for the problem (that is, who's to blame), as well as who is responsible for solving the problem. The typology includes four models (see Table 10.1). The first is the *moral* model, which suggests that people are responsible for both their problems and solutions, and suggests that people need proper motivation in order to improve the situation. The *enlightenment* model holds that people are responsible for their problems, but they are not responsible for the solutions. In this case, people are viewed as unwilling or unable to provide solutions and need discipline in order to do so. The third model is the *compensatory* model. This model does not hold people responsible for their problems, but does hold them responsible for the solutions. People are seen "as having to compensate for the handicaps or obstacles imposed on them by their situation with a special kind of effort, ingenuity, or collaboration with

Table 10.1 Components of Four Helping Models

	Moral Model	Enlightenment Model	Compensatory (Enpowerment) Model	Medical Model
Responsibility	individual alone is responsible for creating and solving own problems	individual is responsible for problems, but not responsible for solutions	individual is not responsible for problems, but is responsible for solutions	individual is not responsible for problems or solutions
Help	if it occurs, it is in the form of motivation, such as reminding individual of own fate and responsibility (in the form of rewards and punishments for appropriate behavior)	emphasis is on enlightening individual as to true nature of problem and difficult actions needed to deal with it	to empower/assist individual to better deal with the environment; individual is seen as deserving opportunities or resources	received by or accepted from experts
Strength	compels individual to take unequivocal stance toward life; if individual does not like situation, he or she is responsible for changing it and should not wait for others' help	a basis of coping if unable to control what is experienced as undesirable on own part; allows individual to credit promises of change on external agencies, rather than own word	allows individual to direct energy outward to solve problems, without blaming self for existence of problems; individual must be assertive and is given credit for devising solutions	allows individual to claim and accept help without being blamed for weaknesses/problems
Weakness	can lead to belief that the world is just and that all is possible; individual victim is responsible for what happens to him or her	can lead to fanatical/obsessive concern with problems and reconstruction of life around behaviors/relations designed to help deal with problems; individual required to accept negative image of self and a strong degree of submission to agents of social control	individual who solves problems he or she did not create may feel great pressure (alienation) and develop negative view of world	individual is seen as ill or incapacitated, is expected to accept this state, and is exempt from his or her ordinary social responsibilities; fosters dependence

others" (Brickman et al., 1982, p. 371). In order for the people to develop solutions, they need to be empowered. Thus this model might be called an *empowerment* model. Hughes (1988) suggests that one problem with the compensatory model is that people may become upset and alienated from having to solve problems that were not necessarily of their own making. He also suggests that, compared to dependency, alienation may be the lesser of two evils. The *medical* model, the fourth model of the typology, suggests that people are neither responsible for the problems nor the solutions. In this case, those with the problems are seen as needing treatment. This model assumes that experts are best suited for identifying the problem and providing the appropriate treatments. One problem resulting from the use of the medical model is that those with the problems may become dependent upon those with the solutions.

The choice of how to provide an educational intervention will vary depending upon the helping model used. Basing a family life education program upon the wrong model can mean failure for the intervention. In specific situations, some models may be more effective or efficient than in other situations. Two models that are commonly used (Hughes, 1988) in developing interventions for families are the compensatory (empowerment) and the medical models. Thus, both will be analyzed in more detail.

Compensatory (Empowerment) Model

There are several assumptions underlying empowerment. First, the empowerment model assumes that experts work in conjunction with those believed to have problems in order to identify both the problems (or needs) and the solutions. Empowerment enhances the possibilities for people to control their own lives, including the ability of people to influence individuals and organizations that affect their lives and the lives of those about whom they care (Hughes, 1988; Rappaport, 1981). Cochran (1986b) suggests that empowerment is based on a nondeficit model, that is, one that assumes that all individuals, families, and communities have strengths upon which they can build.

A second assumption of the empowerment model is that people are cognitive of their needs, their values, and their own goals and that these can be put into action. The corollary of this assumption is that "experts" are not the only source of information for identifying needs or identifying solutions. Thus helpers should act more as collaborators rather than as experts within programs designed to enhance the quality of life for individuals across the life span. For the family life educator this means asking questions such as, "What can we do together to address this problem?" or "How can I be of help?"

A third assumption of this model is that diversity is useful and adaptive (Hughes, 1988). Rappaport (1981) has noted that empowerment should be based on divergent reasoning, since divergent reasoning encourages diversity through the support of many different local groups, rather than one centralized social agency or institution. Rappaport argues that centralized groups that control resources and use convergent reasoning attempt to homogenize people and suggest that there are standardized ways in which people should live their lives. The implication for family life education is that rather than providing "The" answer, the profession provides a variety of answers to ways to live out one's life across the life span. A second implication is that problems, needs, issues and the solutions or needed information are identified in concert with those who are the targets of education efforts.

It is further noted by Hughes (1988) that there are other assumptions of the empowerment model based on Berger and Neuhaus's (1977) concern that help is most effective when it is provided by small, intimate social institutions. It is asserted that people find meaning in their lives through their families, neighborhoods, churches, and voluntary organizations. These social institutions can be the best at providing the appropriate assistance that people need in their lives. Cochran (1986b) notes that one method for reaching people within an empowerment model is to facilitate informal resource exchanges among individuals and groups, perhaps at the neighborhood level. An implication for the family life education profession is that an effective method of reaching people, particularly to maintain knowledge and skills across a longer term, would be the development of support groups that encourage and support behavioral change. Another implication might be to help people learn how to develop support systems throughout the life span so that when necessary, they can call upon other people for the types of information, motivation, and resources necessary to help them through a particular troublesome time. Empowerment thus includes components aimed at strengthening individuals' or families' networks and environments, and developing a sense of community throughout the life cycle.

Hughes (1988) further notes another assumption based upon Cochran's (1986a) work: that empowerment can be at several different levels of analysis. The range includes the individual's own sense of well-being, enhancement, or subjective quality of life through various changes in the objective environment, through improvement and strengthening of the more immediate social environment (such as the family or other intimate relationships), through larger networks (such as kinship groups or neighborhoods), on to such things as community action at a larger level. The implication for life-span family life education is that the development of an integrated program considers the most appropriate intervention level. Programs should perhaps be multilevel in their focus. A more comprehensive program might work at developing the individual's sense of well-being while working at strengthening kinship ties. Another program might help individuals help strengthen their families while at the same time working for community empowerment, so that ways to support the strengthening of families within that community might be identified.

Several reasons for choosing the compensatory model, such as allowing the people with the problems to engage their energies outward, working toward solutions, and building community, are suggested by Hughes (1988). Wright and Rosenblatt (1988) maintain that building community is an important aspect of family life education. Since families do not exist in isolation, families ought to be encouraged and educated in ways of seeking help and support when needed from their relatives, neighbors, and community groups. This reciprocal relationship has important implications for the family life education profession; that people across the life span can be made aware of their need for community, and communities can become sensitive to the fact that throughout their lives, people need community.

Medical Model

Life-span family life education interventions founded upon the medical model are based on different assumptions. In this case, the educators identify the needs of individuals and families and develop the appropriate treatments to correct these deficits. The medical model and resulting programs assume that individuals are not responsible for their problems; rather, people are seen as victims of forces beyond their control. From the perspective of this model, family life educators, as trained experts, can help individuals best and most efficiently by giving them solutions to their problems.

Like empowerment, the medical model may also operate at different levels of analysis. For example, a program might consider individuals in isolation from their environments and provide answers on overcoming a particular problem, such as a communication deficit, parenting problems, or alienation from kinship systems, families, or communities.

A program could also have a family wellness approach, enhancing families through giving appropriate preventative treatments allowing the prevention of problems. The medical model could also take a community health approach, contending that individuals and families in the community can be strengthened by strengthening the community. At this level of analysis, the professionals would work at strengthening larger groups and providing insight so that communities, neighborhoods, schools, and social agencies could provide an environment in which healthy families could develop. Regardless of the level of analysis, the professional uses her or his insight and expertise to develop models of the needs that are critical and strategies to overcome these deficits.

Across the life span, there may be many situations where the medical model could prove to be effective. It may also be more time efficient. The empowerment model assumes collaborative work between individuals and the educators. This may be time consuming and may encounter resistance from people. It may be difficult to find enough time to work on identifying needs and solutions, and the needs identified by a target population may be felt needs or demands, and may be different than those identified by community leaders or experts. It may also be the case that those most in need do not have the time, energy, or the creativity to identify the exact problem and solutions, and are in need of expert help. Perhaps after they have been helped, empowerment schemes may become more appropriate. Hughes (1988) notes that the medical model is more appropriate for severely dysfunctional families or incapacitated communities. Individuals or groups that are blocked and have become immobilized are perhaps in desperate need of help. In this case, experts are in the best position to provide treatment allowing people to get to a healthier state. Then they can start to make progress on their own. But in these situations, with severely dysfunctional families or incapacitated communities, family life education would probably be most effective if used in conjunction with other helping professions, such as therapists, social service agencies, rural development specialists, or social action programs.

Building Integrated Family Life Education Programs Across the Life Span

Several recommendations can be made concerning the development of life-span family life education based upon the information presented in this chapter and the experience of the authors. The first step toward building an integrated family life education program is needs assessment, or identifying exactly what issues are critical. First of all, educators should know the needs that are critical for individuals at various points of the life span (McKillip, 1987). In addition, it is clear that quality family life education is built upon a foundation of careful conceptualizations and rigorous research (Kaplan & Hennon, 1990). Regardless of the skills of the educator, the program is only as good as its content and this is only as good as the research and theory on which it is based. Thus, in addition to linking programs to actual needs, basing the intervention on strong theory and research is required. Even if the program is needs-based, theoretically solid, and based on sound research, it may have little value if it does not reach the target audience at the right time and in the right way. Educators must constantly consider the best methods to reach people so that they might learn. Family life educators must also continually ask, "Did this intervention work?" "Did it make a difference?" The importance of evaluating family life education programs must not be underestimated (Kaplan & Hennon, 1990). As McKillip (1987) notes, "nothing would aid the identification of solutions more than the existence of hard-headed impact assessment of current programming" (p. 13). Because of their importance, each of the above points will be further elaborated.

Needs Assessment: The Foundation for Education

Integrated family life education interventions start with needs assessments. How do educators identify what exactly should be taught? Or, if one has expertise in some particular subject matter, with whom should it be shared (Hennon & Brubaker, 1982)? The question of needs assessment is sticky and certainly is not value free (McKillip, 1987). Exactly how are "needs" defined? If needs are defined as requirements for survival, then there are fewer needs. If, however, needs are defined as having the potential to improve the quality of life, enhance interpersonal relationships, and help people to feel better, then the range of potential needs is broadened. For example, does one need a red, convertible BMW with MFT PHD on the license plate, or just some type of safe transportation? What if the BMW was the reward promised to oneself for the financial and social deprivation endured while pursuing an advanced degree? During hard times and while feeling depressed, the "car" was always there as a goal. Does this symbolic value make it a more justifiable emotional health need?

In addition to referring to the Framework for Life-Span Family Life Education (Arcus, 1987) to sensitize themselves to potential developmental needs of individuals and families in their communities, how can family life educators keep abreast of critical educational needs? Cooperative Extension is a logical place to begin. Specialists can conduct high quality needs assessments of families in their own states or regions. Through combined effort, national assessments can be conducted to identify critical needs across the life span. These identified needs should be shared throughout the family life education profession. Rigorous sampling procedures must be used, and good survey, social indicator analysis, focus group assessments, or other techniques must be followed if reliance is to be placed on the assessments (McKillip, 1987). Diverse family types and life-styles across the life span must be reached. The profession should be able to identify: (a) what is needed; (b) what is desired that would be helpful; and (c) what is desired, but less critical.

McKillip (1987), based upon the work of Bradshaw (1972), distinguishes between four types of expectations that support judgments of need. These are: (a) normative need, an expectation based upon an expert definition of adequate level of performance; (b) felt need, those expectations that one has for his or her own outcomes; (c) expressed need, or expectation for outcomes based upon the behavior of the target population through the use of services or education available; and (d) comparative need, the expectations that are based upon the performance of persons or groups other than the target person or group. In this last instance, the target population is considered to have a problem if it uses a service less or more than others, or if its scores diverge significantly from the average for the population on a performance measure.

Wants can be defined as something people are willing to pay for, in time, money, or other units of value. Demands, "something people are willing to march for" (McKillip, 1987, p. 16), differ from wants in that the target population, rather than the educator, originates and presents the demand. In many cases, "needs" involve the recognition of a problem by an observer. A need is more dispassionate than a demand. "Objective" indicators of a need are frequently used. As McKillip (1987) points out: "The person that another believes to be in need may neither recognize a problem nor use a solution. Many of the more familiar techniques of need identification share this drawback: they are aimed at helping *observers* identify problems that a target population has" (p. 17). Perhaps the family life education profession has cause both to inform people across the life span as to their *needs,* as well as to *solutions* to these needs.

Sharing with other professionals the information obtained through need analysis can occur via various modes, including journal publications, newsletters, electronic bulletin boards, direct mailings, and at conferences. An emphasis should be placed on conducting quality needs assessment research. Moreover, this research has to be conducted often, as needs change over time.

While practitioners may assess needs, often this appears to be poorly done. For example, how valid is it to have a focus group consisting of "regulars" (those who typically attend programs) to identify needs? A statement of family needs in some particular geographical area may therefore be based on a small and biased sample. Moreover, what influence, if any, do one's vested interests play in the reporting of needs identified? It is likely that poor needs assessments results in: (a) people with the most critical needs not being represented, (b) people not adequately identifying their needs, and (c) a systematic underrepresentation of diverse families and individuals and their identified needs. The methodology chosen, as well as value judgments, will likely affect the types of needs identified.

Surveys and community forums provide a ready source of felt needs, that is, those that depend upon the target population for insight into its own problems (McKillip, 1987). The needs identified by the target population and "key informants" may not match. For instance, the authors recently read the results of a rather sophisticated needs assessment conducted to review existing human needs and of the public perception of needs within the service area of a particular organization. The responses of key informants, selected because of their expertise with community issues due to their positions as community leaders and/or as social service providers, showed the following rank-ordered needs based on seriousness of each: substance abuse, employment, crime prevention, basic material needs/shelter, housing, delinquency prevention, mental health services, education, household violence, and planning/coordination of services.

The households sampled in this same community identified the following prioritized list of serious problems: recreation shortage, affordable housing, lack of affordable medical care, drug abuse, public transportation, child day-care shortage, pollution, crime, alcoholism, under/unemployment. While the report notes that the key informants and household survey instruments are different and cannot be compared directly, it also points out that it is clear that the household survey respondents' perceptions of needs within their neighborhoods differ significantly from those of the key informants'. Of the five most important issues, only two are on both lists. Going from the key informants to the households, substance abuse drops from first to fourth and housing increases from fifth to second. The other three important issues for households are on the bottom half (of 25 issues) of the key informants' rank order, and three issues (concern for crime, basic material needs, education) drop dramatically in the households' ranking. Less dramatic but sizable decreases are seen for mental health services and family violence. If you were presented with this needs analysis and asked to develop an appropriate family life education program for this community, to be funded by and requiring the support of key agencies and people, what would you do?

A balance is required between self-identified needs versus those that are identified through other procedures such as emerging basic or applied research, analyzing use of services, social indicator analysis, or the collective wisdom and experience of family life educators and other experts. On the other hand, if people do not understand that they have a need or can benefit by acquiring information on a particular topic, they are not likely to seek education. While programs can be offered, of even greater importance is for individuals to benefit from these programs. A balance is desired between offering programs to meet needs as identified by professionals, versus meeting those felt and requested by families and individuals. On deciding upon this balance, sometimes critical and hard decisions have to be made. But also, sometimes creative insight can lead to innovative and beneficial programming. For example, does learning more about cake decorating lead to a higher quality of family life? Does color analysis lead to better family financial management and thus greater family cohesion? Sometimes, both desired topics of high interest and critical issues that are sensitive and difficult for people to admit they need or understand the relevance of, can be covered in the same program. Perhaps educators addressing the topics requested or needs that are self-identified, might help people to see that other needs, which have not been explicitly identified, can also be met.

Besides conducting needs assessments, other sources used to identify important skills and knowledge for improving the quality of family life across the life span include the collective wisdom of experts and the basic and applied research published in professional journals and books. Programs can then be developed to help people acquire appropriate skills and knowledge. Basic and applied research identifies the interrelationships among skill and knowledge variables that can lead to better parenting, improved communication, enrichment of the marriage, management of stress, and the like. Research has also identified the characteristics of strong, competent, resilient, and healthy families (Lewis, Beavers, Gossett, & Phillips, 1976; McCubbin, Thompson, Pirner, & McCubbin, 1988; D. Olson et al., 1983; Stinnet & DeFrain, 1985; Walsh, 1982). This rich source of information must be consistently monitored and used to keep abreast with the field. Educators must be consumers of this data base, and be trained to read and select relevant research critically as the bases of their programming. This knowledge, used in conjunction with awareness of current family life trends and needs assessments, can help the profession best meet the needs of families and their members.

Grounding Family Life Education in Theory and Research

Educators must keep up to date on current theories about human development and families across the life span. Family life education should be firmly grounded in theoretical models (Kaplan & Hennon, 1990). Educators should be able to justify, on theoretical grounds, the objectives for their programs, exactly why the types of skills or knowledge being taught are important, and how these will contribute to strengthening the family, improving the quality of life, or the plasm of the marriage. Family life educators should always be able to articulate the theoretical basis for each family life education program developed.

As noted above, educational efforts must be tied to the current research about individuals and families at various points of the life span. It is unethical for family life education programs to be based upon out-of-date information or to teach information that is perhaps invalid. Not only should the family life educator be current with the research in the field by attending conferences, reading quality applied journals in the human development and family areas, but also by exploration into more basic research.

Educators should also be abreast of the latest findings concerning effective and efficient teaching and learning modalities, techniques, and methodologies in family life education. Are particular workshops, models, or interventions presented in the most efficient or effective manner, or are educators caught in a "rut" because they have discovered a program that they like?

The relationship between research and family life education is reciprocal, that is, not only should family life education be based upon solid research, but family life education can drive research. The kinds of issues that families bring up, the kinds of problems that need to be solved, the kinds of things that family life educators run into on a day-to-day basis, can be the "grist" for researchers to mill. This is similar to the ideal Cooperative Extension model, which is designed to provide those individuals working on the front lines (such as 4-H agents and Extension Home Economists) current research knowledge to help people solve problems. The issues that people are bringing to those on the front lines are than fed back to the researchers and Extension Specialists in order for research to be conducted on the issues of concern.

Professional organizations are places for this same kind of exchange to take place. Greater informal exchange, at annual conferences and through professional journals and newsletters, between educators and researchers and also with counselors and therapists, can improve the whole field, bringing new insights and new solutions, new paradigms and new conceptual frameworks. These innovations can benefit everyone, including most specifically those individuals and families who are the focus of all it is that family life educators do.

Evaluation: Was the Program Effective?

The importance of rigorous assessments of interventions cannot be overemphasized. Only in such ways will the whole family life education field be advanced, as well as the programs of each individual family life educator. In an integrated program, considerations for evaluating the program are made during the conceptualization and development of the program, and are not "tacked on" at the end.

A question always to be asked, is "How do I know that this particular intervention, this particular program, this particular workshop, has any value?" "Happiness indicators"—asking participants if they liked an experience or thought they benefited from it—are not an effective means to evaluate a program's usefulness and impact. Longitudinal studies, pre-post designs, use of control groups, follow-up studies, in-depth interviews, perhaps even ethnographic and case studies, are important (see Conner, 1981; Fitz-Gibbon & Morris, 1987; Giblin et al., 1985; and King, Morris, & Fitz-Gibbon, 1987, for some excellent examples).

Important outcomes to be identified are any resulting positive *or* negative changes in behavior, attitudes, values, skills, and knowledge related to participating in the program. How long-lasting was this change? Did it have an effect that improved the quality of one's life or marriage? Over what period of time? Was the benefit felt by more than one person in the family? What were the negative consequences of making changes? What was the cost-benefit ratio of negative to positive outcomes? Were the objectives of the program achieved? Were these objectives ambitious enough to effect real change and developed with enough specificity to be measured and evaluated? Was too much promised? (See the discussion earlier in this chapter concerning the "promise" of family life education.)

Questions like these, and also perhaps, cost analysis (Thompson, Rothrock, Strain, & Palmer, 1981), have to be pursued in assessing the effectiveness and impact of family life education across the life span. Good designs are important for both summative and formative evaluations (Fitz-Gibbon & Morris, 1987). Not only should the educator be able to produce a defensible public statement summarizing the program's accomplishments, but the use of rigorous evaluation design during a program's formative period provides opportunities to assess the effectiveness of the program (or selected subcomponents). Formative evaluation allows persuasion of self and staff to constantly scrutinize and rethink assumptions and activities underlying the program. Good evaluation designs can help in conducting small-scale pilot studies and testing newly developed program components. This, in turn, helps inform decisions among possible alternative courses of action and to settle controversies about the more effective ways to install programs (Fitz-Gibbon & Morris, 1987).

Not everyone is trained to do this type of evaluative research. Does that mean, as a profession, that educators give up trying to assess program effectiveness? Does it mean that, as a profession, education based on "blind faith" is acceptable? The answer is absolutely "No." It does mean, however, that the profession should strive to advance the state of its art by better preparing its members to appreciate the importance of, and being equipped to do, the types of evaluation studies required. It means integrating programs—including the evaluation— and then utilizing the results to "fine tune" programs so they are more effective for specific target populations at specific points in the life span.

The need for evaluation also creates opportunities for collaborative research. Professionals who are primarily educators can work closely with those who are primarily researchers. The expertise of each can be combined to plan, implement, and evaluate family life education programs. As "canned" programs are developed for marketing or distribution, they should first be thoroughly evaluated, and then reevaluated periodically in the field.

Linking Family Life Education to Counseling and Therapy

The relationship between family life education and counseling should be explored and built upon as appropriate. A simple dichotomy might be that counseling, or therapeutic, models are to help change a person's paradigm. That is, to help change the way the world is viewed. Therapy and counseling can also be said to help change a personality aspect. Education, on the other hand, is providing knowledge that somehow can allow people to make informed decisions about their lives. Another way of conceptualizing this difference might be that therapeutic interventions or counseling are provided after the fact; that is, after a problem has developed.

Family life education is preventative in orientation and is therefore more a primary, than secondary or tertiary, intervention. However, these distinctions often become blurred in reality (Guerney, 1977; Guerney & Maxson, 1990; L'Abate & Weinstein, 1987). Some of what is done under the rubric of education may in fact be therapeutic in nature, and some of what occurs in therapy may in fact be educational. Recently, some professionals have described psychoeducational approaches, a blending of information and therapy (see for example, Boss, 1988; Guerney, & Maxson, 1990; Kaplan & Hennon, 1990; and L'Abate & Weinstein, 1987). Looking at the methods used in therapy, the way that therapy is done, and the goals of therapy and counseling can help inform family life educators about what may be appropriate techniques, skills, and methods of working with groups, and the kinds of interventions that may or may not work. The skills and theories of therapy can therefore be valuable assets to educators.

The therapy field can also be a rich source to be mined in a different vein. Not only should the research done by people typically known as family relations researchers be consulted by educators, but the therapy literature should also be readily consulted. This knowledge base can provide a rich source of insight into family process, and therefore what education can do to help strengthen families.

Having professional ties with counselors and therapists can facilitate working together with a family, groups of families or children, or individuals. A two-pronged approach may be more beneficial than just one modality or the other. An example might be dealing with the often reported decline in marital satisfaction that takes place over the life cycle. While therapy may be able to help that situation, so might education. Perhaps therapists are helping couples in the community who are experiencing concerns about the quality of their marriages. More effort could be directed at helping individuals in becoming educated to help prevent such drops in marital satisfaction from occurring in the first place. Therapist can team up with educators to provide a wider range of effective interventions that families and individuals can find helpful. They can also refer clients to each other. Therapists can direct people to educational programs, and educators can refer people to therapy as necessary.

Reaching the Public

Family life education must be sensitive to different learning styles as well as different needs that develop across the life span. Family life education should be based upon pedagogical models that are sensitive to different needs, different interests, and different ways of learning at various ages and interest points. Certain people are more apt to learn at specific times. Individuals currently involved in the transition to parenthood will probably be more interested in learning good parenting skills than are individuals with grown children. A 16-year-old who is not sexually active and who plans to attend college might be less interested in parenting education than in other issues, such as getting along with one's own parents or life course planning. While family life education may, in some situations, encompass programs of a more general nature (e.g., strengthening families, time management), those keyed to target groups facing specific issues (e.g., drug abuse, runaways) or transitions (e.g., first-time parenthood, adoption) are also important.

It is important to consider the methods used to reach families and their members over various points of the life span. For example, some researchers indicate that young families want to acquire information by use of learn-at-home packets (Hennon & Peterson, 1981). Other researchers indicate that older individuals benefit from television shows, radio programs, and newspapers (Burton & Hennon, 1980). Age-paced newsletters seem effective for parents (Cudaback, Darden, Nelson, O'Brien, Pinsky, & Wiggins, 1985). Others gain much by attending face-to-face meetings, and by taking materials home to be used in a more private setting (Hennon, Mayer, & Burton, 1981; Seltzer, Litchfield, Lowy, & Levin, 1989). While some people use self-help books, others prefer interpersonal contact, while still others like to share information in group settings. Emerging technologies and delivery mediums include cable television, audio- and videotapes, satellite transmitted teleconferences, computer programs, laser discs, and electronic bulletin boards. All of these possibilities should be considered when developing family life education for a particular target group. Not only should the need for the subject matter be carefully considered, but the characteristics of the target population also require attention. In this way the program can be customized for specific segments of the population.

How often do family life educators assess the learning styles of those seeking to be educated? Perhaps more attention should be given to identifying the learning styles and preferences of the target group, whether unwed mothers, families impacted by unemployment, families being relocated, individuals facing retirement, or those having lost a spouse through divorce or death. While assessing learning styles and preferences prior to program implementation may be time-consuming and cumbersome, it may vastly improve the program's effectiveness. Much emphasis has been placed on individualized learning within the schools. Do family life educators provide individualized learning opportunities both in and out of school settings? These are important questions to be asked and answered as the profession expands.

Potential Limitations of Family Life Education

The educator should be aware of his or her limitations regarding a particular subject matter at a particular point in the life span. How knowledgeable the educator is regarding a particular subject is the obvious place to start. Serious scholarship and constant updating is required by educators. The profession cannot advance beyond the limits of the knowledge of those providing the education.

Awareness of one's values and biases concerning family life across the life span is important. Personal values may be shared during educational sessions, but they should probably be identified as such. It is important for individual family life educators to be aware of gut-level reactions to certain kinds of families, problems, genders, life-styles, sexual orientations, or personal appearances. It is necessary for the educator to be cognizant about her or his responses in the classroom or community, as well as the values held regarding how families ought to be, how they should not be, and how they work. This is important self-knowledge. It will help in assessing the subject matter, target groups, and types of individuals that are not approached in relatively value-neutral ways. It also helps in understanding one's impact on those participating in the program. In other words, self-assessment can help in the recognition of concomitant learning (e.g., what the student learns in addition to what the instructor intends) occurring during educational efforts.

Family life educators should be aware of the limitations of what it is they are attempting. How much change is really possible? Is too much, or perhaps too little, expected? What type of follow-up exists? Are the appropriate motivation and encouragement for change provided over time? Are refresher courses offered? Are naturally occurring or other support groups being tapped to help sustain personal and family growth? Is a more active role on the part of the family life educator needed? Have individuals, families, and/or communities been empowered? Is the educator inappropriately applying a medical or enlightenment model when an empowerment helping model would be more appropriate, or vice versa?

There are limitations on what is known about individual growth, family life, and relationships. How good is the research? How valid are the generalizations? Caution must be exercised to avoid overgeneralizations in family life education. Are the "principles" espoused firmly based on scientific (or other) evidence? Social science research may have severe limitations, in terms of generalizability, the quality of the research, the way variables are measured, and in the kind of concepts being used. Family life educators need to be aware of such limitations; thus training as critical consumers of research is a must. Being an educator is not mutually exclusive from being a researcher. Solid research provides the data base for the family life educator. It is on this foundation that programs rest. Theoretical and empirical knowledge must be acquired, either through combining one's own scholarship with the extant research, or by perusing the literature. Therefore, educators must be: (a) trained to be critical consumers of theory; (b) able to develop useful theories and conceptual frameworks; (c) critical consumers and judges of research; and (d) able to understand and interpret the stated limitations, as well as those not identified, in reports of research. In other words, rather than just precipitously accepting the "received" word about families, educators should strive both critically to assess knowledge and to generate (within the bounds of respectable scholarship) new concepts, configurations, and useful insights concerning family relations.

Summary

This chapter attempts to inform the reader about contemporary and future directions in life-span family life education. It begins with the understanding that family life education is preventative in nature with the objectives of (a) helping people gain knowledge about concepts and principles that are relevant to family living, (b) exploring personal attitudes and values, and (c) developing interpersonal skills. The content and possible uses of the Framework for Life-Span Family Life Education are noted. This framework is utilized to highlight some major directions, issues, and limitations in the practice of family life education for children, adolescents, and adults. Next, the chapter discusses the development of integrated life-span family life education programming. It reviews helping models for life-span family life education, noting specifically the characteristics of both the empowerment and the medical models. The potential for sharing the results of needs assessments are discussed, with attention given to the different types (normative, felt, expressed, comparative, wants, and demands) of needs. The importance for grounding education in high quality theory and research is stressed, as is the potential reciprocal nature of education and research. Ties with counseling and therapy are also noted. Summative and formative evaluation designs are part of the integrated family life education model. The urgency of conducting rigorous and insightful assessments of family life education across the life span is emphasized. Various ways of reaching the public with critical information at the appropriate times across the life span are noted. The chapter ends with a caution about "knowing your limits" concerning family life education.

It is hoped that the information presented in this chapter will be useful in helping both novice and experienced educators establish quality integrated educational programming to meet the needs of individuals and families across the life span. Family life education has become established as a profession. Its future depends upon how well its individual members, independently and in concerted action, can meet the needs of individuals and families, as defined by both those audiences as well as by those who control the purse strings and can set policy. This chapter discusses some current trends in family life education, noting both strengths and some shortcomings. Its strengths can be built upon, and creative use of resources can lead to even better life-span family life education in the future.

11

Marital Therapy in the Twenty-First Century

ANTHONY P. JURICH
CANDYCE S. RUSSELL

When one is asked to look into the future, it is always a difficult, yet challenging, task. One must look at past history, examine present conditions, and extrapolate into future trends. Even when historical trends and contemporary conditions are clear, the science of prediction requires an element of art in order to build a future that is not yet here. This makes the science of prognostication less than perfect and less than science.

This task is especially difficult when trying to predict the future of marital therapy. First, the field of marital therapy is relatively new and does not have a long and extensive past history. Consequently, recurring cycles of change are hard to identify because the field hasn't been around long enough to give us a complete picture of the pendulum swings that are part of every profession's history. Since we have only part of the picture, we don't know if the present theories and practices are part of a continued period of growth, a plateau phase, or the crest of a creative wave that will soon turn downward.

Second, marital therapy, of its nature, is reactive. As marital therapists, we react to the families that come into our office. As a profession, we react to the changes in the world that affect marriages. For example, if the economy of the country takes a downturn, marital therapists will, of necessity, see more couples whose problems will have a strong financial component. This will necessitate a greater understanding of financial decision making on the part of the marital therapist. Our profession changes in response to changes in the marriages we treat, which are in turn changed by societal changes. At each juncture there is an additional potential layer of error introduced into the art of prognostication.

Finally, it is very debatable as to which conditions will have the greatest impact on the profession of marital therapy. Changes in the structure of the American family will most assuredly affect the field of marital therapy. However, will it affect it *more* than a decision by the insurance industry to get out of the business of mental health entirely or a mandate of the government to include marriage and family therapy services as a service area on all insurance policies? All of these would affect the field of marital therapy. The relative effect, however, is open to debate. In addition, many of these decisions are political in nature and therefore are open to the vicissitudes of politics, a field notorious for its *lack* of predictability. The bottom line is, although we are about to gaze into the crystal ball, the image in the crystal is hazy and a great deal of detail may be difficult to distinguish.

The Crossroads of Political Realities

Of all the factors affecting the practice of marital therapy in the 21st century, politics is perhaps the least predictable. There are a series of decisions that will be made in the next 10 years that will have a major impact upon both the form and the viability of the profession of marital therapy. Most of these political decisions center around the realities of money. If we enter into a severe or prolonged economic depression, the face of marital therapy in particular, and the entire mental health field in general, will change. Programs at the federal, state, and local level will be cut or trimmed back, keeping couples who need professional assistance from having access to marital therapy. Utilizing Maslow's "Hierarchy of Needs" in *A Theory of Human Motivation* (1943), government policy will be directed more toward the physical needs of its people, rather than their psychosocial needs. Because marital therapy is a relatively recent field, competing with more established fields of psychotherapy, such as psychiatry or psychology, there is more probability that marital therapy will be "pushed out of the nest" of the therapeutic community. While the growing political presence of such organizations as the American Association for Marriage and Family Therapy lessens the likelihood of such a consequence, such threats remain a possibility if an economic depression were long enough and severe enough.

Under such a scenario, the government would likely try to get out of the business of providing services while at the same time requiring that more professionals be regulated. Whereas the government may wish to minimize the level of need, that would be hard to do after three decades of research into psychosocial problems and the dissemination of that information to the public. The populace is much more aware of such issues as domestic violence, depression, and out-of-control children and is better educated about the role of marital therapy in the successful resolution of those difficulties. Mental health consumer groups are springing up daily. It would not be easy for the government to withdraw support for needed services.

Therefore, despite a tightening economic situation, governmental bodies will be pressured to continue to confront mental health issues. Presently, there is a great deal of pressure from those who have been disenfranchised from the health care system to push the government in the United States to consider a system of socialized medicine similar to that which exists in Canada. This has been countered by the United States government in the form of several health care insurance bills that would leave health care, including mental health and consequently marital therapy, in the hands of the private sector while, at the same time, mandating specific problem areas and providers who would have to be covered under all insurance plans. This is the essence of such bills as the Kennedy-Waxman health care initiative. This would keep the government from providing direct services, while regulating the private sector in its provision of needed services. Such a plan would most likely prohibit insurers from abandoning mental health needs. There would also be a renewed effort to work with corporate America in providing for the mental health needs of their work force through such plans as managed health care systems.

Such a trend in the mental health field would have a major impact on the way marital therapists conduct their business. In all likelihood, the trend of marriage and family therapists' being licensed by states will be continued. This will mean a greater demand for educational preparation at a time when money from governmental sources for education is likely to decrease and competition for educational funds is likely to increase (Stone & Archer, 1990). This will pressure accrediting bodies both to raise standards to meet licensing requirements and to find alternative paths to degree completion in order to survive financially. New marital therapists will find the competition for good schools and excellent training to be tougher and more expensive. However, there will also be alternative educational opportunities from secondary sources as paths to licensure. For the consumer of marital therapy, this will mean a greater assurance that professional standards have been met by certified professionals. If alternative paths to credentialing are allowed, however, the public may still not be sure of professional competence. It will get better, but it will still be a long way from ideal.

Marital therapists will spend more of their time leaving a paper trail for insurance companies and government vendors. As insurance becomes a primary method of payment, more marital therapists will have to fill out more forms and become acquainted with both the jargon and the regulations of the insurance industry. Because this industry is based so heavily upon the medical model, marital therapy will have more of the trappings of medical service. This will require a diagnosis that will need as much specificity as possible. Therefore, marital therapists will have to increase their assessment skills and become acquainted with other models of illness and dysfunction, especially those put forth by the medical community. Therapy will also be pressured to be time-limited. In a medical model, specific types of care most often have specific treatment deadlines. Marital therapy does not lend itself well to this type of time limitation. Seldom can the marital therapist predict that therapy will be completed in "two months" or "four to six sessions." Often, the couple's presenting complaint, upon which the initial diagnosis is based, isn't even the real reason for their seeking therapy. They may be hiding their true problem, or they may not even be aware that there is an underlying problem. Despite these limitations, the insurance industry often requires a specific treatment plan with a time line elaborated. Health maintenance organizations (HMOs) will often sign for no more than six sessions. We believe that this will increase interest, among marital therapists, in short-term or time-limited treatment of marital difficulties. It will also emphasize the importance of termination issues and termination sessions. Of necessity, marital therapists will adjust their treatment as best they can to accommodate their clients' ability to pay.

Insurance company demands will also require marital therapists, as well as all mental health professionals, to demonstrate their therapeutic effectiveness and to hold themselves more accountable for providing therapeutic success. This means that, in a time of declining resources in the area of social services, *more* effort must be spent on including research in our clinical agenda. This is not an easy task. Gottfredson (1987) has pointed out that clinicians respond to an entirely different reward system than do researchers or academicians. A clinician may receive little or no reward for conducting a research project. In fact, since such an endeavor may take time away from his or her clinical activities, the clinician may find him- or herself chastised by an administrator for spending time on a research project that would be rewarded if that same clinician were an academician.

Some researchers have even suggested that researchers and clinicians, in fact, may have different personality types. Rushton, Murray, and Pavnonen (1983) found researchers to be achievement-oriented "investigative types," who possess such personality traits as ambition, endurance, dominance, and independence, while clinicians were more support-oriented "social types," who exhibited such personality traits as sociability, extroversion, and supportiveness. Furthermore, as Caro (1971) points out, researchers approach an examination of a clinical treatment program with a critical perspective, while practitioners consider a strong value commitment and belief in the program to be essential. Therefore, clinicians and researchers may approach the evaluation of a program of marital therapy very differently. Add to this the fact that good research design in the evaluation of marital therapy may conflict with the clinical ethics of the therapy itself (Jurich & Russell, 1985), and the reader can see that asking clinicians to produce research is indeed a very difficult task.

The press from insurance companies to demonstrate therapeutic effectiveness and the pressure from both the public and private sector to be more timely, accurate, and responsive (Saluter, 1989), will influence the profession of marital therapy to produce more research to document the effectiveness of its therapeutic techniques. This will encourage the field to broaden its definition of research to include qualitative, as well as quantitative, research and to identify which interventions are most effective for which presenting problems (Gurman & Kniskern, 1986). It will also encourage clinic directors to commit to a research program and reward clinicians for their research efforts (Stone & Archer, 1990). This will require a continued, and perhaps improved, linkage between research and practice in academic and postdegree training programs that train marital therapists. It may also promote greater cooperation between academicians and researchers and marital therapists in the field as meaningful research questions are identified and research projects designed. Academicians and clinical marital therapists will be called upon jointly to collect and analyze data and then disseminate results to the profession, to insurance companies, and to the public. We believe the increased call for accountability will promote collaboration between academic and applied clinicians in marital therapy as we move toward the 21st century.

Broad Societal Trends

More stable and more predictable than the vicissitudes of the political arena are the broad societal trends that we have witnessed over the past several decades. From past trends we can, with some insight, project into the world of the 21st century. While some of these trends are highly speculative, some are better grounded in demographic statistics.

The Graying of America

One of the most solid trends is that the population of the United States is growing older, both in terms of longevity and in the proportion of the population above the age of 65 (Glick, 1984). This trend poses several interesting scenarios for marital therapists. Marriages will have the potential to last a long time (Brubaker, 1986; 1990a). This may prompt some couples who would have "stuck their marriages out" for a shorter duration of time to seek a divorce when faced with the prospect of another 40 years of marital distress (Brubaker, 1990b). Therefore, marital therapists will be helping couples deal with "the long haul" and will be teaching coping strategies that can be used across multiple stressors, rather than *just* in the immediate crisis situation. Couples will have to be reminded that they will each change over time and that the nature of their relationship will also change over the years. While this caveat has always been important for couples to understand, it will become increasingly important as the couple faces the potential for a *very* long marriage that may last well beyond their seventieth birthdays.

The aging of the American population also means that more clients of an advanced age will be seeking the services of a marital therapist. Doing premarital therapy with a young couple in which neither partner has ever been married, is fairly standard practice for most marital therapists. What happens when the couple is in their sixties and has already been through one or more marriages? The life cycle changes described by Duvall (1957) for the newly married are quite different if the newly married or remarried are in their sixties (Brubaker, 1990b). The mind-set most therapists hold of who seeks premarital therapy services will have to be drastically altered. The marital therapist will have to incorporate a new understanding of adult development and aging into ideas about premarital therapy. We will have to broaden our perspective to include knowledge about the aging process and problems that aging couples encounter (Brubaker, 1985). The present generation of "older citizens" has never accepted therapy as well as the next generation of aged has (Sporakowski, 1988). Therefore, the increase in the aging cohort, together with the greater acceptance of therapy among that population should bring far more aging marital cases into therapy.

Marital therapists will also encounter more young or middle-aged couples whose marital difficulties include their relationships with aging parents (Brubaker, 1986, 1990a, 1990b). Many of these couples will feel an emotional and financial burden with respect to their aging parents (Saluter, 1989; R. Weiss, 1987). Such decisions as whether or not to put an aging parent in a nursing home can rip a couple to shreds. Even those aging parents who have achieved a degree of affluence will place stress upon a middle-aged couple who is attempting to be responsive to both their families of origin and their family of procreation (Giordano, 1988). The tensions of being the "Sandwich Generation" (D. Miller, 1981) will often erupt in the form of marital problems. Marital therapists of the 21st century will have to learn how to recognize when the presenting marital complaints of the couple have their roots in the Sandwich Generation phenomenon. Marital therapists will have to develop an increasing awareness of problems of the aging population and their children and will need to develop intergenerational approaches for coping with such situations (Sporakowski, 1988). Marital therapy that deals with the issues of four or five generations, all of whom may still be alive, will become a necessity in the 21st century.

Ethnic and Cultural Diversity

The American culture is really a "society of subcultures, and family structures and functions are likely to be different from place to place" (R. Weiss, 1987, p. 484). Despite the validity of this statement, many in the "dominant culture" tend to minimize their concerns and behave as if their perspective on life, their values, and their priorities are universally shared (Crawley, 1988). The reality, however, is that we are a very *diverse* culture and that we are becoming more, not less, diverse.

Ethnic and racial minorities will continue to increase as a proportion of the total population (Saluter, 1989; Wetzel, 1989). In addition to these trends, there will be more diversity due to the influence of international families, both migrating to and visiting our country (Stone & Archer, 1990). In addition, the prevalence of mass media in our culture introduces us to a cultural variety that many of us would never otherwise experience in person. One might argue the accuracy of many of these cultural images in the mass media and whether they contribute to or damage the cause of diversity. However, at least these images raise the question of diversity and make it more difficult to ignore anything that isn't defined as the cultural norm. Despite the increase in conservatism and racism that sought to eliminate diversity in the 1980s (Crawley, 1988), cultural and ethnic diversity will increase as we go into the 21st century.

Marital therapists must become aware of cultural and ethnic diversity and alter their methods in order to accommodate to what the client couple brings into the therapeutic relationship. In addition to the racial, ethnic, and cultural differences couples bring to the therapeutic situation, there are also differences in religion, geographical region of the country, sexual preference, and physical capabilities. The old conventional wisdom of therapy stipulated that the best therapist to provide therapy to a client from a "minority" background was someone who shares that background. Therefore, the conventional wisdom would tell us to send a black couple to a black therapist, a Catholic couple to a Catholic therapist, a gay couple to a gay therapist, and a handicapped couple to a handicapped therapist. Neither of us believes that this is necessary, functional, or even possible to do. Certainly the field of marital therapy is lacking in diversity along all of these lines and needs to recruit more members who are different from the "cultural norm." Any efforts in this direction should be applauded and we believe that the field of marital therapy will become much more racially, ethnically, and otherwise diverse than it presently is. Such similarities between client couples and therapists may be necessary in some cases and desirable in others. We believe, however, that *all* marital therapists must and will become more sensitive to cultural diversity over a variety of dimensions as we move toward the 21st century. We must move from "numerical diversity to an interactive pluralism" (Mooney, 1989, p. A15). We believe that, with a systemic view guiding the field of marital therapy, the field will move toward this goal.

Attention to ethnicity in the early 1980s made marital therapists aware of the great variety of beliefs about how spouses should relate to one another, but did so by offering generalizations about specific ethnic groups (e.g., McGoldrick, Pearce, & Giordano, 1982). Therapists were encouraged first to learn about their own ethnic background and then to explore the values and beliefs of one or two different ethnic groups. While the intent was not to contribute to stereotyping, the approach failed to sensitize therapists to the great diversity that exists *within* ethnic groups (e.g., Hardy, 1990).

More recent efforts to sensitize therapists to diversity have gone beyond ethnicity to include a large variety of cultural orientations. Celia Falicov (1988) defines *culture* as

> those *sets of shared world views and adaptive behaviors derived from simultaneous membership in a variety of contexts,* such as ecological setting (rural, urban, suburban), religious background, nationality and ethnicity, social, class, gender-related experience, minority status, occupation, political leanings, migratory patterns and stage of acculturation, or values derived from belonging to the same generation, partaking of a single historical moment, or political ideologies. (p. 336)

Within this perspective, each couple represents a "unique cultural niche." The therapist's job is to understand the worldview that emanates from that niche. Increasingly, marital therapists will learn how to ask questions that will identify how a particular couple is "similar to and different from" any of the *several* cultural groups to which they belong.

Most marital therapists will broaden their knowledge base of racial, cultural, ethnic, and other diversities. However, understanding differences between general groups of people may not be enough. The marital therapist will also have to alter his or her methods of gathering information, criteria for assessment, and techniques of intervention (e.g., Boyd-Franklin, 1990). Therefore, marital therapists of the future will spend more time listening to their clients' perceptions of their world. If we are to be truly sensitive to cultural diversity, we must seek to understand each marital couple through their eyes and use, as our starting point, their definition of the situation. This fits with the "constructivist" perspective of therapy (e.g., M. White & Epstein, 1990) wherein the therapist seeks to understand the spouses' unique perspectives and "ways of being." Increasing awareness of cultural diversity within the profession is likely to co-occur with increasing attention to the constructivist viewpoint in marital therapy as we enter the 21st century.

Some practical implications go beyond the purely theoretical implications for the marital therapist. Sporakowski (1988) points out that, in some cultures, couples may feel much more comfortable having therapy done in their home, rather than a clinic or an office. Part of the therapeutic accommodation to cultural diversity may be a home visit, conducting therapy in the home, or labeling the session a "meeting" (Boyd-Franklin, 1990) rather than a therapy session. In other cultures, especially those with strong boundaries between the generations, in-home therapy would be highly problematic. We are not suggesting that one form of marital therapy should take preference over the other. What we see for the future is a greater diversity of delivery systems and delivery styles to match the diverse cultural needs of the clients.

A therapist working with marital couples also needs to examine his or her own views and prejudices about the couples with whom he or she works. A marital therapist who feels uncomfortable working with a couple of a certain race, ethnicity, nationality, or religion, must be personally honest enough to be open to his or her own feelings. Some therapists who can comfortably work with a homogeneous couple have problems with a biracial, mixed ethnic, or dual-religion couple. Some therapists find it difficult to work with a physically or mentally handicapped couple, or a couple with a different sexual orientation than their own. We believe that, in the future, such self-awareness will be emphasized in training programs and that marital therapists of the future will be better able to recognize hidden or covert prejudices, better able to go to a supervisor to request help with the case, and better able to transfer a case with which they cannot work to another therapist with minimal damage to either the client couple or the therapist. We hope marital therapists of the future will be able to accept and work with diversity. Being optimistic, we think they will.

Gender Issues

Several broad societal trends have centered around the issue of gender. While the proportion of males and females in the population has remained relatively constant, the roles they play, both within the family and in the larger society, have changed significantly (Shehan & Scanzoni, 1988). With the advent of mechanization and the creation of many jobs that require no brute force or physical power, women have been able to compete with men on a more equal plane in the work place. The women's movement, the discovery of more effective methods of birth control, and a mass media that communicated the value of gender equality changed much of the world in which we live. Four significant trends that impact marriage and marital therapy as a result of these events are: (a) increasing numbers of women in the work force, (b) changes in spousal roles, (c) changes in parenting roles, and (d) the development of the men's movement.

Changes in the work force. Since the end of World War II, the percentage of women in the work force has increased by 20% (Rix, 1987). Moreover, the percentage of married women with husbands living in the home who are in the paid labor force has risen to more than 50%, and the number of mothers of school-aged children who now work outside the home has increased to more than 67% (Ritzer, 1986). This is quite a change from the philosophy of "a mother's place is in the home." While the conservative political policies of the 1980s tried to discourage mothers' working, such factors as the divorce rate, the fact that women began having babies later, and the harsh economic realities of trying to maintain the family's standard of living have led to increasing numbers of women, wives, and mothers entering the paid work force (Shehan & Scanzoni, 1988). For the marital therapist of the 21st century, therapy must recognize the press for equality between the sexes and the struggle many couples are having and will continue to have surrounding family hierarchies and gender roles. More couples will come into therapy with attempts to establish an equalitarian relationship, despite many cultural hostilities to that idea and against the tide of previous learning from their families of origin. Future marital therapists must be sensitive to these gender issues, while at the same time sorting out their own hidden and not-so-hidden agendas. Marital therapists will have to be aware of their own biases and guard against becoming too prescriptive in their therapy, while at the same time making covert gender assumptions more overt and inviting the couple to question and discuss those assumptions. There will be more dual-worker couples where both spouses hold a job, and dual-career couples where both spouses pursue a career that demands both high levels of training and commitment to a developmental path over time (Rapaport & Rapaport, 1971). This will present problems of time management, household task negotiation, and resource allocation. Any of these issues can create problems for a couple, but if navigated successfully, can also be a source of strength for the relationship. Marital therapists will increasingly be asked to help navigate through these uncharted waters.

Changes in spousal roles.   Traditionally, the woman in the family was supposed to be the sexual partner of her husband and caretaker of domestic duties. Not only have women been less reluctant to enter into the work force, but they have also chosen to attach less importance to the "state of being married" for much of their personal fulfillment (R. Weiss, 1987). The age of marriage has gone up (Saluter, 1989), while the age of puberty has decreased, as has the age at first intercourse (Bachrach & Horn, 1987). More adult women will never marry and fewer women are remarrying after a divorce (Norton & Moorman, 1987). In addition, when a woman does find a male partner she will often cohabit with him, rather than get married (Tanfer, 1987). Fewer women are confining their sexual life to a marriage specifically. In addition, marriage is looked upon as just one form of a woman's fulfillment, and not the only form. This is quite a change from the male-dominated nuclear family, in which the woman had to do as she was told or be banished from the most important thing in her life, her marriage. The marital therapist of the 21st century will see more couples for relationship therapy who aren't married. Cohabiting couples will more frequently use the services of marital therapists. Likewise, marital therapists will see more premarital cases in which sex is not a dream of the future but is instead an ongoing reality of the present. More single people will seek a marital therapist for guidance on how to develop and maintain an intimate relationship. Marital therapists will also encounter more intergenerational conflict over these matters, as two or even three generations of the same family push for conformity to their own standards. The marital therapist must be aware of his or her feelings on these matters and help clients to find their own solution*s.*

Changes in parenting roles.   Demographic patterns show that women are having fewer children and are waiting to have those they do have until later in life (Shehan & Scanzoni, 1988). More women are *choosing* to have children, rather than feeling obligated to have them (G. Bauer, 1986). It is important to recognize that, even with these statistics, there are still groups of women in the culture who have a large number of children early in life (Fox, 1986; Wetzel, 1989). For many of the couples seeking marital therapy in the 21st century, however, it is hoped that their children will be planned after a long period of mutual consideration. By choosing to have children rather than conceiving out of obligation or tradition, these couples are more likely to approach child care as a mutual endeavor for both husband and wife (Shehan & Scanzoni, 1988). This mutual undertaking may have some positive effects upon the spousal dyad as well as the child. The wife-mother is freed from sole parental obligation; the husband-father can explore the nurturing side of himself; and the baby has the benefit of two genuine parents. However, such an arrangement can also bring about conflict. These new shared parenting roles are likely to be ambiguous and not well defined. These ambiguities are likely to include division of labor and role differentiation (Boss, 1987; Hanson & Johnson, 1979). The marital therapist will have to help spouses define the new shared parenting roles that are so different from the ones they learned in their families of origin.

One pattern, which some women employ in attempting to resolve the cognitive dissonance created by expectations of career, marriage, and parenthood is to attempt to become "superwoman" and do it all. For these women, life becomes one long series of expectations. Frequently, women first express this overload of roles by presenting with complaints about their marriages. The marital therapist of the 21st century needs to be aware of this pattern and needs to involve both partners in reevaluating family roles. Working with both spouses as a team to cope with this overload helps the spouses feel like colleagues instead of adversaries.

The men's movement. As women have pointed out the liabilities of their stereotyped gender role, men have begun to recognize the liabilities of their stereotyped gender role. Men are responding to the feminist critique and are discussing what it means to be a man, to be a husband, and to be a parent. This effort will lead to an expanded appreciation for the role of support and nurturance in the lives of men and the cost to men of living in a system that expects a narrow range of expressed emotion, dominance, autonomy, and productivity (Meth & Pasick, 1990). Marital therapists of the future will be challenged to listen more carefully to the expanding consciousness and identity of both genders in order to appreciate more fully the impact upon the evolving marital relationship. Marital therapists will play a role in raising consciousness about men's ways of being, not only through marital therapy itself but also through support groups for men. In this way the male quest for gender expression will follow a trail blazed by women in the quest for raising consciousness.

Work and Occupations

Much of the country, and particularly the youth of America, are increasingly materialistic and focus upon the means to achieve their goals of ownership and possessions (Stone & Archer, 1990). College student values over the past 20 years have shifted away from altruism and service careers, with their intrinsic reward systems, toward careers that lead to more material comfort and wealth, an extrinsic reward system (Astin & Green, 1987). Consequently, young couples as well as presently middle-aged couples have placed enormous expectations on and have invested time and energy in their careers. Feelings of self-worth for *both* spouses may derive more from career rewards and advancement than from marriage (Sporakowski, 1988). This is a powerful rival to the marital relationship. Recently, one spouse in therapy described her husband's job as an "affair." She said, "I can cope with another woman but how do I cope with his computer?" This emphasis on working for pay in order to accrue material possessions belittles home chores and parenting duties. The marital therapist of the future will see many conflicts centering around rivalries between spouses' jobs and fights over who has to do the valueless work around the house. More and more, spouses are fusing their self-worth with their jobs. Therefore, the interaction among work, marital, and family roles with each spouse's identity will become an issue as we march into the 21st century.

The marital therapist must also prepare to deal with the fallout of such a dual-career or dual-work life-style. Because work outside the home is *so* valuable, many women will return to the work force as soon as they can after giving birth to their children (R. Weiss, 1987). This introduces the necessity of day care and the frequent backwash of guilt experienced by the mother or father or both (Sporakowski, 1988). Such guilt can create distance in a marriage or become blame directed at the other spouse. Such couples will seek marital therapy for a problem that has its genesis in work and parenting issues. Because the demands of work are so different from one generation to the next, the grandparental generation will not understand the work demands of the parental generation (Saluter, 1989), and will often exacerbate the guilt the parents feel about their parenting style. This may necessitate the marital therapist's involving both generations to cope with a problem that was first labeled a spousal dispute.

Family Trends

While all of the trends mentioned above affect the family, there are some trends that specifically influence family structure and function. The most obvious trend is the high divorce rate (Farber, 1987). Although in recent years the divorce rate has begun to stabilize, it remains high (Saluter, 1989). R. Weiss (1987) believes that marriage is being viewed with increasing ambivalence by the young adults of today, who find marriage to be increasingly close to cohabitation in its structure and function. In fact, several researchers and theorists have suggested that divorce and successive changing of marital partners may now be considered a "Normal Life Process," when viewed from a life cycle perspective (Ahrons & Rodgers, 1987; Farber, 1987; Kaslow & Schwartz, 1987). This perspective calls into question cultural myths about divorce that insist on placing blame and locating responsibility with one of the former spouses (Sporakowski, 1988). While this perspective removes the "pathology" from divorce and remarriage, it sets up a system that has some liabilities, when compared with the marriage that lasted for the duration of the spouses' lives. In such a system, the couple will rely on friends for short-term help, professionals for long-term help, and kin for "not much more than a shared celebration on family holidays" (R. Weiss, 1987, p. 467). With the family and friends shut off from helping the couple cope with serious difficulties, the professional marital therapist may become the couple's only resource. The therapist needs to understand the nature of the couple's problems from their perspective. If the couple feels very little sense of obligation to each other, they may fit into the "divorce as a normal life process decision" group of people. In this case pursuing ultimate causality and blame will result only in further unhappiness and do little for the couple's reunification (J. Bernard, 1981). For the marital therapists of the 21st century, helping the couple on the brink of divorce will become more common. In some cases, we can help them back away from the brink by rediscovering a sense of interpersonal commitment. In other cases, we must accept their decision, even if we disagree with it, and help them go on with the rest of their life cycle. This may mean rehearsing for the single life and reentering the "dating game." For others, it may be a review of what went wrong in their first marriage and an exploration of what to avoid or change in future relationships. In any case, the marital therapist of the future cannot judge the success or failure of therapy by the couple's remaining together or divorcing. Success may be a successful divorce.

One fallout of a culture that has a high divorce rate is the existence of many single parents. From 1970 to 1987, single-parent households rose from 5% to 8.1% (U.S. Bureau of the Census, 1987). While this represents a larger group of clients for family therapists, it also may produce work for marital therapists. Young adults raised in single-parent families often have problems with members of the opposite sex as they begin to date and marry (Hetherington, Cox, & Cox, 1977). Such individuals will come to a marital therapist, either alone or with spouse, and display a set of attitudes and emotions that have their genesis not in the marital dyad, but in the single-parent family of origin. Another time when a marital therapist may be called on to help a single-parent family is when the single parent starts dating again. The entire dating experience becomes fraught with extra complications because the potential spouse must not only consider becoming a new spouse but also becoming an instant parent. This becomes especially difficult if the children are in their teens and are themselves dating. The marital therapist of the future will face more of these circumstances and must learn to help the couple distinguish tensions that comes from within the dyadic relationship from those that impinge from outside.

Once the couple proceeds to marriage, new challenges appear. The marital therapist must now help the remarried couple cope with the blended family. Sager, Brown, Crohn, Engel, Rodstein, & Walker (1983) suggest that negotiations between spouses are indeed difficult with demands coming from one or more sets of children, two previous spouses, the courts, the community, and eight sets of grandparents. A marital therapist needs to help the remarried couple through this maze of relationships to strengthen their marital dyad. Because of his or her distance from the system, the marital therapist is in a position to lend a note of objectivity to the family in the midst of a very complicated series of interactive patterns. All the demographics seem to indicate an increase in this type of family for the future (Sporakowski, 1988).

Another family pattern that is likely to continue to impact marriages is the one in which adult children are still living at home (Wetzel, 1989). These children are typically of two types: "The Neverleavers," who are either afraid to get out into the world on their own or know that they can't approach the standard of living given to them by their parents if they were on their own, or the "Boomerangers," who have tried to make it on their own but have returned to their parents' home. The presence of adult children in the home greatly disrupts the parents' expectations for a "post-parental" phase of marriage (Duvall, 1957). Consequently, this family structure can be highly stressful for the parents' marriage. The marital therapist must be aware of the potential for such stress and be prepared to help the couple separate their issues with an unlaunched adult child from their issues with one another.

The functioning of large numbers of families is strongly impacted by chronic problems that are often intergenerational in nature and that have attracted a great deal of media attention. Whether the rise in clients presenting with these problems indicates a greater prevalence or better reporting procedures and a greater cultural awareness is open to debate. However, families who experience addictions (Rahdert, 1988), who resort to violence (Finkelhor, Gelles, Hotaling, & Straus, 1983), or who have experienced sexual abuse (Meiselman, 1978) are all on the rise and flooding the offices of marital therapists. There is little sign of these social problems abating any time in the near future. Screening for addictions, codependency, and violence within the marital relationship or within the family of origin will need to become more systematic in the early stages of treatment. Training programs are responding to this need with their curricula (Commission on Accreditation, 1988), and we expect that marital therapists will proceed with treatment with greater confidence as treatment models for these issues become articulated more clearly (e.g., Bepko & Krestan, 1985; Curtois, 1988; LoPiccolo & Friedman, 1988; Stith, Williams, & Rosen, 1990) and treatment programs become systematically evaluated through outcome data. We also believe the profession will play a role in responding to the popular press by introducing complexity into their use of such concepts as "codependent" and "dysfunctional family." Increasingly, client couples will come to therapy familiar with such concepts through self-help literature, but will need help in identifying patterns that are specific to their relationship and in taking responsibility for their part in those patterns.

The 21st century will present several challenges to marital therapy. These include political pressures, changes in demography, and changes in family structure. We must be sensitive both to the larger systems in which the couple is embedded and to the individuals within the dyad. As we face the challenges of the 21st century, we will need to coordinate our services with other health care providers. Who, in the early eighties, could have foretold the AIDS epidemic that was to sweep the country? This scourge, which so devastates us (Macklin, 1988), also unites us as professionals. Cooperation among a wide variety of professionals—relationship therapists, physicians, social workers, politicians, and attorneys—will be needed to address the complex needs of clients. While this is a dramatic example, the need for cooperation among the professions is a common one. It is in this spirit of cooperation and coordination that we turn ourselves to the 21st century, to the new challenges that lie ahead.

12

State and Federal Initiatives in Family Policy

Lessons From the Eighties, Proposals for the Nineties

STEVEN K. WISENSALE

Historically, family policy has been an elusive concept in the United States. Although it first surfaced in European policy debates in the early forties (Kamerman & Kahn, 1978; Myrdal, 1941), its development in the United States has been both slow and disjointed, to say the least. According to Kamerman and Kahn (1989), the concept was first mentioned in the United States in the 1960s (N. Cohen & Connery, 1967; Moynihan, 1968; A. Schorr, 1968), vigorously debated in the 1970s (Kahn & Kamerman, 1975; Kamerman & Kahn, 1976, 1978; Keniston, 1977), both rejected and embraced in the early 1980s (Dempsey, 1981; Steiner, 1981) and then later incorporated in policy debates toward the end of the decade (Anderson & Hula, 1989; Cherlin, 1988; Edelman, 1987; Moynihan, 1986).

The reasons for America's inconsistent pattern with respect to family policy can be traced to at least four important factors. First, a decentralized political system has placed much policy-making power in the hands of state government. This is particularly true in relation to the family. For, despite the growth in federal power over the past 50 years, family law in particular still remains predominantly a state responsibility. Thus there is much variation across states in terms of marriage and divorce laws, levels of income maintenance and other types of economic support, and access to day care and family leave—to cite but a few examples.

A second factor contributing to the United States's approach to family issues is its long history of embracing incrementalism as part of the policy-making process. Commonly referred to as "muddling through" (Lindblom, 1959), this approach tends to choose small-ticket items over large-ticket items (Kamerman & Kahn, 1989), Band-Aids over tourniquets, and quick fixes over long-range planning. For example, Medicare, a health program for the elderly that passed in 1965, came 30 years after national health insurance for all was proposed. Similarly, SSI (Supplemental Security Income), a special economic support program for the extremely poor and disabled, is little more than residue from a much broader Family Assistance Plan (FAP) that was first introduced in the early 1970s. And although a national day-care bill nearly passed in 1971, it took another 18 years to see a very limited version of the original adopted, prompting one of its staunchest supporters to declare victory but to describe it as little more than "a good beginning" (Senator Chris Dodd, cited in Spivack, 1990). In short, family policy, like all U.S. policy initiatives, is subjected to a very slow incremental process that often produces acceptable patchworks instead of beautiful quilts.

The third factor concerns a cultural heritage and value system that places individualism above collectivism. With respect to family policy, this is most clearly manifested in numerous social policies that are geared to individuals rather than to families. One becomes eligible for a program according to one's individual characteristics or specific needs, not according to the characteristics or needs of the family of which one is a part. In order for the family to become the unit of eligibility instead of the individual, there usually must be evidence of some sort of malfunction, dysfunction, inadequacy, or disorganization. AFDC (Aid to Families with Dependent Children), food stamps, Medicaid, and Head Start all serve as examples of programs that view the family as the unit of eligibility, but only when poverty is the criterion employed. Thus, compared to many European and Scandinavian countries, the United States, due to its focus on individual needs, simply lacks universal access to family-oriented policies.

And last, the fourth factor that helps to explain the United States's inconsistency with respect to family policy can be traced to the fact that we are an extremely pluralistic society that can neither agree on the definition of "family," nor reach a consensus on the specific goals of family policy. Simply put, while we may agree with Kamerman and Kahn's (1989) definition of *family policy* ("what the government does to and for families") (p. 581), we cannot always agree on what we mean by a family, let alone agree on what actions government should take in the first place. Therefore, argues Steiner (1981), what we have in family policy is little more than "a theme in search of a definition" (p. 19).

Whether or not these four factors will continue to play a major role in the development of family policy is, of course, an unknown. All indications, however, are that a major policy shift occurred in the 1980s that has given families a legitimate position on the political agenda. How and why this shift occurred, and where it may be taking us as a nation, is the subject of this chapter. What follows is a discussion of major national trends, examples of significant state and federal initiatives directed toward families, an outline of important lessons learned from the eighties, and a checklist of specific policy proposals that should be explored in the nineties.

Major National Trends in the Eighties

In addition to the four factors discussed above, the development of comprehensive family policy has been complicated over the past 10 years by major changes demographically, politically, economically, and in the American family. Each is discussed briefly below.

Demographic Changes

Two significant demographic trends that became particularly visible in the 1980s were in the areas of ethnicity and aging. With respect to the former, it is clear that the nation is evolving into a multiracial, multicultural, and multilingual society. It is estimated, for example, that Hispanics experienced a 16% national growth rate between 1980 and 1985, compared to a 3% growth rate for the nation as a whole (Latin American Research, 1987). Hispanics tend to be younger, poorer, have more children, and drop out of high school at a greater rate than non-Hispanics (Center on Budget and Policy Priorities, 1988).

Concerning the latter trend, it is clear that the nation is aging. Not only has the 65 or older group grown to 15% of the entire population, but estimates are that the 85 years and older population will double between 1980 and 2000 (American Association of Retired Persons,

1988). Such a change has not only placed greater demands on our long-term health care system, but on the family as well. Therefore, women, who tend to be the primary caregivers, can expect to spend more years caring for an aging parent than for a dependent child. In 1900, for example, a woman spent 19 years with a child and only 9 with a parent. Today she will spend 17 years caring for a dependent child and 18 years assisting an elderly parent (House Select Committee on Aging, 1987). And, as will be the case with changing ethnicity, the aging of the population will affect both the family's structure and its function well into the future.

Political Changes

Politically, the 1980s witnessed several major changes. Ronald Reagan was elected President and promptly shifted major policy-making responsibilities from the federal government to the states. The New Federalism of the eighties became the antithesis of the New Deal of the 1930s.

In Congress, traditional liberals found themselves outnumbered and incapable of reversing a tide of Republican policy initiatives and White House budget cuts. In the meantime, the 1990 Census results revealed that the population is shifting to the conservative South and West, and thus Congress will be apportioned accordingly. Traditionally liberal states, such as New York and Pennsylvania, will lose three and two congressional seats, respectively, while California will pick up seven seats and Florida will add four. Advocates for a national family policy as well as proponents of family-oriented legislative proposals cannot afford to ignore these developments.

Equally important, there also have been major changes in the U.S. Supreme Court. Reagan's appointments of O'Connor, Scalia, and Kennedy, combined with Bush's appointment of Souter and Thomas, have transformed a traditionally liberal court to one of conservatism. And, of the two liberals remaining on the court, they are either in their late seventies or early eighties. This ongoing change, which was initiated during the Reagan administration, will also eventually impact on families to a greater or lesser degree.

Economic Changes

Several major economic trends in the 1980s can be identified. First, the middle class declined. According to the National Conference of

State Legislatures (1989), four times the number of Americans fell out of the middle class as climbed above it. In addition, the gap between rich and poor widened significantly in the eighties. By 1989, the gap was wider than at any time since the Census Bureau began collecting such data in 1947 (National Conference of State Legislatures, 1989). Second, the need for two incomes to support families increased considerably during the 1980s. Based on a report issued by the California Assembly Human Services Committee (1987), nearly 35% more two-parent families would live below the poverty line if one spouse were not employed. In the meantime, the most vulnerable families, those with single parents, increased in number during the 1980s (Edelman, 1987).

And third, in economic terms, young families were hit especially hard during the eighties. While median income rose 4% for families with a household head at least 35 years of age, it declined 3% for 25- to 35-year-old heads of households and by 24% for 15- to 24-year-old household heads (Children's Defense Fund, 1988).

The Changing Family

Major changes in the American family that began prior to the 1980s continued throughout the decade. Although the divorce rate stabilized during the eighties, the actual number of persons divorcing continued to rise (Day & Bahr, 1986). This development, in turn, contributed to the increase in single-parent households headed by females, which experienced the largest growth rate of any one family type. Further, female-headed households are expected to increase 23% to 25% during the last 15 years of the century (Evans, 1987; Federal Register, 1986). Another contributing factor to the growth of this family type has been teen pregnancy. Although the actual numbers of births to teens is declining, the percentage of children born out of wedlock is increasing, especially among black and Hispanic teens (Moore, 1986).

Two other important facts from the eighties are indicative of the changing family. First, it is aging. Whereas in 1963, 25% of people over the age of 45 had a surviving parent, by 1980, 40% of people in their late fifties had at least one surviving parent (National Retired Teachers Association-American Association of Retired Persons, 1984). As a result, and for the first time in American history, the average married couple has more parents than children (Preston, 1984).

The other important fact concerns the increasing labor force participation rate among women. Almost 75% of all women 18 to 44 years of age are in the labor force and nearly 50% of all women with young children also work and thus require some form of child care (U.S. Bureau of the Census, 1987). In addition, almost 62% of all women between the ages of 45 and 54 now work, as do 42% of those who fall into the 53- to 64-age range (U.S. Department of Labor, 1984). It is precisely these two groups of middle-aged females, consisting primarily of adult daughters and daughters-in-law, who are most likely to provide the necessary care to the disabled parent or husband. The policy implications of these national trends have not been overlooked. Legislators, fully aware of major demographic, economic, and political changes and their corresponding impact on families, have put forth important initiatives at both the state and federal levels to address many of the issues that emerged over the past ten years. Specific proposals introduced, and strategies employed by policymakers to meet the challenges confronting today's families, are discussed in detail below.

State Initiatives in Family Policy

With respect to state initiatives in family policy, the 1980s become significant for at least two reasons. First, despite the fact that some family issues surfaced more than 50 years earlier, the nation held its first ever White House Conference on Families (WHCF) in 1980. Conceived by President Carter and held in three different cities (Los Angeles, Minneapolis, and Baltimore) during the last six months of his term, the WHCF submitted 60 recommendations that addressed such issues as child care, alcohol and drug abuse, the mentally and physically handicapped, abortion, care of the elderly, and family impact analysis. Although the Conference often got bogged down in semantics and few, if any, problems were resolved, it did create an open atmosphere for debate and assisted in getting family policy on the political agenda.

In the 12 years since the conference, there has been a constant flow of research literature that is related to family policy. Cherlin (1988), Diamond (1983), Genovese (1984), Moynihan (1986), Moroney (1986), Noble and Sussman (1987), Peden and Glahe (1986), Steiner (1981), and Zimmerman (1988) have all made significant contributions to the field. Numerous courses on family policy have been initiated at various colleges and universities throughout the country, and at least two journals, *Policy Studies Review* (1989) and *Family Relations* (1991) recently included special symposia on family policy. In addition, throughout the decade, both the federal and state governments introduced legislation, created task forces, and established study commissions that targeted the needs of families.

A second reason why 1980 was particularly significant for the growing interest in family policy can be traced to the election of Ronald Reagan. A strong advocate for reduced powers and budgets in Washington, Reagan's version of New Federalism was designed to place greater responsibility on the shoulders of state government for addressing many of the nation's domestic problems. Thus, by early 1981, most of the enthusiasm that still remained from the White House Conference on Families—a conference that called for national action—was deflected away from Washington and directed toward state legislatures. Aware that Washington would not move on many issues, states began to act unilaterally to meet the needs of families.

Despite the fact that states have a long history of involvement in family issues, until recently most of the discussion on family policy has been confined to the national level. With the exception of Wisensale (1989), Zimmerman (1988), and Zimmerman and Owens (1989), state efforts in family policy have been largely ignored in the literature. However, in a recent survey to which 42 states responded, Wisensale (1990) found that 28 had made a special effort to focus on the family during a legislative session within the previous two years. Twenty-four states had created special task forces (13) or commissions (11) during the same time period to focus on the needs of families. Seven states created both. These included very broad categories, such as Maryland's Commission on the Family and Minnesota's Council on Children and Families, as well as those with a more narrow focus, such as Maine's Adolescent Pregnancy Task Force and Georgia's Special Study Committee on Homeless Families.

But perhaps the most precise measure of a state's commitment to families is represented by the quantity and quality of the legislation adopted. According to the National Conference of State Legislatures (1989), the four policy areas in particular that states have chosen to address during the past decade have been (a) work and family issues; (b) child welfare; (c) family health policy; and (d) teen pregnancy. Each of these is discussed in some detail below.

Work and Family Issues

Because more women, and particularly mothers, are entering the work force on a full-time basis than at any time since World War II, greater pressure has been placed on policymakers at the state level to address family needs in at least two ways: family leave and child care. With respect to the former, the United States had no statutory provision for maternity or parental leave until the late eighties. Of the 28 states that introduced some form of parental or family leave legislation in 1987, only 4 (Connecticut, Rhode Island, Oregon, and Minnesota) enacted such laws. All were gender-neutral, each included a job guarantee upon the return to work, and none were paid. Connecticut's policy allowed for 24 weeks of leave, applied to state employees only, and was intergenerational. That is, employees could take time off to care for a child or an aging parent. The other bills ranged in length from 13 weeks in Rhode Island to 6 in Minnesota, applied to both the public and private sectors, and were not intergenerational in structure.

Since 1987, 10 other states have adopted parental or family leave bills. Seven of them (Maryland, Maine, North Dakota, Oklahoma, Pennsylvania, West Virginia, and Wisconsin) are intergenerational while the others (Tennessee, Vermont, and Washington) limit leaves to caring for children. One state, Massachusetts, has failed to enact family leave to date, but represents the only governing body in the nation to propose paid leave. Massachusetts' strategy is to apply the Temporary Disability Insurance (TDI) model to family caregiving. Under such a policy, the family, instead of the individual, would be viewed as "disabled" and the principal caregiver would qualify for leave and some sort of wage replacement (Wisensale, 1990).

Concerning the other work and family issue, child care, that has caught the attention of state lawmakers, three major themes dominate the policy process: affordability, accessibility, and quality (National Conference of State Legislatures, 1989). In addressing each of these, states employ a variety of policy options, including special subsidies, tax credits or deductions, loans and grants, resource and referral services, and targeted training programs for child care workers.

In more specific terms, Alaska, California, Massachusetts, Minnesota, New York, and Rhode Island attack the affordability question by providing money for state child care programs on a sliding scale (Gnezda, 1987). At least nine states (California, Connecticut, Florida, Michigan, New York, Pennsylvania, Texas, Rhode Island, and Wisconsin) provide special funding to assist teen parents with day care in order that they may complete high school (National Conference of State Legislatures, 1989).

About 15 states tackle the accessibility question by using tax incentives to encourage employers to assist with the provision of child care. Both Connecticut and Oregon, for example, offer direct tax deductions to employers. Other states such as Arizona, California, Florida, and New Mexico employ tax credits or deductions for start-up or equipment costs in on-site facilities (Sonnier, 1989).

In addressing the quality issue, states have usually chosen one of two major routes: increased salaries or special training programs for child care workers. While Connecticut, Maine, Maryland, Massachusetts, Minnesota, New Jersey, and Pennsylvania have followed the first route, Rhode Island and New York have chosen the second (Gnezda, 1989). Recently, however, Connecticut has combined its strategy of increased salaries with a special cable television training series for child care providers.

Child Welfare

According to a 1988 survey, state legislature activities toward the end of the decade tended to focus more on children and child welfare legislation than on the family as a whole. For example, between 1986 and 1988 alone, some 32 states passed more stringent child abuse and neglect laws, 31 states passed more stringent child support enforcement bills, and 30 states passed some form of child care and early education legislation (S. Wisensale, 1990).

Two states in particular have been very aggressive in attempting to meet the needs of children. New York, for example, announced in 1988 that the next 10 years would be declared the "Decade of the Child." This policy initiative, according to Governor Mario Cuomo, represents a new age of accountability for public investments in children. Guaranteeing that children will receive top priority in budgeting decisions over the next decade, the centerpiece of the policy is the new $261 million-a-year Liberty Scholarship program. Consisting of three major parts, the scholarships will provide full nontuition assistance to 94,000 lower income students at colleges throughout the state, counsel 60,000 potential dropouts starting in the seventh grade, and increase the amount of tuition assistance for college and university students.

Rhode Island has followed a similar course. Modeled after Eugene Lang's "I Have a Dream," and strongly endorsed by then Governor

Edward D. Di Prete in 1990, Rhode Island's "Children's Crusade for Higher Education" will offer full state-college scholarships for low-income pupils from the third grade through high school. Although any third grader may enroll, the program is aimed primarily at about 3,200 students who come from low-income families. In return for the promise of college scholarships, students and parents must sign a contract that permits the state to monitor report cards and asserts that students will avoid drugs and teen pregnancy, obey the law, and meet strict academic requirements.

To fund the program, corporations, foundations, and schools are being asked to contribute the initial $10 million to a special trust fund in order to begin the program by September 1991. The state, in turn, will be expected to contribute $3.2 million a year, bringing the fund, with interest, to about $50 million after 10 years. It is estimated that 1,200 students who successfully complete the program each year will attend college. Another 1,200 students will enter special vocational training programs that will also be covered under the plan.

Clearly, both New York and Rhode Island have made major commitments to children. Whether or not their efforts will have a positive impact on the family in general, and children in particular, remains to be seen. However, the decision to emphasize the child more than the family represents one political strategy that other state policymakers may or may not want to emulate. Such an approach may produce mixed reactions among researchers as well. For example, Kamerman and Kahn (1989) argue that all family policy initiatives should center the debate on how to do better by children rather than on what is wrong with families. On the other hand, Scanzoni (1989) argues that the interests of adults should not be separated from those of children in the formulation of family policy.

Teen Pregnancy

As statistics continue to show, the United States has the highest rates of teenage pregnancy, birth, and abortion of all Western industrialized nations. Each year more than 1 in 10 American girls become pregnant before their 20th birthday (Maggard, 1985). This pattern of early parenting, in turn, produces a variety of major consequences, including low educational achievement, high unemployment, more single-parent households, greater welfare dependency, and numerous health problems such as an increase in low-birth-weight babies, a rise in infant mortality, and a higher rate of child abuse than the rest of the population.

The federal government did not address teen pregnancy until 1978. Other than passing what later became an ineffective teenage pregnancy prevention bill (The Adolescent Family Life Act) and creating a series of "just say no to sex" campaigns, it has done little since. Therefore, states have been forced to bear the burden of the problem in at least two ways: a loss of human resources and a corresponding increase in welfare expenditures.

Primarily because of limited action in Washington concerning teen pregnancy, we have witnessed a pattern of increased legislative activity at the state level. According to the National Conference of State Legislatures (1989), much of this has occurred within the past three years. For example, by 1987 only 9 states had enacted and 23 had introduced legislation geared toward teen pregnancy. By 1990, however, 38 states had enacted and 48 states had introduced such legislation. In addition, at least one third of the states have established special task forces to study the issue more closely and make policy recommendations.

Of the legislation that has been enacted, two specific trends can be clearly identified. The first concentrates on coordinating services and programs for pregnant as well as parenting teens. The second trend utilizes schools as target areas for various prevention strategies. These usually take the form of school-based health clinics and day-care facilities for student parents.

Three states have been particularly active in both of these areas. New Jersey, for example, has created the School-Based Youth Services Program that provides pregnant and parenting teens with job training, child care, health care, counseling, and family-life education. Maryland's system of Family Support Centers attempts to prevent additional unplanned pregnancies among existing teen mothers, and Connecticut's Teen Pregnancy Prevention Program consists of five demonstration sites that focus on family-life education, mentoring, tutoring, peer pressure, and a sophisticated advertising campaign.

Three legislative issues revolving around teen pregnancy that are especially controversial are (a) financial liability; (b) the dispensing of contraceptives; and (c) parental consent/notification for abortion services. Regarding the first issue, six states (Georgia, Idaho, Maine, Texas, Virginia, and Wisconsin) have passed laws holding parents financially responsible for the offspring of their children. Concerning the second issue, seven states (Georgia, Illinois, Iowa, Kentucky, North Carolina, South Carolina, and Wisconsin) have passed legislation that specifically prohibits the dispensing of contraceptives to minors in schools or local health clinics. In relation to the third issue of controversy, 13 states passed legislation requiring either parental consent or notification prior to a teen getting an abortion (National Conference of State Legislature, 1989). However, a recent U.S. Supreme Court case upheld the teenager's right to an abortion, but also confirmed the right of a state to maintain a judicial by-pass procedure. Under such a procedure, the teen must first appear before a judge who determines whether or not she is sufficiently mature to make an abortion decision without parental involvement.

Family Health Policy

As was learned from the discussion on work and family issues, child welfare policy and teenage pregnancy prevention programs, in which states have been held more accountable during the past 10 years for solving these problems, so it is with respect to family health care. Simply put, medical indigence has become the number one health issue on state legislative agendas. The reasons are obvious. Rising costs and limited resources have forced states to reduce access to health services. For example, in 1975 about 63% of persons with incomes below the federal poverty level qualified for Medicaid; by 1986, the number dropped to 41% (National Conference of State Legislatures, 1989). But the problem appears particularly acute when viewed from the perspective of human beings instead of Medicaid dollars.

A 1987 survey concluded that nearly 37 million Americans are without some form of health insurance. Of those, about half are under age 25 and 31% are under age 19. Almost 80% are employed at least part-time or are the dependents of employed persons. More than one third of the 37 million uninsured have incomes below the federal poverty level and nearly 44% of all uninsured children live in such families. In addition, more than 78% of the uninsured population are white, but almost one third of all Hispanics and 22% of all blacks are uninsured. Not insignificant is the fact that a greater proportion of the uninsured live in the western and southern states of the country, which typically lack the financial resources necessary to meet the health care needs of their lower income citizens (Short, Monheit, & Beauregard, 1987).

Legislative attempts to address the problem of the medically indigent have included new financing mechanisms, the targeting of special groups, and more emphasis being placed on equal access to services. While almost all states are attacking this problem in one form or another, three in particular can be singled out for putting forth what some would consider to be innovative policies.

Massachusetts, for example, passed the first bill in the nation that was designed to ensure health coverage for about 600,000 uninsured residents. Enacted in April 1988, but not to take effect until 1992, the law requires businesses to make health insurance available to their employees. The bill also offers small businesses special incentives to participate as well (Marcus, 1990).

New Jersey recently created the Uncompensated Care Trust Fund. Under this model, each hospital adds a special surtax to patient bills to cover uncompensated hospital care. In 1989, this rate was 10%, which in turn produced about $500 million in revenues. The trust fund is then distributed to hospitals according to their respective levels of uncompensated care. The objective is to create both fair competition in setting prices and in patient access (King, 1989).

Finally, Oregon has enacted perhaps the most controversial piece of legislation yet, concerning the medically indigent. In 1989, the State began to rank medical procedures according to their importance so that government-funded health insurance could serve the greatest number of people at the most reasonable cost. Medicaid reimbursement would be cut off for all ailments and services that fall below a predetermined line drawn through the list of medical procedures. Commonly referred to as the first legislative attempt at health rationing, the Oregon plan is expected to cover an estimated 77,000 more people than under the existing Medicaid program (Veatch, 1991).

While states continue to wrestle with the issue of universal access to health care, two additional points should be kept in mind. First, health care services for low-income uninsured people have always been a state, not a federal, responsibility—even prior to the election of Ronald Reagan. The second point to emphasize is that the recently released Pepper Commission Report (1990) recommends that the federal government should assume greater responsibility for meeting the health care needs of the uninsured and the long-term care needs of the elderly. To what extent Congress adopts the recommendations of the Pepper Commission may ultimately determine the future of health care policy at the state level.

Other State Initiatives

There are, of course, other family policy issues that were addressed by the states throughout the eighties. These include domestic violence, homeless families, welfare reform, AIDS, mental health, and parent education. One state, Connecticut, became the first in the nation to pass a comprehensive family policy package. Enacted in 1987, the 16 bills covered four major categories: economic self-sufficiency (job training); supportive services (family leave); maternal and child health (pregnant teens); and family stability (assisting "at risk families") (Wisensale, 1989).

Although other states have not followed in Connecticut's footsteps during the past three years, California appears ready to move in that direction during the nineties (California Assembly Human Services Committee, 1987). But whether or not family policy initiatives will continue at the state level depends on at least two important factors. First, will the executive branch continue to follow a policy of New Federalism? If so, more action will be expected from states and less from Washington. And second, to what extent will individual states be able to harness economic resources to address the needs of families? This becomes particularly problematic during periods of economic downturn when families are in greatest need of government assistance. Such developments as prolonged recessions could eventually force the hand of the federal government, as occurred during the 1930s.

Federal Initiatives in Family Policy

The federal government's interest in the family can be identified early in our history. The U.S. Supreme court case of *Reynolds v. U.S.* in 1878, which outlawed polygamy, and the adoption of AFDC in 1935, which addressed the economic needs of families, are two classic examples. It was, however, Jimmy Carter's Nine-Point Plan on the Family, and a call for the nation's first White House Conference on Families, that ultimately gave family policy legitimacy—both politically and academically.

By the time Ronald Reagan was elected in 1980, political interest in the family was clearly divided between the liberal wing of the Democratic party on the one hand, and the conservative right wing of the Republican party on the other. What B. Berger and Berger (1983) referred to as "the war over the family," and Steiner (1981) labeled as "the battle to capture the higher moral ground," had emerged in the early eighties in the form of major political confrontations over such issues as day care, family leave, teen pregnancy, abortion, welfare reform, and health care.

But clearly, it was the Reagan Administration itself that created the parameters for political debate and policy development during the eighties. With respect to family policy in particular, the administration issued two important documents that are most representative of its position on the family. The first, *The Family: Preserving America's Future* (United States Executive Office of the President, 1986), was a 52-page report issued by the White House Working Group on the Family. The second, Executive Order 12606 (United States Executive Office of the President, 1987), was issued by President Reagan. It mandated that all executive-level agencies apply some form of family impact analysis prior to implementing legislation or creating special programs. Both documents had at least three themes in common: first, it is implied throughout, that liberal Democratic policies of the past inflicted severe harm to the American family; second, that the rights of the family are superior to the state, and therefore, it should be protected from government intrusion at all costs; and third, that when government does intervene in family affairs, it should be undertaken by that level of government closest to the people.

Equally relevant to this discussion is the fact that the family served as the focal point of debate on three major legislative initiatives during the eighties. These included child care, family leave, and welfare reform.

Child Care

Although the United States came extremely close to passing a comprehensive child care bill in 1971, only to see it vetoed by President Nixon, it took nearly 20 years to get the issue back on the political agenda. Consistently opposed by the Reagan and Bush administrations throughout the 1980s on the grounds that taxpayers should not pay for the middle class's baby-sitters, a national child care bill finally passed in the fall of 1990 as part of the deficit reduction and budget reconciliation agreement.

Originally designed by Senator Chris Dodd (D-CT) in 1986, the final version more closely resembled a proposal sponsored by Republican Senator Orrin Hatch (UT) and Representative Nancy Johnson (R-CT).

For example, instead of the $2.5 billion funding package that Dodd and his supporters argued for, they got $750 million. Dodd's demands for federal health and safety standards for child care providers was also defeated. Instead, states have been given the option to establish such standards. Similarly, Dodd's desire for federally funded training programs for child care providers was also dropped, as was an effort to expand the Head Start program. Today, due to low funding, less than 20% of children eligible for the program actually participate (National Conference of State Legislatures, 1989).

The one provision added to the original Dodd bill also happened to be the centerpiece of the counter-proposal put forth by Bush and the Republicans. It called for a special tax credit for low- and moderate-income families in need of child care services. In the end, despite Senator Dodd and other Democrats declaring victory, Republican Representative Nancy Johnson of Connecticut put the matter in perspective. "Its key ideas are Republican," she said. "I would like to get equal credit" (Spivack, 1990, p. 4).

Family Leave

Compared to other nations, the United States has been slow in developing a national family leave policy. About 135 other nations have enacted such legislation. As was discussed previously, most of the political activity in this area has been confined to state legislatures. However, that is not to say that proposals have not surfaced in Congress. Between 1985 and 1990 at least four family leave bills were introduced. By early 1992, however, only one bill remained, its fate unknown.

H.R. 770, the Family and Medical Leave Act, was introduced in the House on February 2, 1989 by Representatives William Clay (D-MO), Marge Roukema (R-NJ), and Patricia Schroeder (D-CO). It was cosponsored by more than 120 other representatives. Almost simultaneously, Chris Dodd (D-CT) introduced S. 345, the Senate version of the bill, with 15 Senators as cosponsors. Although it passed easily through both houses, President Bush promptly vetoed the measure on June 29, 1990, as he had promised.

Had President Bush signed the bill or had Congress overridden his veto, it would have included the following provisions: a 12-week period of leave for the care of a child or dependent adult, job security, and applicable to those in firms of 50 or more employees. It would have been unpaid and a physician's written certification would have been required prior to taking the leave.

In vetoing the legislation, President Bush stated his belief that the federal government should not mandate personnel policies for private corporations. His stance was strongly endorsed by more than 170 trade associations, professional societies, private corporations, and various conservative citizen groups (Rausch, 1991).

Welfare Reform

Efforts to reform the welfare system during both the Nixon and Carter administrations tended to fall short of expectations. However, in 1988, after more than three years of policy development, public hearings, and deliberations, Congress completed action on welfare reform legislation in the final days of the 100th Congress. On October 13th, President Reagan signed the Family Support Act of 1988 into law.

Directed specifically at welfare families, the law consists of six major provisions or titles. Title I requires states to withhold child support dollars from an absent parent's paycheck. Title II creates a new education, training, and employment program known as JOBS. Title III provides child care for JOBS participants and guarantees 12 months of transitional medical coverage for individuals choosing to leave the welfare roles for employment. Title IV mandates that all states must offer AFDC to impoverished two-parent families and institute a mandatory work requirement of at least 16 hours a week for one of the parents (workfare). Title V authorizes up to 10 demonstration sites of in-home early childhood development programs. And Title VI contains various miscellaneous provisions, including a requirement that states implement measures to detect fraudulent AFDC applications.

Designed primarily by Senator Daniel Patrick Moynihan (D-NY), the purpose of the Family Support Act is to promote self-sufficiency and discourage welfare dependency. However, many questions remain unanswered. Will workfare produce marketable skills for its participants? Is the funding sufficient enough to lift families out of welfare? And, will the reforms be managed well at the state level?

Other Federal Initiatives

In addition to the three initiatives discussed above, Congress moved on other legislation in the 1980s that at least contained some provisions directed toward families. For example, The Adoption Assistance and Child Welfare Act of 1980 (P.L. 96-272) requires that states make "reasonable efforts" to keep families together through the provision of family-based services. The Omnibus Budget Reconciliation Act of 1986 created new categories of persons eligible for Medicaid, including pregnant women and very young children whose incomes fall below the poverty level. Furthermore, as of July 1, 1990, all states must provide Medicaid coverage of prenatal care services to pregnant women with family incomes up to 100% of the federal poverty level.

There were at least three other pieces of legislation that deserve recognition. The 1987 Stewart B. McKinney Homeless Assistance Act guaranteed, among other things, that local residency requirements could not be used to deny homeless children access to public schools. The Child Abuse Prevention, Adoption and Family Services Act of 1988 establishes the funding of programs that prevent and treat alcohol- and drug-related child abuse and neglect. And the Medicare Catastrophic Coverage Act of 1988 contained provisions to assist family caregivers by paying for respite care of chronically dependent Medicare recipients. However, under pressure from groups of irate elderly citizens who protested the Act's funding mechanism, Congress repealed the law and did not include the respite care provision when the bill was restructured.

There was at least one other important family policy initiative that was put forth during the 1980s. On May 17, 1989, two weeks prior to his death, Representative Claude Pepper (D-FL) introduced "The Pepper Package for Keeping America's Families Together." Consisting of seven separate bills, the package included such provisions as long-term home care for the chronically ill of all ages; establishing the Social Security Administration as an independent agency; creating strict standards for board and care homes; a restitution program for fraud victims; a "Young Americans Act," modeled on the Older Americans Act of 1965; and the "School Completion and Incentives Act." To date, however, none of the bills has moved much beyond their original committees.

And finally, a discussion of federal policy initiatives should not conclude without some mention of the U.S. Supreme Court. Although most family issues are usually decided in state courts, the 1980s witnessed a two-way shift in the direction of the U.S. Supreme Court. First, new appointments by Reagan and Bush have produced a court that is significantly more conservative. And second, the Court's willingness to take on more family-oriented cases appears to be growing (Spakes, 1985). Within the last two years alone, it has handled cases that dealt with such issues as a teenager's right to an abortion (*Hodgson v. Minnesota* and *Ohio v. Akron Center*), child abuse (*De Shaney v. Winnebago County Department of Human Services*), and, for the first time, a right to die case (*Cruzan v. Missouri*).

In the Hodgson case, the court strengthened parental authority (even if a couple is divorced), but also upheld the right of judicial by-pass, thus allowing teens to seek permission for an abortion from a judge instead of a parent. In the De Shaney case, the court ruled that a publicly funded social service agency cannot be held accountable for child abuse if it does not have custody of the child. Here, too, parental authority was strengthened. However, in the Cruzan case the Court ruled that the authority of the state supersedes that of the family in right-to-die cases unless the incompetent individual has left behind clear and convincing evidence of his or her wishes under such circumstances.

There is no indication that the Supreme Court's growing interest in family issues will reverse itself in the near future. Surrogate parenting and more abortion cases will surely appear on the Court's docket in the years ahead. And, most important perhaps, the remaining liberals on the Court are also its oldest members who will most likely be replaced by conservatives. Therefore, many important family issues will be decided within a judicial framework created by Reagan and perpetuated by Bush.

Lessons From the Eighties, Proposals for the Nineties

The evidence is clear that family policy emerged in the 1980s as a significant political issue. From the convening of the White House Conference at the conclusion of the Carter Administration to the passage of day-care legislation in the early years of the Bush Administration, policymakers have learned a number of important lessons that should help them develop new proposals throughout the nineties.

In more specific terms, at least six lessons from the eighties can be identified and discussed. First, it was learned that family policy, like other areas of American public policy, is not immune to incrementalism. Policy initiatives related to families tend to move slowly and are limited in scope. This was best illustrated in the discussion of the nation's first day-care bill that passed in the fall of 1990. In short, we prefer small-ticket items over large-ticket items.

A second lesson learned was that Reagan's adoption of New Federalism shifted even more responsibility for families from the federal government to the states. While this resulted in several innovative policy initiatives in Connecticut, New York, and Rhode Island, other states with fewer resources were less responsive.

Third, it was learned that the issue of family policy itself is highly politicized, creating much tension between the conservative right and the liberal left. It (family policy) can easily become, argue Kamerman and Kahn (1989), a vehicle for achieving other goals. Thus some may contend, for example, that the Family Support Act of 1988 was little more than a vehicle used to reform a rapidly deteriorating welfare system. Whether or not such a strategy was in the best interest of families remains to be seen.

Fourth, we learned that the private sector is interested in the well-being of families but does not want policies dictated to it by government. More than 170 organizations representing private interests openly opposed the Family and Medical Leave Act and President Bush, in his veto message, reiterated his belief that the federal government should not mandate the personnel policies of private corporations. The private sector, concerned primarily about profits, is on record for opposing other family-oriented policy initiatives as well—both at the state and federal levels.

Fifth, the eighties taught us that there may be a developing conflict between generations. The formation of AGE (Americans for Generational Equity) in 1985 and works by Binstock (1983), Callahan (1987), Longman (1987), Preston (1984), and Wisensale (1988) have all addressed this issue. In an aging society, ask Richman and Stagner (1986), will children become a treasured resource or forgotten minority? Claude Pepper's family policy package, discussed earlier in this chapter, was an attempt to respond to this very important policy question. Whether or not other shifts toward more intergenerational policies will ultimately drive us toward a comprehensive family policy is still open for debate.

And finally, we learned in the 1980s that the U.S. Supreme Court became more conservative and took a greater interest in family issues. "The court may be old fashioned, it may be slow, and it may be inconsistent," argues Patricia Spakes (1985), "but no attempt at designing a national family policy can ignore its role" (p. 186). And although it is pure speculation at this point, it appears that this particular court will serve as guardian of the traditional family, despite dramatic social changes already afoot.

Based on what we learned from the eighties, we should now direct our attention toward the nineties. Six proposals are put forth here that deserve to be openly discussed within the public policy forum. First, it is essential that we recognize the importance of national leadership in establishing a family policy agenda. Because many states are incapable of curing social ills, we need political leaders at the national level who are willing to go forward with specific policy proposals to address the needs of families. In short, substance must replace rhetoric; legislative action must replace campaign slogans. But to be more precise, we need a President who is willing to call a second White House Conference on Families and use it as a springboard for policy development.

Second, we need to create universal access to health care. Presently, almost 37 million Americans are without health insurance. This deficiency is particularly harmful to pregnant women and newborns. National leaders must recognize that health care is also a family issue and therefore must take steps to replicate the Massachusetts model on universal health care.

Third, we need a new national housing policy directed toward lower and middle-income families. The Reagan Administration's moratorium on housing must be lifted so homelessness can be eradicated, so low-income families can find adequate shelter, and so more middle-income families can purchase their own homes.

Fourth, future policies need to be more intergenerational in structure. Claude Pepper's family policy package, which called for a "Young Americans Act" to coincide with the Older Americans Act of 1965, as well as his "Medical Long-Term Home Care Catastrophic Protection Act," which called for home health care for dependent individuals of all ages, should be adopted. More important, similar intergenerational policy initiatives should be proposed in the future.

Fifth, work and family issues must be placed near the top of our national political agenda. The recently passed child care bill needs to be expanded, as does Head Start, which serves only 20% of eligible children. We also need a national family leave policy that includes some form of wage replacement. Unpaid leave is little more than symbolic politics conveniently employed by politicians at election time to harvest female votes. Equally important, the private sector must become more sensitive to the needs of families. Too few corporations have instituted policies designed to support families and too many corporate representatives have lobbied against profamily legislation. This must change. And finally, whatever policies we adopt in relation to families, it is imperative that they reflect an understanding of the growing diversity in family structure. We can no longer afford to live in the nineties and dream in the fifties. For clearly, the family is changing and policymakers are being called upon to respond accordingly. For example, on May 26, 1989, the Danish legislature voted to revise the nation's marital laws and allow unmarried couples (homosexuals, not heterosexuals) to have the same rights (adoption excepted) as married couples. In the United States this concept has only surfaced at the local government level, with seven communities adopting "domestic partnership" ordinances within the past five years (Heckart, 1990).

Whether or not similar policies should be adopted by state or federal legislators is an open question. But one thing is certain, the day of reckoning on this issue as well as many other issues discussed in this chapter is rapidly approaching. Our responsibility then is twofold: to become better informed on the issues, and to participate actively in the debate.

References

Ahrons, C., & Bowman, M. (1982). Changes in family relationships following divorce of an adult child: Grandmothers' perceptions. *Journal of Divorce, 5,* 49-68.

Ahrons, C., & Rodgers, R. (1987). *Divorced families: A multidisciplinary developmental view.* New York: Norton.

Aldous, J. (1978). *Family careers: Developmental change in families.* New York: John Wiley.

Allen, K. R. (1987). Integrating a feminist perspective into family studies courses. *Family Relations, 37,* 29-35.

Ambert, A. (1988). Relationships with former in-laws after divorce: A research note. *Journal of Marriage and the Family, 50*(3), 679-686.

American Association for Protecting Children. (1988). *Highlights of official child neglect and abuse reporting 1986.* Denver: American Humane Association.

American Association of Retired Persons. (1988). *National survey of caregivers: Summary of findings.* Washington, DC: American Association of Retired Persons, and Hartford, CT: The Travelers Companies Foundation.

Ammerman, R. T. (1990). Etiological models of child maltreatment. *Behavior Modification, 14,* 230-254.

Anderson, E., & Hula, R. (Eds.). (1989). Symposium: Family policy. *Policy Studies Review, 8*(3), 573-716.

Andresen, S. (1990). *The indivisible split: Exploring the relationship between former spouse interactions and stepfamily functioning.* Unpublished doctoral dissertation, University of Missouri-St. Louis.

Anspach, D. (1976). Kinship and divorce. *Journal of Marriage and the Family, 38,* 323-330.

Antonovsky, A. (1979). *Health, stress and coping.* San Francisco: Jossey-Bass.

Arcus, M. (1987). A framework for life-span family life education. *Family Relations, 36,* 5-10.

251

Arcus, M., Moss, J. J., & Schvaneveldt, J. (in press). The nature of family life education. In J. Schvaneveldt, M. Arcus, & J. J. Moss (Eds.), *Handbook of family life education,* (Vol. 1). Newbury Park, CA: Sage.

Astin, A. W., & Green, K. C. (1987). *The American freshman: Twenty-year trends.* Los Angeles: University of California, Higher Education Research Institute.

Atkinson, J., & Huston, T. L. (1984). Sex role orientation and division of labor early in marriage. *Journal of Personality and Social Psychology, 46,* 330-345.

Avery, C. E., & Lee, M. R. (1964). Family life education: Its philosophy and purpose. *Family Life Coordinator, 13,* 27-37.

Azar, S. T., Robinson, D. R., Hekimian, E., & Twentyman, C. (1984). Unrealistic expectations and problem-solving ability in maltreating and comparison mothers. *Journal of Consulting and Clinical Psychology, 52,* 687-691.

Bachrach, C. A., & Horn, M. C. (1987). *Married and unmarried couples, U.S. 1982* (Vital and Health Statistics, Series 23, No. 15). Washington, DC: Government Printing Office.

Bagarozzi, D. A., & Rauen, P. (1981). Premarital counseling: Appraisal and status. *American Journal of Family Therapy, 9,* 13-30.

Bailyn, L., & Schein, E. (1976). *Life/career considerations as indicators of quality of employment. Measuring work quality for social reporting.* Beverly Hills, CA: Sage.

Baker, L. G., Jr., & Darcy, J. B. (1970). Survey of family life and sex education programs in Washington secondary schools and development of guidelines for statewide coordinated programs. *Family Coordinator, 19,* 228-233.

Baltes, P. B., Reese, H. W., & Lipsitt, L. P. (1980). Life-span developmental psychology. *Annual Review of Psychology, 3,* 65-110.

Bane, M. J. (1979). Marital disruption and the lives of children. In G. Levinger & O. C. Moles (Eds.), *Divorce and separation* (pp. 276-286). New York: Basic Books.

Barnes, G. E., Greenwood, L., & Sommer, R. (1991). Courtship violence in a Canadian sample of male college students. *Family Relations, 40,* 37-44.

Barnes, H., & Olson, D. H. (1983). Parent-adolescent communication and the Circumplex Model. *Child Development, 56,* 438-447.

Barnes, H., & Olson, D. H. (1985). Parent-adolescent communication scale. In D. H. Olson, H. I. McCubbin, H. Barnes, A. Larsen, M. Muxen, & M. Wilson (Eds.), *Family inventories* (pp. 51-66). St. Paul: University of Minnesota, Family Social Science.

Bauer, G. L. (1986). *The family: Preserving America's future.* Washington, DC: White House Working Group on the Family.

Bauer, W. D., & Twentyman, C. (1985). Abusing, neglectful and comparison mothers' responses to child-related and non-child-related stressors. *Journal of Consulting and Clinical Psychology, 53,* 335-343.

Beavers, W. B., & Hampson, R. B. (1990). *Successful families: Assessment and intervention.* New York: Norton

Beavers, W. B., & Voeller, M. N. (1983). Family models: Comparing and contrasting the Olson's Circumplex Model and the Beavers' Systems Model. *Family Process, 22,* 250-260.

Belknap, J. (1989). The sexual victimization of unmarried women by nonrelative acquaintances. In M. Pirog-Good & J. Stets (Eds.), *Violence in dating relationships* (pp. 205-218). New York: Praeger.

Belsky, J. (1980). Child maltreatment: An ecological integration. *American Psychologist, 35,* 320-335.

Belsky, J. (1984). The determinants of parenting: A process model. *Child Development, 55*, 83-96.

Belsky, J. (1985). Experimenting with the family in the newborn period. *Child Development, 56*, 407-414.

Benjamin, L. S. (1977). Structural analysis of a family in therapy. *Journal of Counseling Clinical Psychology, 45*, 391-406.

Bepko, C., & Krestan, J. A. (1985). *The responsibility trap: A blueprint for treating the alcoholic family.* New York: Free Press.

Berardo, F. M. (1990). Family research in the 1980s: Recent trends and future directions. *Journal of Marriage and the Family, 52*(4), 809-817.

Berger, B., & Berger, P. (1983). *The war over the family: Capturing the middle ground.* Garden City, NY: Anchor.

Berger, P. L., & Neuhaus, R. J. (1977). *To empower people: The role of mediating structures in public policy.* Washington, DC: American Enterprise Institute for Public Policy Research.

Bernard, J. (1971). *Women and the public interest.* Chicago: Aldine, Atherton.

Bernard, J. (1981). The divorce myth. *Personnel and Guidance Journal, 60*(2), 67-71.

Bernard, J. L., Bernard, S. L., & Bernard, N. L. (1985). Courtship violence and sex-typing. *Family Relations, 34*, 573-576.

Best, F. (1980). *Flexible life scheduling.* New York: Praeger.

Billingham, R. E., & Sack, A. R. (1987). Conflict tactics and the level of emotional commitment among unmarrieds. *Human Relations, 40*, 59-74.

Binstock, R. (1983). The aged as scapegoat. *The Gerontologist, 23*, 136-143.

Bird, G. W., Stith, S., & Schladale, J. (1991). Psychological resources, coping strategies, and negotiation styles as discriminators of violence in dating relationships. *Family Relations, 40*, 45-50.

Blake, J. (1989). *Family size and achievement.* Berkeley: University of California Press.

Blau, F., & Ferber, M. (1986). *The economics of women, men, and work.* Englewood Cliffs, NJ: Prentice-Hall.

Block, J. H., Block, J., & Gjerde, P. (1986). The personality of children prior to divorce: A prospective study. *Child Development, 57*, 827-840.

Block, M., & Sinnot, J. (1979). *The battered elder syndrome: An exploratory study.* Unpublished manuscript, University of Maryland, College Park.

Bohannon, P. (1970). *Divorce and after: An analysis of the emotional and social problems of divorce.* Garden City, NY: Anchor.

Bohen, H. H. (1984). Gender equality in work and family. *Journal of Family Issues, 5*, 254-272.

Bonkowski, S. (1989). Lingering sadness: Young adults' response to parental divorce. *Social Casework, 70*(4), 219-223.

Booth, A. (1987). The state of the American family. *Journal of Family Issues, 8*, 429-430.

Booth, C. L., Mitchell, S. L., Barnard, K. E., & Spieker, S. J. (1989). Development of maternal skills in multiproblem families: Effects on the mother-child relationship. *Developmental Psychology, 25*, 403-412.

Boss, P. G. (1987). Family stress. In M. B. Sussman & S. K. Steinmetz (Eds.), *Handbook of marriage and the family* (pp. 695-721). New York: Plenum.

Boss, P. G. (1988). *Family stress management.* Newbury Park, CA: Sage.

Boss, P. G., & Greenberg, J. (1984). Family boundary ambiguity: A new variable in family stress theory. *Family Process, 23*, 535-546.

Boswell, D. M. (1969). Personal crisis and the mobilization of the social network. In J. C. Mitchell (Ed.), *Social networks in urban situations* (pp. 245-296). Manchester, UK: Manchester University Press.

Bourgeois-Pichat, J. (1987). The unprecedented shortage of births in Europe. *Population and Development Review, 12,* 2-25.

Boyd-Franklin, N. (1990, October). *Empowering black families.* Paper presented at the Annual Conference of the American Association for Marriage and Family Therapy, Washington, DC.

Breines, W., & Gordon, L. (1983). The new scholarship on violence. *Signs: Journal of Women in Culture and Society, 8,* 490-531.

Brickman, P., Rabinowitz, V. C., Karuza, J., Jr., Coates, D., Cohn, E., & Kidder, L. (1982). Models of helping and coping. *American Psychologist, 37,* 368-384.

Briere, J., & Runtz, M. (1988a). Multivariate correlates of childhood psychological and physical maltreatment among university women. *Child Abuse & Neglect, 12,* 331-341.

Briere, J., & Runtz, M. (1988b). Symptomatology associated with childhood sexual victimization in a nonclinical sample. *Child Abuse & Neglect, 12,* 51-59.

Brim, O. (1959). *Education for child rearing.* New York: Russell Sage.

Brody, E. M. (1985). Parent care as normative family stress. *The Gerontologist, 25,* 19-29.

Brody, E. M., Kleban, M. H., Johnsen, P. T., Hoffman, C., & Schoonover, C. B. (1987). Work status and parent care. *The Gerontologist, 27,* 201-208.

Brody, E. M., & Schoonover, C. B. (1986). Patterns of parent-care when adult daughters work and when they do not. *The Gerontologist, 26,* 372-381.

Brody, G., Neubaum, E., & Forehand, R. (1988). Serial marriage: A heuristic analysis of an emerging family form. *Psychological Bulletin, 103,* 211-222.

Bronfenbrenner, U. (1974). *Is early intervention effective? A report on longitudinal evaluations of preschool programs* (Vol. 2). Washington, DC: Department of Health, Education and Welfare, Office of Child Development.

Bronfenbrenner, U. (1979). *The ecology of human development: Experiments by nature and design.* Cambridge, MA: Harvard University Press.

Brookfield, S. (1986). *Understanding and facilitating adult learning.* San Francisco: Jossey-Bass.

Browne, A., & Finkelhor, D. (1986). Initial and long-term effects: A review of the research. In D. Finkelhor (Ed.), *Sourcebook on child sexual abuse* (pp. 180-198). Beverly Hills, CA: Sage.

Brubaker, T. H. (1985). *Later life families.* Beverly Hills, CA: Sage.

Brubaker, T. H. (1986). Developmental tasks in later life. *American Behavioral Scientist, 29,* 381-388.

Brubaker, T. H. (1990a). Continuity and change in later life families: Grandparenthood, couple relationships and family caregiving. *Gerontology Review, 3,* 24-40.

Brubaker, T. H. (1990b). Families in later life: A burgeoning research area. *Journal of Marriage and the Family, 52,* 959-981.

Bulik, C. M., Sullivan, P. F., & Rorty, M. (1989). Childhood sexual abuse in women with bulimia. *Journal of Clinical Psychiatry, 50,* 460-464.

Bumpass, L. (1984). Children and marital disruption: A replication and update. *Demography, 21,* 71-82.

Bumpass, L. (1985). Some characteristics of children's second families. *American Journal of Sociology, 90,* 608-662.

Bumpass, L. (1990). What's happening to the family? Interactions between demographic and institutional change. *Demography, 27,* 483-489.

Bumpass, L., & McLanahan, S. (1989). Unmarried motherhood: Recent trends and black-white differences. *Demography, 26,* 279-286.

Bumpass, L., Sweet, J., & Cherlin, A. (1989). *The role of cohabitation in declining rates of marriage* (NSFH Working Paper 5). Madison: University of Wisconsin, Center for Demography and Ecology.

Bumpass, L. L., & Sweet, J. A. (1989). Children's experience in single-parent families: Implications of cohabitation and marital transition. *Family Planning Perspectives, 21*(6), 256-260.

Bureau of National Affairs. (1986). *Work and family: A changing dynamic.* Washington, DC: Author.

Burgess, R. L., Anderson, E. A., Schellenbach, C. J., & Conger, R. D. (1981). A social interactional approach to the study of abusive families. In J. P. Vincent (Ed.), *Advances in family intervention, assessment and theory* (Vol. 3). Greenwich, CT: JAI Press.

Burke, P. J., Stets, J. E., & Pirog-Good, M. A. (1988). Gender identity, self esteem and physical and sexual abuse in dating relationships. *Social Psychology Quarterly, 51,* 272-285.

Burkhart, B. R., & Stanton, A. L. (1988). Sexual aggression in acquaintance relationships. In G. W. Russell (Ed.), *Violence in intimate relationships* (pp. 43-65). Great Neck, NY: PMA Publishing.

Burr, W. F. (1973). *Theory construction and the sociology of the family.* New York: John Wiley.

Burton, J. R., & Hennon, C. B. (1980). Consumer concerns of senior citizen center participants. *Journal of Consumer Affairs, 14,* 366-381.

Butler, J. R., & Burton, L. M. (1990). Rethinking teenage childbearing: Is sexual abuse a missing link? *Family Relations, 39,* 73-80.

Cain, B. S. (1988). Divorce among elderly women: A growing social phenomenon. *Social Casework, 69,* 563-568.

Cain, B. S. (1989). Parental divorce during the college years. *Psychiatry, 52,* 135-146.

Caldwell, B. M. (1985). What is quality child care? In B. Caldwell & A. Hilliard (Eds.), *What is quality child care?* (pp. 1-16). Washington, DC: National Association for the Education of Young Children.

Caldwell, J. (1980). Mass education as a determinant of the timing of the fertility decline. *Population and Development Review, 6,* 225-256.

California Assembly Human Services Committee. (1987). *The changing American family to the year 2000: Planning for our children's future.* Sacramento: California General Assembly.

Callahan, D. (1987). *Setting limits: Medical goals in an aging society.* New York: Simon & Schuster.

Campbell, A., Converse, P. E., & Rodgers, W. L. (1976). *The quality of American life.* New York: Russell Sage.

Carnes, P. (1989). *Contrary to love: Helping the sexual addict.* Minneapolis, MN: CompCare Publications.

Caro, F. (1971). Issues in the evaluation of social programs. *Review of Educational Research, 41,* 87-114.

Cate, R. M., Henton, J. M., Koval, J. E., Christopher, F. S., & Lloyd, S. A. (1982). Premarital abuse: A social psychological perspective. *Journal of Family Issues, 3,* 79-90.

Center on Budget and Policy Priorities. (1988). *Shortchanged: Recent developments in Hispanic poverty, income and employment.* Washington, DC: Author.

Cheatham, H., & Stewart, J. (Eds.). (1990). *Black families.* New Brunswick, NJ: Transaction Books.

Chenoweth, L., & Maret, E. (1980). The career patterns of mature American women. *Sociology of Work and Occupations, 7,* 222-251.

Cherlin, A. (1981). *Marriage, divorce, remarriage.* Cambridge, MA: Harvard University Press.

Cherlin, A. (1988). (Ed.). *The changing American family and public policy.* Washington, DC: Urban Institute Press.

Children's Defense Fund. (1988). *A children's defense budget: FY-1989—An analysis of our nation's investment in children.* Washington, DC: Author.

Chiriboga, D. (1982). Adaptation to marital separation in later and earlier life. *Journal of Gerontology, 37,* 109-114.

Christensen, K. E., & Staines, G. L. (1990). Flextime. *Journal of Family Issues, 11,* 455-476.

Cicirelli, V. G. (1983). A comparison of helping behavior to elderly parents of adult children with intact and disrupted marriages. *The Gerontologist, 23*(6), 619-625.

Clarke, J. (1984). *The family types of neurotics, schizophrenics and normals.* Unpublished doctoral dissertation, University of Minnesota, Family Social Science, St. Paul.

Cochran, M. (1986a, April). *Family matters: Evaluation of a parental empowerment process.* Paper presented at the National Extension Family Life Specialists' Workshop, Purdue University, West Lafayette, IN.

Cochran, M. (1986b). The parental empowerment process: Building on family strengths. In J. Harris (Ed.), *Child psychology in action* (pp. 12-23). Cambridge, MA: Brookline Books.

Cochran, M. (1988). Parental empowerment in family matters: Lessons learned from a research program. In D. R. Powell (Ed.), *Parent education as early childhood intervention* (pp. 23-50). Norwood, NJ: Ablex.

Cohen, J. (1979). Male roles in mid-life. *Family Coordinator, 28,* 465-471.

Cohen, N., & Connery, M. (1967). Government policy and the family. *Journal of Marriage and the Family, 29,* 6-17.

Cohen, S., & Wills, T. A. (1985). Stress, social support and the buffering hypothesis. *Psychological Bulletin, 98,* 310-357.

Cole, P. M., & Woogler, C. (1989). Incest survivors: The relation of their perceptions of their parents and their own parenting attitudes. *Child Abuse & Neglect, 13,* 409-416.

Coleman, D. H., & Straus, M. A. (1990). Marital power, conflict and violence in a nationally representative sample of American couples. In M. A. Straus & R. Gelles (Eds.), *Physical violence in American families* (pp. 287-304). New Brunswick, NJ: Transaction Books.

Coleman, J. S. (1987). Families and schools. *Educational Researcher, 16,* 32-38.

Commission on Accreditation for Marriage and Family Therapy Education. (1988). *Manual on accreditation.* Washington, DC: Author.

Conner, R. (Ed.). (1981). *Methodological advances in evaluation research.* Beverly Hills, CA: Sage.

Consortium for Longitudinal Studies. (1983). *As the twig is bent: Lasting effects of preschool programs.* Hillsdale, NJ: Lawrence Erlbaum.

Constantine, L. (1986). *Family paradigms.* New York: Guilford.

Conte, J. R., & Berliner, L. (1988). The impact of sexual abuse on children: Empirical findings. In L. E. A. Walker (Ed.), *Handbook on sexual abuse of children* (pp. 72-93). New York: Springer.

Cooney, T. M. (1988). Young adults and parental divorce: Exploring important issues. *Human Relations, 41,* 805-822.

Cooney, T. M., Smyer, M. A., Hagestad, G. O., & Klock, R. (1986). Parental divorce in young adulthood: Some preliminary findings. *American Journal of Orthopsychiatry, 56,* 470-477.

Crawley, B. (1988). Black families in a neo-conservative era. *Family Relations, 37,* 415-419.

Crittenden, P. (1988). Family and dyadic patterns of functioning in maltreating families. In K. Browne, C. Davies, & P. Stratton (Eds.), *Early prediction and prevention of child abuse* (pp. 161-189). New York: John Wiley.

Crnic, K. A., & Greenberg, M. T. (1990). Minor parenting stresses with young children. *Child Development, 61,* 1628-1637.

Croake, J. W., & Glover, K. E. (1977). A history and evaluation of parent education. *Family Coordinator, 26,* 151-158.

Cudaback, D., Darden, C., Nelson, P., O'Brien, S., Pinsky, D., & Wiggins, E. (1985). Becoming successful parents: Can age-paced newsletters help? *Family Relations, 34,* 271-275.

Curtois, C. A. (1988). *Healing the incest wound: Adult survivors in therapy.* New York: Norton.

Daniels, P., & Weingarten, K. (1982). *Sooner or later: The timing of parenthood in adult lives.* New York: Norton.

Darling, C. A. (1987). Family life education. In M. B. Sussman & S. K. Steinmetz (Eds.), *Handbook of marriage and the family* (pp. 815-833). New York: Plenum.

Day, R. D., & Bahr, S. J. (1986). Income changes following divorce and remarriage. *Journal of Divorce, 9*(3), 75-88.

DeKeseredy, W. S. (1988). *Woman abuse in dating relationships: The role of male peer support.* Toronto: Canadian Scholars Press.

DeLissovoy, V. (1978). Parent education: White elephant in the classroom? *Youth & Society, 9,* 315-338.

DeMaris, A. (1990). The dynamics of generational transfer in courtship violence: A biracial exploration. *Journal of Marriage and the Family, 52,* 219-231.

Demo, D., & Acock, A. (1988). The impact of divorce on children. *Journal of Marriage and the Family, 50,* 619-648.

Dempsey, J. (1981). *The family and public policy: The issue of the 1980s.* Baltimore, MD: Brookes.

Derdeyn, A. P. (1985). Grandparent visitation rights: Rendering family dissension more pronounced? *American Journal of Orthopsychiatry, 55,* 277-287.

DeShane, M., & Brown-Wilson, K. (1981). Divorce in late life: A call for research. *Journal of Divorce, 4*(4), 81-91.

Diamond, I. (Ed.). (1983). *Families, politics, and public policy: A feminist dialogue on women and the state.* New York: Longman.

Dickie, J. R., & Gerber, S. C. (1980). Training in social competence: The effect on mothers, fathers, and infants. *Child Development, 51,* 1248-1251.

Dokecki, P. R., & Moroney, R. M. (1983). To strengthen all families: A human development and community value framework. In R. Haskins & D. Adams (Eds.), *Parent education and public policy* (pp. 40-64). Norwood, NJ: Ablex.

Douglass, R. L. (1988). *Domestic mistreatment of the elderly: Towards prevention.* Washington, DC: Criminal Justice Services.

Douglass, R. L., & Hickey, T. (1983). Domestic neglect and abuse of the elderly: Research findings and a systems perspective for service delivery planning. In J. Kosberg (Ed.), *Abuse and maltreatment of the elderly* (pp. 115-133). Littleton, MA: PSG.

Duncan, G., & Hoffman, S. (1990). Welfare benefits, economic opportunities, and out-of-wedlock births among black teenage girls. *Demography, 27,* 519-535.

Dunst, C. J., & Trivette, C. M. (1988). A family systems model of early intervention with handicapped and developmentally at-risk children. In D. R. Powell (Ed.), *Parent education as early childhood intervention* (pp. 131-179). Norwood, NJ: Ablex.

Dutton, D. G. (1988). *The domestic assault of women.* Boston: Allyn & Bacon.

Duvall, E. (1957). *Family development.* Philadelphia: J. B. Lippincott.

Easterlin, R. (1980). *Birth and fortune.* New York: Basic Books.

Edelman, M. W. (1987). *Families in peril: An agenda for social change.* Cambridge, MA: Harvard University Press.

Egeland, B., Jacobvitz, D., & Sroufe, L. A. (1988). Breaking the cycle of abuse. *Child Development, 59,* 1080-1088.

Eisenstadt, J. W., & Powell, D. R. (1987). Processes of participation in a mother-infant program as modified by stress and impulse control. *Journal of Applied Developmental Psychology, 8,* 17-37.

Elder, G. H., Jr. (1977). Family history and the life course. *Journal of Family History, 2,* 279-304.

Emery, B., Cate, R., Henton, J., & Andrews, D. (1988, November). *Perceived legitimizing factors in premarital violence.* Paper presented at the meeting of the National Council on Family Relations, Atlanta, GA.

Emery, B. C. (1983). *Factors contributing to violence in dating relationships.* Unpublished master's thesis, Oregon State University, Corvallis.

Emery, B. C., Lloyd, S. A., & Castleton, A. (1989, November). *Why women hit back: A feminist perspective.* Paper presented at the National Council on Family Relations Annual Meeting, New Orleans.

Emery, R. (1988). *Marriage, divorce, and children's adjustment.* Newbury Park, CA: Sage.

Epstein, N. B., Baldwin, L., & Bishop, D. S. (1983). The McMaster Assessment Device (FAD). *Journal of Marriage and Family Counseling, 9,* 171-180.

Espenshade, T. (1985). Marriage trends in America. *Population and Development Review, 11,* 193-245.

Evans, A. (1987). *Families at risk* (Report No. IB 87017). Washington, DC: Education and Public Welfare Division, Congressional Research Service.

Falicov, C. J. (1988). Learning to think culturally. In H. A. Liddle, D. Breunlin, & R. C. Schwartz (Eds.), *Handbook of family therapy training and supervision* (pp. 335-357). New York: Guilford.

Faller, K. C. (1990). *Understanding child sexual maltreatment.* Newbury Park, CA: Sage.

Family Relations. (1991). Family policy [Special collection], *40*(2), pp. 139-217.

Farber, B. (1987). The future of the American family: A dialectical account. *Journal of Family Issues, 8,* 431-433.

Farley, R. (1988). After the starting line: Blacks and women in an uphill race. *Demography, 25,* 477-495.

Federal Register. (1986, September 30). Vol. 51, p. 189. Washington, DC: Government Printing Office.

Ferree, M. M. (1991). Beyond separate spheres: Feminism and family research. In A. Booth (Ed.), *Contemporary families: Looking forward, looking back* (pp. 103-121). Minneapolis, MN: National Council on Family Relations.

Fethke, C. (1989). Life-cycle models of saving and the effect of the timing of divorce on retirement economic well-being. *Journal of Gerontology: Social Sciences, 44,* S121-S128.

Finch, J., & Groves, D. (Eds.). (1983). *A labour of love: Women, work, and caring.* Boston: Routledge, Chapman & Hall.

Finkelhor, D. (1982). Sexual abuse: A sociological view. *Child Abuse & Neglect, 6,* 95-102.

Finkelhor, D., & Baron, L. (1986). High-risk children. In D. Finkelhor (Ed.), *Sourcebook on child sexual abuse* (pp. 15-59). Beverly Hills, CA: Sage.

Finkelhor, D., Gelles, R. J., Hotaling, G. T., & Straus, M. A. (Eds.). (1983). *The dark side of families: Current family violence research.* Beverly Hills, CA: Sage.

Finkelhor, D., Hotaling, G., Lewis, I. A., & Smith, C. (1990). Sexual abuse in a national survey of adult men and women: Prevalence, characteristics, and risk factors. *Child Abuse & Neglect, 14,* 19-28.

Finkelhor, D., & Yllo, K. (1985). *License to rape: Sexual abuse of wives.* New York: Free Press.

Firebaugh, G. (1990). *A framework for linking societal and individual change using data from repeated surveys.* Unpublished manuscript, Pennsylvania State University, University Park.

Fischer, J. L., Sollie, D. L., & Leslie, L. (1990). *Structural, interactional and exchange characteristics of social networks during the transition to marriage.* Unpublished manuscript, Texas Tech University, Lubbock.

Fischer, J. L., Sollie, D. L., Sorell, G. T., & Green, S. (1989). Marital status and career stage influences on social networks of young adults. *Journal of Marriage and the Family, 51,* 521-534.

Fitz-Gibbon, C. T., & Morris, L. L. (1987). *How to design a program evaluation.* Newbury Park, CA: Sage.

Follingstad, D. R., Wright, S., Lloyd, S., & Sebastian, J. A. (1991). Sex differences in motivations and effects in dating violence. *Family Relations, 40,* 51-57.

Form, W. (1979). Comparative industrial sociology and the convergence hypothesis. *Annual Review of Sociology, 5,* 1-25.

Fournier, D. (1980, May). *Strengthening the premarital dyad: Some effective strategies in marriage preparation.* Paper presented at the Building Family Strengths Conference, Lincoln, NE.

Fox, G. L. (1986). The family context of adolescent sexuality and sex roles. In G. K. Leigh & G. W. Peterson (Eds.), *Adolescents in families* (pp. 179-204). Cincinnati, OH: Southwestern Publishing.

French, A. P., & Guidera, B. J. (1974). *The family as a system in four dimensions: A theoretical model.* Paper presented at the American Academy of Child Psychology, San Francisco.

Friedl, E. (1975). *Women and men: An anthropologist's view.* New York: Holt, Rinehart & Winston.

Friedman, D. E. (1990). Corporate responses to family needs. *Marriage and Family Review, 15,* 77-98.

Frieze, I. H., & Browne, A. (1989). Violence in marriage. In L. Ohlin & M. Tonry (Eds.), *Family violence* (pp. 163-218). Chicago: University of Chicago Press.

Frisch, R. (1978). Population, food intake and fertility. *Science, 99,* 22-29.

Frude, N. (1982). The sexual nature of sexual abuse. *Child Abuse & Neglect, 6,* 211-223.

Furstenberg, F. (1990). Divorce and the American family. *Annual Review of Sociology, 16,* 379-403.

Furstenberg, F., & Nord, C. W. (1985). Parenting apart: Patterns of childrearing after marital disruption. *Journal of Marriage and the Family, 47,* 893-905.

Fusfeld, D. (1973). The basic economics of the urban and racial crisis. In J. Huber & P. Chalfant (Eds.), *The sociology of American poverty* (pp. 43-70). Cambridge: Schenkman. (Original work published 1968)

Galinsky, E. (1981). *Between generations: The six stages of parenthood.* New York: Time-Life Books.

Galinsky, E. (1991). The private sector as a partner in early care and education. In S. L. Kagan (Ed.), *The care and education of America's young children: Obstacles and opportunities* (pp. 131-153) (Nineteenth yearbook of the National Society for the Study of Education, Part I). Chicago: University of Chicago Press.

Galinsky, E., & Hooks, W. (1977). *The new extended family: Day care that works.* New York: Houghton Mifflin.

Galston, W. (1990). *Putting children first* [Monograph]. Washington, DC: Public Policy Institute.

Gander, A. M., & Jorgensen, L. B. (1990). Post divorce adjustment: Social supports among older divorced persons. *Journal of Divorce, 13,* 37-52.

Ganong, L., Coleman, M., & Brown, G. (1980). Perceptions and attitudes of marriage and family life by adolescents in intact, single-parent, and reconstituted families. *Adolescence, 16,* 281-288.

Ganong, L., Coleman, M., & Mapes, W. D. (1990). A meta-analytic review of family structure stereotypes. *Journal of Marriage and the Family, 52,* 287-297.

Garbarino, J. (1977). The human ecology of child maltreatment. *Journal of Marriage and the Family, 39,* 721-727.

Geffner, R., & Pagelow, M. D. (1990). Victims of spouse abuse. In R. T. Ammerman & M. Hersen (Eds.), *Treatment of family violence* (pp. 113-135). New York: John Wiley.

Gelles, R. J., & Conte, J. R. (1990). Domestic violence and sexual abuse of children: A review of the research in the eighties. *Journal of Marriage and the Family, 52,* 1045-1058.

Gelles, R. J., & Conte, J.R. (1991). Domestic violence and sexual abuse of children: A review of the research in the eighties. In A. Booth (Ed.), *Contemporary families:*

Looking forward, looking back (pp. 327-340). Minneapolis, MN: National Council on Family Relations.

Genovese, R. (Ed.). (1984). *Families and change: Social needs and public policies.* New York: Praeger.

Gershuny, J., & Robinson, J. P. (1988). Historical changes in the household division of labor. *Demography, 25,* 537-552.

Giblin, P., Sprenkle, D. H., & Sheehan, R. (1985). Enrichment outcome research: A meta-analysis of premarital, marital, and family interventions. *Journal of Marital and Family Therapy, 11,* 257-271.

Giele, J. A. (1988). Gender and sex roles. In N. Smelser (Ed.), *Handbook of sociology* (pp. 291-326). Newbury Park, CA: Sage.

Gilbert, M. K., & Benokraitis, N. V. (1989). The Family and Medical Leave Act. *Family Perspective, 23,* 57-73.

Giordano, J. A. (1988). Parents of the baby boomers: A now generation of young-old. *Family Relations, 37,* 411-414.

Gladstone, J. (1988). Perceived changes in grandmother-grandchild relations following a child's separation or divorce. *The Gerontologist, 28,* 66-72.

Glass, J. (1990, April). *Housewives and employed wives: Demographic and attitudinal change, 1972-1986.* Paper presented at the annual meeting of the Population Association of America, Toronto.

Glenn, N. D. (1987). Continuity versus change, sanguineness versus concern: Views of the American family in the later 1980s. *Journal of Family Issues, 8,* 348-354.

Glick, P. C. (1984). American household structure in transition. *Family Planning Perspectives, 16,* 205-211.

Gnezda, T. (1989). *State fiscal policies for child care and early childhood education* (State Legislative Report 12, No. 7). Denver: National Conference of State Legislatures.

Goldstein, M. Z. (1989). Elder neglect, abuse and exploitation. In L. J. Dickstein & C. C. Nadelson (Eds.), *Family violence: Emerging issues of a national crisis* (pp. 101-124). Washington, DC: American Psychiatric Press.

Goode, W. (1963). *World revolution and family patterns.* New York: Free Press.

Goodnow, J. J. (1988). Parents' ideas, actions, and feelings: Models and methods from developmental and social psychology. *Child Development, 59,* 286-320.

Goody, J. (1976). *Production and reproduction.* Cambridge: Cambridge University Press.

Goody, J. (1983). *The development of family and marriage in Europe.* Cambridge: Cambridge University Press.

Gordon, T. (1970). *Parent-effectiveness training: The "no-lose" program for raising responsible children.* New York: Wyden.

Gottfredson, G. D. (1987). Employment setting, specialization, and patterns of accomplishment among psychologists. *Professional Psychology: Research and Practice, 18,* 452-460.

Gottman, J. M. (1979). *Marital interaction.* New York: Basic Books.

Gove, W., & Shin, H. (1989). The psychological well-being of divorced and widowed men and women: An empirical analysis. *Journal of Family Issues, 10,* 122-144.

Gove, W. R., Style, C. B., & Hughes, M. (1990). The effect of marriage on the well-being of adults. *Journal of Social Issues, 11,* 4-35.

Gray, M., & Coleman, M. (1985). Separation through divorce: Supportive professional practices. *Child Care Quarterly, 14*(4), 248-261.

Greenblat, C. S. (1983). The salience of sexuality in the early years of marriage. *Journal of Marriage and the Family, 45,* 289-299.

Greenhalgh, S. (1990). Toward a political economy of fertility. *Population and Development Review, 16,* 85-106.

Greenwald, E., & Leitenberg, H. (1990). Posttraumatic stress disorder in a nonclinical and nonstudent sample of adult women sexually abused as children. *Journal of Interpersonal Violence, 5,* 217-228.

Griffin, S., Weeks-Kirk, S., & Coleman, M. (1985). Stepfamilies: Awareness and attitudes of preschool children. *Early Child Development and Care, 19,* 281-290.

Guerney, B. (1977). *Relationship enhancement: Skill training programs for therapy, problem prevention, and enrichment.* San Francisco: Jossey-Bass.

Guerney, B., Jr., & Maxson, P. (1990). Marital and family enrichment research: A decade review and look ahead. *Journal of Marriage and the Family, 52,* 1127-1135.

Gurman, A. S., & Kniskern, D. P. (1986). Research in the process and outcome of marriage and family therapy. In S. Garfield & A. E. Bergin (Eds.), *Handbook of psychotherapy and behavior change* (3rd ed.) (pp. 565-626). New York: John Wiley.

Haas, J. (1990). Gender equality and social policy. *Journal of Family Issues, 11,* 401-423.

Hagestad, G. (1988). Demographic change and the life courses: Some emerging trends in the family realm. *Family Relations, 37,* 405-410.

Hagestad, G., & Smyer, M. (1982). Dissolving long term relationships: Patterns of divorcing in middle age. In S. Duck (Ed.), *Personal relationships. 4: Dissolving personal relationships* (pp. 155-188). New York: Academic Press.

Hall, F. S., & Hall, D. T. (1979). *The two-career couple.* Reading, MA: Addison-Wesley.

Halpern, R., & Larner, M. (1988). The design of family support programs in high-risk communities: Lessons from the Child Survival/Fair Start initiative. In D. R. Powell (Ed.), *Parent education as early childhood intervention* (pp. 181-207). Norwood, NJ: Ablex.

Hamilton, A., Stiles, W. B., Melowsky, F., & Beal, D. G. (1987). A multilevel comparison of child abusers with nonabusers. *Journal of Family Violence, 2,* 215-225.

Handy, E. S., & Pukui, M. (1978). *The Polynesian family system in Ka'u Hawaii.* Rutland, VT: Charles E. Tuttle.

Hanson, D. A., & Johnson, V. A. (1979). Rethinking family stress theory: Definitional aspects. In W. R. Burr, R. Hill, F. I. Nye, & I. L. Reis (Eds.), *Contemporary theories about the family: General theories and theoretical orientations* (Vol. 1, pp. 582-603). New York: Free Press.

Hardy, K. (1990, March). *Challenging the myth of sameness.* Paper presented at the Family Therapy Networker Conference, Washington, DC.

Harmin, D., & Brim, O. G., Jr. (1980). *Learning to be parents: Principles, programs and methods.* Beverly Hills, CA: Sage.

Harrison, B., & Bluestone, B. (1988). *The great u-turn.* New York: Basic Books.

Harry, J. (1976). Evolving sources of happiness for men over the life cycle: A structural analysis. *Journal of Marriage and the Family, 38,* 289-296.

Hart, H. (1933). Changing attitudes and interests. In *President's Research Committee on Social Trends,* (pp. 382-442). New York: McGraw-Hill.

Hayghe, H. V. (1990, March). Family members in the work force. *Monthly Labor Review,* pp. 14-19.

Health and Welfare Canada. (1989). *Child sexual abuse overview: A summary of 26 literature reviews and special projects.* Ottawa: Family Violence Prevention, Social Services Program Branch, Health and Welfare, Canada.

Heckart, K. (1990). *Domestic partnership laws in seven communities.* Unpublished manuscript, University of Connecticut, School of Family Studies, Storrs.

Heinecke, C. M., Beckwith, L., & Thompson, A. (1988). Early intervention in the family system: A framework and review. *Infant Mental Health Journal, 9,* 111-141.

Hennon, C. B. (1983). Divorce and the elderly: A neglected area of research. In T. H. Brubaker (Ed.), *Family relationships in later life* (pp. 149-172). Beverly Hills, CA: Sage.

Hennon, C. B., & Brubaker, T. H. (1982, October). *Family life education in community settings: Who wants to know what and if you know something, to whom do you teach it?* Roundtable presented at the National Conference on Family Relations, Washington, DC.

Hennon, C. B., Mayer, R. N., & Burton, J. R. (1981). Empirical support for and evaluation of an intervention model for elderly consumers. *Journal of Consumer Studies and Home Economics, 5,* 13-21.

Hennon, C. B., & Peterson, B. (1981). An evaluation of a family life education delivery system for young families. *Family Relations, 30,* 387-394.

Henton, J., Cate, R., & Emery, B. (1984). The dependent elderly: Targets for abuse. In W. H. Quinn & G. A. Hughston (Eds.), *Independent aging: Family and social systems perspectives* (pp. 149-162). Rockville, MD: Aspen.

Henton, J. M., Cate, R. M., Koval, J. E., Lloyd, S. A., & Christopher, F. S. (1983). Romance and violence in dating relationships. *Journal of Family Issues, 4,* 467-482.

Hetherington, E. M., Cox, M., & Cox, R. (1977). The aftermath of divorce. In J. J. Stevens, Jr., & M. Matthews (Eds.), *Mother-child, father-child relations.* Washington, DC: National Association for the Education of Young Children.

Hey, R., & Neubeck, G. (1989). Family life education. In D. H. Olson & S. Hansen (Eds.), *2001: Preparing families for the future* (pp. 15-16). Minneapolis, MN: National Council on Family Relations.

Hickey, T., & Douglass, R. L. (1981). Mistreatment of the elderly in a domestic setting: An exploratory study. *American Journal of Public Health, 71,* 500-507.

Hicks, M., & Platt, M. (1970). Marital happiness and stability: A review of research in the sixties. In C. Broderick (Ed.), *A decade of family research and action 1960-1969.* Minneapolis, MN: National Council on Family Relations.

Hill, R. (1949). *Families under stress.* New York: Harper & Row.

Hill, R. (1964). Methodological issues in family development research. *Family Process, 3,* 186-206.

Hill, R. (1970). *Family development in three generations.* Cambridge, MA: Schenkman.

Hill, R., & Aldous, J. (1969). Socialization for marriage and parenthood. In D. A. Goslin (Ed.), *Handbook of socialization theory and research* (pp. 885-950). Chicago: Rand McNally.

Himes, N. (1970). *Medical history of contraception.* New York: Schocken.

Hochschild, A. (1989). *The second shift: Inside the two-job marriage.* New York: Viking.

Hof, L., & Miller, W. R. (1980). Marriage enrichment. *Marriage & Family Review, 3,* 1-27.

Hoffman, L. W. (1989). Effects of maternal employment in the two-parent family. *American Psychologist, 44,* 283-292.

Hoffman, S., & Duncan, G. (1988). What are the economic consequences of divorce? *Demography, 25,* 641-645.

Hogan, S. (1990). Care for the caregiver: Social policies to ease their burden. *Journal of Gerontological Nursing, 16,* 12-17.

Holahan, C. J., & Moos, R. H. (1986). Personality, coping, and family resources in stress resistance: A longitudinal analysis. *Journal of Personality and Social Psychology, 51,* 389-395.

Hooyman, N. (1983). Elder abuse and neglect: Community interventions. In J. Kosberg (Ed.), *Abuse and maltreatment of the elderly* (pp. 376-390). Littleton, MA: PSG Publishing.

Hotaling, G. T., & Sugarman, D. B. (1986). An analysis of risk markers in husband to wife violence: The current state of knowledge. *Violence and Victims, 1,* 101-124.

Houseknecht, S. (1987). Voluntary childlessness. In M. B. Sussman & S. K. Steinmetz (Eds.), *Handbook of marriage and the family* (pp. 369-395). New York: Plenum.

House Select Committee on Aging. (1987). *Exploding the myth: Caregiving in America.* Washington, DC: Government Printing Office.

Howe, W. J., & Parks, W. (1989). Labor market completes sixth year of expansion in 1988. *Monthly Labor Review, 112,* 3-14.

Huber, J., & Spitze, G. (1983). *Sex stratification: Children, housework, and jobs.* New York: Academic Press.

Huber, J., & Spitze, G. (1988). Trends in family sociology. In N. Smelser (Ed.), *Handbook of sociology,* (pp. 425-448). Newbury Park, CA: Sage.

Hughes, R., Jr. (1988). Empowering rural families and communities. In R. Marotz-Baden, C. B. Hennon, & T. H. Brubaker (Eds.), *Families in rural America: Stress, adaptation and revitalization* (pp. 261-269). St. Paul, MN: National Council on Family Relations.

Hunt, J. G., & Hunt, L. L. (1982). The dualities of careers and families: New integrations or new polarizations? *Social Problems, 29,* 499-510.

Institute for American Values. (1989). What's new: Family leave legislation since 1987. *Family Affairs, 2,* 8.

Isaacs, M. B., & Leon, G. H. (1986). Social networks, divorce, and adjustment: A tale of three generations. *Journal of Divorce, 9,* 1-16.

Jacobson, C., Heaton, T., & Taylor, K. (1989). Childlessness among American women. *Social Biology, 35,* 186-197.

Johnson, B. L. (1980, April). Marital and family characteristics of the labor force. *Monthly Labor Review,* pp. 48-52.

Johnson, C. L. (1988). *Ex-familia: Grandparents, parents, and children adjust to divorce.* New Brunswick, NJ: Rutgers University Press.

Johnson, J. E., & Martin, C. (1985). Parents' beliefs and home learning environments: Effects on cognitive development. In I. E. Sigel (Ed.), *Parental belief systems* (pp. 25-50). Hillsdale, NJ: Lawrence Erlbaum.

Johnson, M. P., & Leslie, L. (1982). Couple involvement and network structure: A test of the dyadic withdrawal hypothesis. *Social Psychology Quarterly, 45,* 34-43.

Jones, E. (1986). *Teenage pregnancy in industrialized countries.* New Haven, CT: Yale University Press.

Jorgensen, S. R. (1981). Sex education and the reduction of adolescent pregnancies: Prospects for the 1980s. *Journal of Early Adolescence, 1, 38-52.*

Jouriles, E. N., Murphy, C. M., & O'Leary, K. D. (1989). Interspousal aggression, marital discord, and child problems. *Journal of Consulting and Clinical Psychology, 57,* 453-455.

Jurich, A. P., & Russell, C. R. (1985). The conflict between the ethics of therapy and outcome research in family therapy. In L. L. Andreozzi & R. F. Levant (Eds.), *Integrating research and clinical practice* (pp. 90-97). Rockville, MD: Aspen.

Kahn, A. J., & Kamerman, S. B. (1975). *Not for the poor alone.* Philadelphia: Temple University Press.

Kalmuss, D. S., & Straus, M. A. (1990). Wife's marital dependency and wife abuse. In M. A. Straus & R. Gelles (Eds.), *Physical violence in American families* (pp. 369-382). New Brunswick, NJ: Transaction Books.

Kamerman, S. B., & Kahn, A. J. (1976). Explorations in family policy. *Social Work, 23*(3), 181-186.

Kamerman, S. B., & Kahn, A. J. (1978). *Family policy: Government and families in fourteen countries.* New York: Columbia University Press.

Kamerman, S. B., & Kahn, A. J. (1989). Family policy: Has the United States learned from Europe. *Policy Studies Review, 8*(3), 581-598.

Kantor, D., & Lehr, W. (1975). *Inside the family.* San Francisco: Jossey-Bass.

Kantor, G. K., & Straus, M. A. (1990). The "drunken bum" theory of wife beating. In M. A. Straus & R. Gelles (Eds.), *Physical violence in American families* (pp. 227-244). New Brunswick, NJ: Transaction Books.

Kaplan, L., & Hennon, C. B. (1990, April). *A social psychology of remarriage: A theoretical foundation for personal reflections.* Paper presented at Celebrate the Family: Sixth Symposium on Building Family Strengths, University Park, PA. (Document 1-90, Family and Child Studies Center manuscript series, Miami University, Oxford, OH.)

Kaslow, F. W., & Schwartz, L. L. (1987). *The dynamics of divorce: A life cycle perspective.* New York: Brunner/Mazel.

Kaufman, J., & Zigler, E. (1987). Do abused children become abusive parents? *American Journal of Orthopsychiatry, 57,* 186-197.

Keith, P. M. (1986). Isolation of the unmarried in later life. *Family Relations, 35,* 389-395.

Kelly, E. L., & Conley, J. J. (1987). Personality and compatibility: A prospective analysis of marital satisfaction. *Journal of Personality and Social Psychology, 52,* 27-40.

Kelly, R. F., & Voydanoff, P. (1985). Work/family role strain among employed parents. *Family Relations, 34,* 367-374.

Kempe, C., Silverman, F., Steele, B., Droegemueller, W., & Silver, H. K. (1962). The battered child syndrome. *Journal of the American Medical Association, 181,* 17-24.

Keniston, K. (1977). *All our children.* New York: Harcourt Brace Jovanovich.

Kerckhoff, R. K. (1964). Family life education in America. In H. T. Christensen (Ed.), *Handbook of marriage and the family* (pp. 881-911). Chicago: Rand McNally.

Kessen, W. (1979). The American child and other cultural inventions. *American Psychologist, 34,* 815-820.

Kessler, R. C., & Essex, M. (1982). Marital status and depression: The importance of coping resources. *Social Forces, 61,* 484-507.

Kilpatrick, D. G., Best, C. L., Saunders, B. E., & Vernon, L. J. (1988). Rape in marriage and dating relationships: How bad is it for mental health? *Annals of the New York Academy of Sciences, 528,* 335-344.

Kimsey, L. R., Tarbox, A. R., & Bragg, D. F. (1981). The caretakers and the hidden agenda I: The caretakers and categories of abuse. *Journal of American Geriatrics Society, 29,* 465-472.

King, J. A., Morris, L. L., & Fitz-Gibbon, C. T. (1987). *How to assess program implementation.* Newbury Park, CA: Sage.

King, M. (1989). *Medical indigency and uncompensated health care costs.* Denver: National Conference of State Legislatures.

Kirk, D. (1968). Population I. The field of demography. In D. Sills (Ed.), *International encyclopedia of the social sciences* (Vol. 12, pp. 342-349). New York: Free Press.

Kitson, G., & Morgan, L. (1990). The multiple consequences of divorce: A decade review. *Journal of Marriage and the Family, 52*(4), 913-924.

Kobasa, S., Maddi, S., & Kahn, S. (1982). Hardiness and health: A prospective study. *Journal of Personality and Social Psychology, 42,* 168-177.

Kosberg, J. I. (1983). The special vulnerability of elderly parents. In J. Kosberg (Ed.), *Abuse and maltreatment of the elderly* (pp. 263-275). Littleton, MA: PSG Publishing.

Koss, M. P. (1988). Hidden rape: Sexual aggression and victimization in a national sample of students in higher education. In A. W. Burgess (Ed.), *Rape and sexual assault* (pp. 3-25). New York: Garland.

Koss, M. P., & Dinero, T. E. (1989). Discriminant analysis of risk factors for sexual victimization among a sample of college women. *Family Relations, 57,* 242-250.

Kraly, E., & Hirschman, C. (1990). Racial and ethnic inequality among U.S. Children: 1940 and 1950. *Social Forces, 69,* 33-51.

Krauss, M. W., & Jacobs, F. (1990). Family assessment: Purposes and techniques. In S. J. Meisels & J. P. Shonkoff (Eds.), *Handbook of early childhood intervention* (pp. 303-325). New York: Cambridge University Press.

Kurdek, L. (1987). Children's adjustment to parental divorce: An ecological perspective. *Advances in Family Intervention, Assessment and Theory, 4,* 1-31.

L'Abate, L., & Weinstein, S. E. (1987). *Structured enrichment programs for couples and families.* New York: Brunner/Mazel.

Lane, K. E., & Gwartney-Gibbs, P. A. (1985). Violence in the context of dating and sex. *Journal of Family Issues, 6,* 45-59.

Langelier, R., & Deckert, P. (1980). Divorce counseling guidelines for the late divorced female. *Journal of Divorce, 3,* 402-411.

Laosa, L. (1983). Parent education, cultural pluralism, and public policy: The uncertain connection. In R. Haskins & D. Adams (Eds.), *Parent education and public policy.* Norwood, NJ: Ablex.

Latin American Research. (1987). *Hispanic agenda: 1990 and beyond.* Denver: Latin American Research and Service Agency.

Lau, E. E., & Kosberg, J. I. (1979). Abuse of the elderly by informal care providers. *Aging, 299-300,* 10-15.

Lavee, Y., McCubbin, H. I., & Patterson, J. M. (1985). The Double ABCX Model of Stress and Adaptation: An empirical test by analysis of structural equations with latent variables. *Journal of Marriage and the Family, 47,* 811-825.

Leary, T. (1957). *Interpersonal diagnosis of personality.* New York: Ronald Press.

Lee, C. (1988). Theories of family adaptability: Toward a synthesis of Olson's Circumplex Model and Beavers' Systems Model. *Family Process, 27*(2), 73-85.

Leff, J., & Vaughn, C. (1985). *Expressed emotion in families.* New York: Guilford.

Lenski, G. (1966). *Power and privilege.* New York: McGraw-Hill.

Lenski, G., & Lenski, J. (1990). *Human societies* (5th ed.). New York: McGraw-Hill.

Leonard, K. E., & Jacob, J. (1988). Alcohol, alcoholism, and family violence. In V. Van Hasselt, R. Morrison, A. Bellack, & M. Hersen (Eds.), *Handbook of family violence* (pp. 383-406). New York: Plenum.

Lerner, R. M. (1984). *On the nature of human plasticity.* New York: Cambridge University Press.

Lerner, R. M. (1986). *Concepts and theories of human development* (2nd ed.). New York: Random House.

Lesthaeghe, R. (1983). A century of demographic and cultural change in western Europe. *Population and Development Review, 9,* 411-435.

Lewis, J. M., Beavers, W. R., Gossett, J. T., & Phillips, V. A. (1976). *No single thread: Psychological health in family systems.* New York: Brunner/Mazel.

Lindblom, C. E. (1959). The science of muddling through. *Public Administration Review, 19*(1), 79-88.

Lloyd, S. A. (1988, November). *Conflict and violence in marriage.* Paper presented at the National Council on Family Relations Annual Conference, Philadelphia.

Lloyd, S. A. (1990). Conflict types and strategies in violent marriages. *Journal of Family Violence, 5,* 269-284.

Lloyd, S. A. (1991). The dark side of courtship. *Family Relations, 40,* 14-20.

Lloyd, S. A., Koval, J. E., & Cate, R. M. (1989). Conflict and violence in dating relationships. In M. Pirog-Good & J. Stets (Eds.), *Violence in dating relationships* (pp. 126-144). New York: Praeger.

Lloyd, S. A., & Zick, C. D. (1986). Divorce at mid and later life: Does the empirical evidence support the theory. *Journal of Divorce, 9,* 89-102.

Locke, H. J., & Wallace, K. M. (1959). Short marital-adjustment and prediction tests: Their reliability and validity. *Marriage and Family Living, 21,* 251-255.

Longman, P. (1987). *Born to pay: The new politics of aging in America.* Boston: Houghton-Mifflin.

LoPiccolo, J., & Friedman, J. (1988). Broad spectrum treatments of low sexual desire: Integration of cognitive, behavioral, and systemic therapy. In S. Lieblum & R. Roson (Eds.), *Sexual desire disorders* (pp. 107-144). New York: Guilford.

Lundberg-Love, P., & Geffner, R. (1989). Date rape: Prevalence, risk factors and a proposed model. In M. Pirog-Good & J. Stets (Eds.), *Violence in dating relationships* (pp. 169-184). New York: Praeger.

Lusk, R., & Waterman, J. (1986). Effects of sexual abuse on children. In K. MacFarlane & J. Waterman (Eds.), *Sexual abuse of young children* (pp. 101-120). New York: Guilford.

Macklin, E. D. (1988). AIDS: Implications for families. *Family Relations, 37,* 141-149.

Maggard, H. (1985). *State legislative initiatives that address the issue of teen pregnancy and parenting.* Denver: National Conference of State Legislatures.

Makepeace, J. M. (1981). Courtship violence among college students. *Family Relations, 30,* 97-102.

Makepeace, J. M. (1983). Life events stress and courtship violence. *Family Relations, 32,* 101-109.

Malamuth, N. M. (1981). Rape proclivity among males. *Journal of Social Issues, 4,* 138-157.

Mannarino, A. P., & Cohen, A. (1986). A clinical-demographic study of sexually abused children. *Child Abuse & Neglect, 10,* 17-23.

Marcus, L. (1990). Universal health insurance in Massachusetts: Negotiating policy compromise. *Journal of Aging and Social Policy, 1/2*(1), 33-59.

Margolin, G., John, R. S., & Gleberman, L. (1988). Affective responses to conflictual discussion in violent and nonviolent couples. *Journal of Consulting and Clinical Psychology, 56,* 24-33.

Margolin, G., John, R. S., & O'Brien, M. (1989). Sequential affective patterns as a function of marital conflict style. *Journal of Social and Clinical Psychology, 8,* 45-61.

Markman, H. J. (1981). Prediction of marital distress: A 5-year follow-up. *Journal of Consulting and Clinical Psychology, 49,* 760-762.

Martin, T. C., & Bumpass, L. (1989). Recent trends in marital disruption. *Demography, 26,* 37-51.

Maslow, A. H. (1943). A theory of human motivation. *Psychological Review, 50,* 370-396.

Mason, K. O., & Lu, Y.-H. (1988). Attitudes toward U.S. women's familial roles, 1977-1985. *Gender and Society, 2,* 39-57.

Mason, R. L. (1977). Family life education in the high schools of Kentucky. *Family Coordinator, 23,* 197-201.

Massey, D. (1990). American apartheid: Segregation and the making of the underclass. *American Journal of Sociology, 96,* 329-357.

Massey, D., & Denton, N. (1987). Trends in the residential segregation of blacks, Hispanics, and Asians: 1970-1980. *American Sociological Review, 52,* 802-805.

Mattox, W. R. (1991). The parent trap. *Policy Review, 55,* 6-13.

McGoldrick, M., Pearce, J. K., & Giordano, J. (1982). *Ethnicity and family therapy.* New York: Guilford.

McCubbin, H. I., Boss, P., Wilson, L. R., & Dahl, P. B. (1981). *Family Coping Inventory (FCI), (Form B).* St. Paul: University of Minnesota, Family Social Science.

McCubbin, H. I., Dahl, B., & Hunter, E. (1975). Residuals of war. *Journal of Family Issues, 31*(4), 161-182.

McCubbin, H. I., Dahl, B., & Hunter, E. (Eds). (1976). *Families in the military system.* Beverly Hills, CA: Sage.

McCubbin, H. I., Dahl, B., Metres, P., Hunter, E., & Plag, J. (Eds.). (1974). *Family separation and reunion.* Washington, DC: Government Printing Office.

McCubbin, H. I., & Figley, C. R. (Eds.). (1983). *Stress and the family: Vol. I. Coping with normative transitions.* New York: Brunner/Mazel.

McCubbin, H. I., Larsen, A., & Olson, D. H. (1987). F-COPES: Family oriented personal scales. In H. I. McCubbin & A. Thompson (Eds.), *Family assessment inventories for research and practice* (pp. 193-207). Madison: University of Wisconsin-Madison.

McCubbin, H. I., & McCubbin, M. A. (1988). Typologies of resilient families: Emerging roles of social class and ethnicity. *Family Relations, 37,* 247-254.

McCubbin, H. I., McCubbin, M. A., & Thompson, A. (1987). Family Hardiness Index. In H. I. McCubbin, A. Thompson, P. Pirner, & M. A. McCubbin (Eds.), *Family types and strengths: A life cycle and ecological perspective* (p. 29). Edina, MN: Burgess MN International.

McCubbin, H. I., Olson, D. H., Lavee, Y., & Patterson, J. M. (1985). *FIT: Family Invulnerability Test.* St. Paul: University of Minnesota, Family Social Science.

McCubbin, H. I., & Patterson, J. M. (1983). Family transitions: Adaptation to stress. In H. I. McCubbin & C. R. Figley (Eds.), *Stress and the family: Vol. I. Coping with normative transitions* (pp. 5-25). New York: Brunner/Mazel.

McCubbin, H. I., Patterson, J., & Glynn, T. (1987). Social Support Index (SSI). In H. I. McCubbin & A. Thompson (Eds.), *Family assessment inventories for research and practice* (pp. 285-302). Madison: University of Wisconsin-Madison.

McCubbin, H. I., & Thompson, A. (1989). *Balancing work and family life on Wall Street: Stockbrokers and families coping with economic instability.* Edina, MN: Burgess MN International.

McCubbin, H. I., & Thompson, A. (1990). *The Family Distress Index.* Madison: University of Wisconsin-Madison.

McCubbin, H. I., Thompson, A., Pirner, P., & McCubbin, M. A. (1988). *Family types and family strengths: A life cycle and ecological perspective.* Edina, MN: Burgess MN International.

McCubbin, M. A. (1990). The Typology Model of Adjustment and Adaptation: A family stress model. *Guidance and Counseling, 5,* 6-22.

McCubbin, M. A., & McCubbin, H. I. (1989a). Theoretical orientations to family stress and coping. In C. R. Figley (Ed.), *Treating stress in families* (pp. 3-43). New York: Brunner/Mazel.

McCubbin, M. A., & McCubbin, H. I. (1989b). The typology model of family adjustment and adaptations. In C. Figley (Ed.), *Family stress and coping* (pp. 3-43). New York: Brunner/Mazel.

McCubbin, M. A., & McCubbin, H. I. (1992). Family coping with health crises: The Resiliency Model of Family Stress, Adjustment and Adaptation. In C. Danielson, B. Hamel-Bissell, & P. Winstead-Fry (Eds.), *Families, health and illness.* St. Louis: C. V. Mosby.

McCubbin, M. A., McCubbin, H. I., & Thompson, A. (1987). Family Hardiness Index. In H. I. McCubbin & A. Thompson (Eds.), *Family assessment inventories for research and practice* (pp. 125-130). Madison: University of Wisconsin-Madison.

McCubbin, M. A., McCubbin, H. I., & Thompson, A. (1988). *Family Problem-Solving Communications Index.* Madison: University of Wisconsin-Madison, Family Stress, Coping and Health Project.

McGillicuddy-DeLisi, A. V. (1985). The relationship between parental beliefs and children's cognitive level. In I. E. Sigel (Ed.), *Parental belief systems* (pp. 7-24). Hillsdale, NJ: Lawrence Erlbaum.

McGoldrick, M., Pearce, J. K., & Giordano, J. (1982). *Ethnicity and family therapy.* New York: Guilford.

McKillip, J. (1987). *Need analysis: Tools for the human services and education.* Newbury Park, CA: Sage.

McLanahan, S. (1991). The two faces of divorce: Women's and children's interests. In J. Huber (Ed.), *Macro-micro linkages in sociology* (pp. 193-207). Newbury Park, CA: Sage.

McLanahan, S., & Adams, J. (1987). Parenthood and psychological wellbeing. *Annual Review of Sociology, 13,* 237-257.

Meiselman, K. C. (1978). *Incest: A psychological study of causes and effects with treatment recommendations.* San Francisco: Jossey-Bass.

Mellor, E. F. (1986, November). Shift work and flextime: How prevalent are they? *Monthly Labor Review,* pp. 14-21.

Meth, R., & Pasick, R. (1990). *Men in therapy: The challenge when men ask for help.* New York: Guilford.

Mey, B. V. (1988). The sexual victimization of male children: A review of previous research. *Child Abuse & Neglect, 12,* 61-72.

Milardo, R. M., Johnson, M. P., & Huston, T. (1983). Developing close relationships: Changing patterns of interaction between pair members and social networks. *Journal of Personality and Social Psychology, 44,* 964-976.

Miller, D. A. (1981). The "sandwich" generation: Adult children of the aging. *Social Work, 26,* 419-423.

Miller, S. A. (1988). Parents' beliefs about children's development. *Child Development, 59,* 259-285.

Mindel, C., Habenstein, R., & Wright, R. (Eds.). (1988). *Ethnic families in America: Patterns and variations* (3rd ed.) (Vol. 3). New York: Elsevier.

Mindick, B. (1986). *Social engineering in family matters.* New York: Praeger.

Mishel, L., & Simon, J. (1988). *The state of working America.* Washington, DC: Economic Policy Institute.

Modell, J., Furstenberg, F., & Hershberg, T. (1976). Social change and transitions to adulthood in historical perspective. *Journal of Family History, 1,* 7-32.

Moen, P. (1985). Continuities and discontinuities in women's labor force activity. In G. H. Elder, Jr. (Ed.), *Life course dynamics* (pp. 113-155). Ithaca, NY: Cornell University Press.

Mohr, J. (1978). *Abortion in America.* New York: Oxford University Press.

Monahan, T. (1955). Is childlessness related to family stability? *American Sociological Review, 20,* 446-456.

Mooney, C. J. (1989, April 12). Stanford University reports strained campus race relations; University of Michigan faculty rejects required course on racism. *Chronicle of Higher Education.*

Moore, K. A. (1986). *Facts at a glance.* Washington, DC: Child Trends.

Moroney, R. (1986). *Shared responsibility: Families and social policy.* New York: Aldine.

Moynihan, D. P. (1968). Foreword. In A. Myrdal (Ed.), *Nation and family.* Cambridge: MIT Press.

Moynihan, D. P. (1986). *Family and nation.* New York: Harper & Row.

Muehlenhard, C. L., & Linton, M. (1987). Date rape and sexual aggression in dating situations: Incidence and risk factors. *Journal of Counseling Psychology, 34,* 186-195.

Myrdal, A. (1941). *Nation and family: The Swedish experiment in democratic family and population policy.* New York: Harper & Brothers.

Nardone, T. J. (1986, February). Part-time workers: Who are they? *Monthly Labor Review,* pp. 13-19.

National Center on Child Abuse & Neglect. (1988). *Study findings: Study of national incidence and prevalence of child abuse and neglect: 1988.* Washington, DC: Department of Health and Human Services.

National Commission on Family Life Education, a task force of the National Council on Family Relations. (1968). Family life education programs: Principles, plans, procedures. *Family Coordinator, 17,* 211-214.

National Conference of State Legislatures. (1989). *Family policy: Recommendations for state action.* Denver: National Conference of State Legislatures.

National Council on Family Relations. (1970). Position paper on family life education. *Family Coordinator, 19,* 186.

National Council on Family Relations. (1984). *Standards and criteria for the certification of family life educators, college/university curriculum guidelines, and content guidelines for family life education: A framework for planning programs over the life span.* Minneapolis, MN: National Council on Family Relations.

National Retired Teachers Association—American Association of Retired Persons. (1984). *National survey of older Americans.* Washington, DC: American Association of Retired Persons.

Newman, M. R., & Lutzker, J. R. (1990). Prevention programs. In R. T. Ammerman & M. Hersen (Eds.), *Children at risk* (pp. 225-248). New York: Plenum.

Noble, J., & Sussman, M. (1987). *Government and family.* New York: Haworth.

Norton, A. J., & Moorman, J. E. (1987). Current trends in marriage and divorce among American women. *Journal of Marriage and the Family, 49,* 3-14.

O'Connell, M. (1990). *Maternity leave arrangements: 1961-85* (Current Population Reports, Report No. 165). Washington, DC: U.S. Department of Commerce.

O'Connell, M., & Bachu, A. (1990). *Who's minding the kids?* (Current Population Reports, Series P-70, No. 20). Washington, DC: U.S. Department of Commerce.

O'Keeffe, D. C. (1990, December 6). Divorced parents becoming norm in today's society. *Columbia Missourian.*

O'Leary, K. D., Barling, J., Arias, I., Rosenbaum, A., Malone, J., & Tyree, A. (1989). Prevalence and stability of physical aggression between spouses: A longitudinal analysis. *Journal of Consulting and Clinical Psychology, 57,* 263-268.

Olson, D. H. (1977). Insider's and outsider's perspectives of relationships: Research strategies. In G. Levinger & H. Rausch, (Eds.), *Close relationships.* Amherst: University of Massachusetts Press.

Olson, D. H. (1986). Circumplex Model VII: Validation studies and FACES III. *Family Process, 25,* 337-351.

Olson, D. H. (1990). *Clinical rating scale for Circumplex Model.* St. Paul: University of Minnesota, Family Social Science.

Olson, D. H., Fournier, D. G., & Druckman, J. M. (1986). *PREPARE, PREPARE-MC and ENRICH inventories* (2nd ed.). Minneapolis, MN: Prepare/Enrich.

Olson, D. H., McCubbin, H. I., Barnes, H., Larsen, A., Muxen, A., & Wilson, M. (1983). *Families: What makes them work?* Beverly Hills, CA: Sage.

Olson, D. H., McCubbin, H. I., Barnes, H., Larsen, A., Muxen, A., & Wilson, M. (1986). *Family inventories.* St. Paul: University of Minnesota, Family Social Science.

Olson, D. H., McCubbin, H. I., Barnes, H., Larsen, A., Muxen, A., & Wilson, M. (1989). *Families: What makes them work* (2nd ed.). Newbury Park, CA: Sage.

Olson, D. H., Portner, J., & Lavee, Y. (1985). *FACES III.* St. Paul: University of Minnesota, Family Social Science.

Olson, D. H., Russell, C. S., & Sprenkle, D. H. (1989). *Circumplex Model: Systemic assessment and treatment of families* (2nd ed.). New York: Haworth.

Olson, D. H., & Wilson, M. (1985). Family satisfaction. In D. H. Olson, H. I. McCubbin, H. Barnes, A. Larsen, M. Muxen, & M. Wilson (Eds.), *Family inventories.* St. Paul: University of Minnesota, Family Social Science.

Parke, R., & Collmer, C. (1975). Child abuse: An interdisciplinary review. In E. M. Hetherington (Ed.), *Review of child development research* (Vol. 5). Chicago: University of Chicago Press.

Parmelee, P. A. (1987). Sex role identity, role performance and marital satisfaction of newly-wed couples. *Journal of Social and Personal Relationships, 4,* 429-444.

Parsons, D. (1984). On the economics of intergenerational control. *Population and Development Review, 10,* 41-54.

Parsons, D., & Goldin, C. (1987). Parental altruism and self-interest: Child labor among late nineteenth century American families. *Economic Inquiry, 27,* 637-659.

Parsons, T. (1943). The kinship system in the contemporary United States. *American Anthropologist, 45,* 22-38.

Parsons, T., & Bales, R. F. (1955). *Family socialization and interaction process.* Glencoe, IL: Free Press.

Peden, J., & Glahe, F. (1986). *The American family and the state.* San Francisco: Pacific Institute for Public Policy Research.

Pepper Commission Report. (1990). Washington, DC: Government Printing Office.

Pillemer, K. (1985). The dangers of dependency: New findings on domestic violence against the elderly. *Social Problems, 33,* 146-158.

Pillemer, K., & Finkelhor, D. (1988). The prevalence of elder abuse: A random sample survey. *The Gerontologist, 28,* 51-57.

Pillemer, K., & Suitor, J. J. (1988). Elder abuse. In V. B. Van Hasselt, R. L. Morrison, A. S. Bellack, & M. Hersen (Eds.), *Handbook of family violence* (pp. 247-270). New York: Plenum.

Pleck, J. H. (1977, May). *Developmental stages in men's lives: How do they differ from women's?* Paper presented at the Conference on Resocialization of Sex Roles: Challenge for the 1970s, Hartland, MI.

Pleck, J. H. (1983). Husband's paid work and family roles: Current research issues. In H. Z. Lopata & J. H. Pleck (Eds.), *Research in the interweave of social roles: Families and jobs* (pp. 251-333). Greenwich, CT: JAI Press.

Pleck, J. H. (1989). Fathers and infant care leave. In E. F. Zigler & M. Frank (Eds.), *The parental leave crisis* (pp. 177-191). New Haven, CT: Yale University Press.

Pleck, J. H. (1990, August). *Family supportive employer policies: Are they relevant to men?.* Paper presented at the annual meeting of the American Psychological Association, Boston.

Pless, B., & Satterwhite, B. (1973). A measure of family functioning and its application. *Social Science Medicine, 7,* 613.

Powell, D. R. (1984). Enhancing the effectiveness of parent education: An analysis of program assumptions. In L. Katz (Ed.), *Current topics in early childhood education* (Vol. 5, pp. 121-139). Norwood, NJ: Ablex.

Powell, D. R. (1988a). Emerging directions in parent-child intervention. In D. R. Powell (Ed.), *Parent education as early childhood intervention* (pp. 1-22). Norwood, NJ: Ablex.

Powell, D. R. (1988b). Support groups for low-income mothers: Design considerations and patterns of participation. In B. Gottlieb (Ed.), *Marshalling social support: Formats, processes, and effects* (pp. 111-134). Newbury Park, CA: Sage.

Powell, D. R. (1990). Home visiting in the early years: Policy and program design decisions. *Young Children, 45,* 65-73.

Powell, D. R. (1991). How schools support families: Critical policy tensions. *Elementary School Journal, 91,* 307-319.

Powell, D. R., & Eisenstadt, J. W. (1988). Informal and formal conversations in parent discussion groups: An observational study. *Family Relations, 37,* 166-170.

Powell, D. R., Zambrana, R., & Silva-Palacios, V. (1990). Designing culturally responsive parent programs: A comparison of low-income Mexican and Mexican-American mothers' preferences. *Family Relations, 39,* 298-304.

Presser, H. (1988). Shift work and child care among young dual-earner American parents. *Journal of Marriage and the Family, 50,* 3-14.

Presser, H. (1989). Can we make time for children? *Demography, 26,* 523-543.

Preston, S. (1984). Children and the elderly in the U.S. *Scientific American, 250,* 44-49.

Preston, S. (1991). Parenthood, work, and women. In J. Huber (Ed.), *Linkages in sociology* (pp. 141-152). Newbury Park, CA: Sage.

Preston, S., & Haines, M. (1991). *Fatal years: Child mortality in late nineteenth century America.* Princeton, NJ: Princeton University Press.

Provence, S., Naylor, A., & Patterson, S. (1977). *The challenge of day care.* New Haven, CT: Yale University Press.

Quinn, M. J., & Tomita, S. K. (1986). *Elder abuse and neglect: Causes, diagnosis, and intervention strategies.* New York: Springer.

Rahdert, F. R. (1988). Treatment services for adolescent drug abusers: Introduction and overview. In E. R. Rahdert & J. Grabowski (Eds.), *Adolescent drug abuse: Analyses of treatment research* (pp. 1-3) (NIDA Research Monograph 77). Washington, DC: Government Printing Office.

Rahe, R. H. (1981). Developments in life change measurement: Subjective life change unit scaling. In B. S. Dohrenwend & B. P. Dohrenwend (Eds.), *Stressful life events and their contexts* (pp. 73-86). New York: Prodist.

Ramey, C. T., Bryant, D. M., & Suarez, T. M. (1985). Preschool compensatory education and the modifiability of intelligence: A critical review. In D. Detterman (Ed.), *Current topics in human intelligence* (pp. 247-296). Norwood, NJ: Ablex.

Rapaport, R., & Rapaport, R. (1971). *Dual career families.* New York: Viking.

Rappaport, J. (1981). In praise of paradox: Social policy of empowerment over prevention. *American Journal of Community Psychology, 9,* 1-25.

Rathbone-McCuan, E. (1980). Elderly victims of family violence and neglect. *Social Casework, 61,* 296-304.

Rausch, F. (1991). *H.R. 770: The Family and Medical Leave Act.* Unpublished manuscript, University of Connecticut, School of Family Studies, Storrs.

Reiss, D. (1981). *The family's construction of reality.* Cambridge, MA: Harvard University Press.

Reiss, D., & Oliveri, M. E. (1980). Family paradigm and family coping: A proposal for linking the family's intrinsic adaptive capacities to its responses to stress. *Family Relations, 29,* 431-444.

Reskin, B. (1991). Labor markets as queues: A structural approach to changing occupational sex segregation. In J. Huber (Ed.), *Macro-micro linkages in sociology* (pp. 170-192). Newbury Park, CA: Sage.

Reskin, B. F., & Hartmann, H. I. (Eds.). (1986). *Women's work, men's work: Sex segregation on the job.* Washington, DC: National Academy Press.

Richman, H., & Stagner, M. (1986). Children in an aging society: Treasured resource or forgotten minority? *Daedalus, 115*(4), 171-189.

Ritzer, G. (1986). *Working: Conflict and change.* Englewood Cliffs, NJ: Prentice-Hall.

Rix, S. (Ed.). (1987). *The American women 1987-88: A report in depth.* New York: Norton.

Rodick, J. D., Henggler, S. W., & Hanson, C. L. (1986). An evaluation of family adaptability, cohesion evaluation scales (FACES) and the Circumplex Model. *Journal of Abnormal Child Psychology, 14,* 77-87.

Rodman, H. (1970). *Teaching about families: Textbook evaluations and recommendations for secondary schools.* Cambridge, MA: Howard A. Doyle.

Rosenbaum, A., & Maiuro, R. D. (1990). Perpetrators of spouse abuse. In R. T. Ammerman & M. Hersen (Eds.), *Treatment of family violence* (pp. 280-309). New York: John Wiley.

Ross, C., Mirowsky, J., & Huber, J. (1983. Dividing work, sharing work, and in-between. *American Sociological Review, 48,* 809-823.

Rossiter, A. (1988). A model for group intervention with preschool children experiencing separation and divorce. *American Journal of Orthopsychiatry, 58,* 387-396.

Rupp, L., & Taylor, V. (1987). *Survival in the doldrums: The American women's rights movement, 1945 to 1960s.* New York: Oxford University Press.

Rushton, J. P., Murray, H. G., & Pavnonen, S. V. (1983). Personality, research creativity, and teaching effectiveness in university professors. *Scientometrics, 5,* 93-116.

Russell, D. (1988). The incidence and prevalence of intrafamilial and extrafamilial sexual abuse of female children. In L. E. A. Walker (Ed.), *Handbook on sexual abuse of children* (pp. 55-71). New York: Springer.

Russell, D. (1982). *Rape in marriage.* New York: Macmillan.

Russell, D., Peplau, L. A., & Cutrona, E. C. (1980). The revised UCLA Loneliness Scale: Concurrent and discriminant validity evidence. *Journal of Genetic Psychology, 142,* 225-238.

Sager, C. J., Brown, H. S., Crohn, H., Engel, T., Rodstein, E., & Walker, L. (1983). *Treating the remarried family.* New York: Brunner/Mazel.

Saluter, A. F. (1989). *Changes in American family life* (Current Population Report, Series P-23, No. 163). Washington, DC: Government Printing Office.

Sawin, M. (1979). The Family Cluster Model of family enrichment. In N. Stinnett, B. Chesser, & J. DeFrain (Eds.), *Building family strengths: Blueprints for action* (pp. 163-172). Lincoln: University of Nebraska Press.

Scales, P. (1986). The changing context of sexuality education: Paradigms and challenges for alternative futures. *Family Relations, 35,* 265-274.

Scanzoni, J. (1989). Alternative images for public policy: Family structure versus family struggling. *Policy Studies Review, 8*(3), 599-609.

Scharlach, A. E., & Boyd, S. L. (1989). Caregiving and employment: Results of an employee survey. *The Gerontologist, 29,* 382-387.

Schneewind, K. A. (1986). *Family psychology: A case for the birth of an overdue psychological discipline.* Paper presented at the Bi-annual Congress of the German Psychological Association, Heidelberg, Germany.

Schoen, R., & Kluegel, J. (1988). The widening gap in black and white marriage rates: The impact of population composition and differential marriage propensities. *American Sociological Review, 53,* 895-907.

Schorr, A. (1968). Family policy in the United States. In *Explorations in social policy.* New York: Basic Books. (Reprinted from *International Social Science Journal, 1962, 14*(3), 452-467)

Schorr, L. (1988). *Within our reach: Breaking the cycle of disadvantage.* Garden City, NY: Doubleday.

Schwartz, P. (1987). The family as a changed institution. *Journal of Family Issues, 8,* 455-459.

Segal, M. (1985). A study of maternal beliefs and values within the context of an intervention program. In E. I. Sigel (Ed.), *Parental belief systems: The psychological consequences for children* (pp. 271-286). Hillsdale, NJ: Lawrence Erlbaum.

Seltzer, J. S., & Bianchi, S. M. (1988). Children's contact with absent parents. *Journal of Marriage and the Family, 50,* 663-677.

Seltzer, M. M., Litchfield, L. C., Lowy, L., & Levin, R. (1989). Families as case managers: A longitudinal study. *Family Relations, 38,* 332-336.

Shank, S. E. (1988, March). Women and the labor market. *Monthly Labor Review,* pp. 3-8.

Sheek, G. W. (1984). *A nation for families.* Washington, DC: American Home Economics Association.

Shehan, C. L., & Scanzoni, J. H. (1988). Gender patterns in the United States: Demographic trends and policy prospects. *Family Relations, 37,* 444-450.

Short, P., Monheit, A., & Beauregard, K. (1987). *Uninsured Americans: A profile.* Rockville, MD: National Center for Health Services Research and Health Care Technology Assessment.

Silverman, P. R. (1977). Widowhood and preventive intervention. In S. H. Zarit (Ed.), *Readings in aging and death: Contemporary perspectives* (pp. 175-182). New York: Harper & Row.

Singer, M. I., Petchers, M. K., & Hussey, D. (1989). The relationship between sexual abuse and substance abuse among psychiatrically hospitalized adolescents. *Child Abuse & Neglect, 13,* 319-325.

Skinner, H. A., Santa-Barbara, J., & Steinhauer, P. D. (1983). The Family Assessment Measure. *Canadian Journal of Community Mental Health, 2,* 91-105.

Slaughter, D. R. (1983). Early intervention and its effects on maternal and child development. *Monographs of the Society for Research in Child Development, 48*(4, Serial No. 202).

Smelser, N. (1959). *Social change in the Industrial Revolution.* Chicago: University of Chicago Press.

Smilkstein, G. (1978). The family APGAR: A proposal for a family function test and its use by physicians. *Journal of Family Practice, 6,* 1231-1239.

Smith, J. (1987). Transforming households: Working class women and economic crisis. *Social Problems, 34,* 416-436.

Smith, M. B. (1968). Competence and socialization. In J. A. Clausen (Ed.), *Socialization and society* (pp. 270-320). Boston: Little, Brown.

Smith, S. J. (1982, March). New worklife estimates reflect changing profile of labor force. *Monthly Labor Review,* pp. 15-20.

Sollie, D. L., & Fischer, J. L. (1988). Career entry influences on social networks of young adults: A longitudinal study. *Journal of Social Behavior and Personality, 3,* 205-225.

Sonnier, C. (1989). *Public/private partnerships in child care.* State Legislative Report 13 (Report No. 33). Denver: National Conference of State Legislatures.

South, S. J., & Spitze, G. (1986). Determinants of divorce over the marital life course. *American Sociological Review, 51,* 583-590.

Spakes, P. (1985). The supreme court, family policy, and alternative family lifestyles: The clash of interests. *Lifestyles: A Journal of Changing Patterns, 7*(3), 170-186.

Spanier, G., & Lewis, R. (1980). Marital quality: A review of the Seventies. *Journal of Marriage and the Family, 42,* 825-839.

Spanier, G. B. (1989). Bequeathing family continuity. *Journal of Marriage and the Family, 51,* 3-13.

Spicer, J., & Hampe, G. (1975). Kinship interaction after divorce. *Journal of Marriage and the Family, 37,* 113-119.

Spickard, P. (1990). *Mixed blood: Intermarriage and ethnic identity in twentieth-century America.* Madison: University of Wisconsin-Madison.

Spitze, G. (1985). The division of task responsibility in U.S. households: Longitudinal change. *Social Forces, 64,* 689-701.

Spitze, G. (1988). Women's employment and family relations: A review. *Journal of Marriage and the Family, 50,* 595-618.

Spitze, G., & Huber, J. (1980). Changing attitudes toward women's nonfamily roles: 1938 to 1978. *Journal of Work and Occupations, 7,* 317-335.

Spitze, G., & South, S. (1985). Women's employment, time expenditure, and divorce. *Journal of Family Issues, 6,* 307-330.

Spivack, M. (1990, October 21). Dodd won only the shell of a child-care bill. *Norwich Bulletin,* p. 4.

Sporakowski, M. J. (1988). A therapist's views on the consequences of change for the contemporary family. *Family Relations, 37,* 373-378.

Starr, R. H., Dubowitz, H., & Bush, B. A. (1990). The epidemiology of child maltreatment. In R. T. Ammerman & M. Hersen (Eds.), *Children at risk* (pp. 23-54). New York: Plenum.

Steele, B. F. (1986). Notes on the lasting effects of early child abuse throughout the lifecycle. *Child Abuse & Neglect, 10,* 283-291.

Steiner, G. (1981). *The futility of family policy.* Washington, DC: Brookings Institution.

Steinmetz, S. K. (1983). Dependency, stress and violence between middle-aged caregivers and their elderly parents. In J. Kosberg (Ed.), *Abuse and maltreatment of the elderly* (pp. 134-149). Littleton, MA: PSG Publishing.

Steinmetz, S. K. (1981, January/February). Elder abuse. *Aging,* pp. 6-10.

Steinmetz, S. K., & Amsden, D. J. (1983). Dependent elders, family stress, and abuse. In T. H. Brubaker (Ed.), *Family relationships in later life.* Beverly Hills, CA: Sage.

Stets, J. E. (1988). *Domestic violence and control.* New York: Springer.

Stets, J. E., & Henderson, D. A. (1991). Contextual factors surrounding conflict resolution while dating: Results from a national study. *Family Relations, 40,* 29-36.

Stets, J. E., & Pirog-Good, M. A. (1989). Patterns of physical and sexual abuse for men and women in dating relationships: A descriptive analysis. *Journal of Family Violence, 4,* 63-76.

Stets, J. E., & Pirog-Good, M. A. (1990). Interpersonal control and courtship aggression. *Journal of Social and Personal Relationships, 7,* 371-394.

Stevens, J. H. (1984). Child development knowledge and parenting skills. *Family Relations, 33,* 237-244.

Stinnet, N., & DeFrain, J. (1985). *Secrets of strong families.* Boston: Little, Brown.

Stith, S., Williams, M. B., & Rosen, K. (1990). *Violence hits home: Comprehensive treatment approaches to domestic violence.* New York: Springer.

St. John-Parsons, D. (1978). Continuous dual-career families. *Psychology of Women Quarterly, 3,* 30-42.

Stoller, E. P. (1983). Parental caregiving by adult children. *Journal of Marriage and the Family, 45,* 851-858.

Stone, G. L., & Archer, J., Jr. (1990). College and university counseling centers in the 1990's: Challenge and limits. *The Counseling Psychologist, 18,* 539-607.

Straus, M. A. (1977). A sociological perspective on the prevention and treatment of wifebeating. In M. Roy (Ed.), *Battered women* (pp. 194-238). New York: Van Nostrand Reinhold.

Straus, M. A., & Gelles, R. J. (1986). Societal change and change in family violence from 1975 to 1985 as revealed by two national surveys. *Journal of Marriage and the Family, 48,* 465-479.

Straus, M. A., & Gelles, R. J. (1990). How violent are American families? Estimates from the national violence resurvey and other studies. In M. A. Straus & R. Gelles (Eds.), *Physical violence in American families* (pp. 95-112). New Brunswick, NJ: Transaction Books.

Straus, M. A., & Smith, C. (1990). Family patterns and child abuse. In M. A. Straus & R. Gelles (Eds.), *Physical violence in American families* (pp. 245-262). New Brunswick, NJ: Transaction Books.

Sugarman, D. B., & Hotaling, G. T. (1989). Dating violence: Prevalence, context and risk markers. In M. Pirog-Good & J. Stets (Eds.), *Violence in dating relationships* (pp. 3-32). New York: Praeger.

Sussman, G. (1982). *Selling mothers' milk.* Urbana: University of Illinois Press.

Tabah, L. (1980). World population trends: A stocktaking. *Population and Development Review, 6,* 355-389.

Takaki, R. (1989). *Strangers from a different shore.* Boston: Little, Brown.

Tan, G. G., Ray, M. P., & Cate, R. (1991). Migrant farm child abuse and neglect within an ecosystems framework. *Family Relations, 40,* 84-90.

Tanfer, K. (1987). Patterns of premarital cohabitation among never-married women in the U.S. *Journal of Marriage and the Family, 49,* 483-498.

Tharp, R. (1989). Psychocultural variables and constants: Effects on teaching and learning in schools. *American Psychologist, 44,* 349-359.

Thompson, L., & Walker, A. J. (1989). Gender in families: Women and men in marriage, work, and parenthood. *Journal of Marriage and the Family, 51,* 845-871.

Thompson, L., & Walker, A. J. (1991). Gender in families: Women and men in marriage, work, and parenthood. In A. Booth (Ed.), *Contemporary families: Looking forward, looking back* (pp. 76-102). Minneapolis, MN: National Council on Family Relations.

Thompson, M. S., Rothrock, J. K., Strain, R., & Palmer, H. (1981). Cost analysis for program evaluation. In R. F. Conner (Ed.), *Methodological advances in evaluation research* (pp. 31-46). Beverly Hills, CA: Sage.

Thornton, A., & Freedman, D. (1983). The changing American family. *Population Bulletin, 38,* 1-44.

Tierney, K. J., & Corwin, D. L. (1983). Exploring intrafamilial child sexual abuse. In D. Finkelhor, R. Gelles, G. T. Hotaling, & M. A. Straus (Eds.), *The dark side of families: Current family violence research* (pp. 102-118). Beverly Hills, CA: Sage.

Tolnay, S. (1987). The decline of black marital fertility in the rural South: 1910-1940. *American Sociological Review, 52,* 111-117.

Tolsdorf, C. (1976). Social network, support and coping: An exploratory study. *Family Process, 15,* 407-417.

Travers, J., Nauta, M., & Irwin, N. (1982). *The effects of a social program: Final report of the Child and Family Resource Program's infant-toddler component.* Cambridge, MA: Abt.

Trepper, T. S., & Barrett, M. J. (1986). Vulnerability to incest: A framework for assessment. In T. S. Trepper & M. J. Barrett (Eds.), *Treating incest: A multiple systems perspective* (pp. 13-26). New York: Haworth.

Truesdell, D. L., McNeil, J. S., & Deschner, J. P. (1986). Incidence of wife abuse in incestuous families. *Social Work, 31,* 138-140.

Uhlenberg, P. (1980). Death and the family. *Journal of Family History, 5,* 313-320.

Uhlenberg, P., & Meyers, M. A. (1981). Divorce and the elderly. *The Gerontologist, 21,* 276-282.

Ulin, R. L. (1977). *Death and dying education.* Washington, DC: National Education Association.

U.S. Bureau of the Census. (1976). *Historical statistics of the United States.* Washington, DC: Government Printing Office.

U.S. Bureau of the Census. (1987). *Households, families, marital status, and living arrangements: March, 1987* (Current Population Reports, No. 417, p. 20). Washington, DC: Government Printing Office.

U.S. Bureau of the Census. (1989a). *The black population in the United States: March 1988* (Current Population Reports, Series P-20, No. 442). Washington, DC: Government Printing Office.

U.S. Bureau of the Census. (1989b). *Statistical abstracts of the United States.* Washington, DC: Government Printing Office.

U.S. Bureau of the Census. (1989c). *Studies in marriage and the family* (Current Population Reports, Special Studies, Series P-23, No. 162). Washington DC: Government Printing Office.

U.S. Department of Labor. (1977). *U.S. working women: A data book.* Washington, DC: Government Printing Office.

U.S. Department of Labor, Bureau of Labor Statistics. (1984). *Employment and earnings.* Washington, DC: Government Printing Office.

U.S. Executive Office of the President. (1986). *The family: Preserving America's future.* Washington, DC: Government Printing Office.

U.S. Executive Office of the President. (1987). *Executive order 12606.* Washington, DC: Government Printing Office.

U.S. House of Representatives. (1989). *U.S. children and their families: Current conditions and recent trends* (A report of the Select Committee on Children, Youth, and Families). Washington, DC: Government Printing Office.

The Vanier Institute of the Family. (1971). *Report of family life education survey, Part II, Family life education in the schools.* Ottawa: Author.

Veatch, R. (1991). An egalitarian argument for rationing. *Aging Today, 9*(6), 9-12.

Vondra, J. I. (1990). Sociological and ecological factors. In R. T. Ammerman & M. Hersen (Eds.), *Children at risk* (pp. 149-170). New York: Plenum.

Voydanoff, P. (1987). *Work and family life.* Newbury Park, CA: Sage.

Voydanoff, P. (1991). Economic distress and family relations: A review of the eighties. In A. Booth (Ed.), *Contemporary families: Women and men in marriage, work, and parenthood* (pp. 429-445). Minneapolis, MN: National Council on Family Relations.

Voydanoff, P., & Kelly, R. F. (1984). Determinants of work-related family problems among employed parents. *Journal of Marriage and the Family, 46,* 881-892.

Walker, A. J., Martin, S. S. K., & Thompson, L. (1987). Feminist programs for families. *Family Relations, 37,* 17-22.

Walsh, F. (Ed.). (1982). *Normal family process.* New York: Guilford.

Waterman, J. (1986). Family dynamics of incest with young children. In K. MacFarlane & J. Waterman (Eds.), *Sexual abuse of young children* (pp. 204-219). New York: Guilford.

Watkins, S. C., Bongaarts, J., & Menken, J. (1987). Demographic foundations of family change. *American Sociological Review, 52,* 346-358.

Wauchope, B. A., & Straus, M. A. (1990). Physical punishment and physical abuse of American children: Incidence rates by age, gender, and occupational status. In M. A. Straus & R. Gelles (Eds.), *Physical violence in American families* (pp. 133-150). New Brunswick, NJ: Transaction Books.

Weingarten, H. R. (1988). Late life divorce and the life review. *Journal of Gerontological Social Work, 12,* 83-100.

Weiss, H. (1989). State family support and education programs: Lessons from the pioneers. *American Journal of Orthopsychiatry, 59,* 32-48.

Weiss, R. S. (1987). On the current state of the American family. *Journal of Family Issues, 8,* 464-467.

Wetzel, J. R. (1989). *American youth: A statistical snapshot.* Washington, DC: W. T. Grant Foundation Commission on Youth.

White, L., & Booth, A. (1985). Quality and stability of remarriages: The role of stepchildren. *American Sociological Review, 50,* 689-698.

White, M., & Epstein, D. (1990). *Narrative means to therapeutic ends.* New York: Norton.

Widom, C. S. (1989). Does violence beget violence? A critical examination of the literature. *Psychological Bulletin, 106,* 3-28.

Wilensky, H. (1961). Orderly careers and social participation. *American Sociological Review, 26,* 521-539.

Williams, L. M., & Finkelhor, D. (1990). The characteristics of incestuous fathers. In M. L. Marshall, D. R. Laros, & H. E. Barbaree (Eds.), *Handbook of sexual assault* (pp. 231-255). New York: Plenum.

Wilson, W. J. (1987). *The truly disadvantaged: The inner city, the underclass, and public policy.* Chicago: University of Chicago Press.

Wisensale, S. (1988). Generational equity and intergenerational policies. *The Gerontologist, 28*(6), 773-778.

Wisensale, S. (1989). Family policy in the state legislature: The Connecticut agenda. *Policy Studies Review, 8*(3), 622-637.

Wisensale, S. (1990). Approaches to family policy in state government: A report on five states. *Family Relations, 39,* 136-140.

Wisensale, S. K., & Allison, M. D. (1988). An analysis of 1987 state family leave legislation: Implications for caregivers of the elderly. *The Gerontologist, 28,* 779-785.

Wood, B. (1987). Survival KIT for the holidays: A grief workshop approach. *Family Relations, 36,* 237-241.

Wolfe, D. A. (1985). Child-abusive parents: An empirical review and analysis. *Psychological Bulletin, 97,* 462-482.

Wolfe, D. A. (1987). *Child abuse: Implications for child development and psychopathology*. Newbury Park, CA: Sage.

Wolfe, D. A., Wolfe, V. V., & Best, C. L. (1988). Child victims of sexual abuse. In V. Van Hasselt, R. Morrison, A. Bellack, & M. Hersen (Eds.), *Handbook of family violence* (pp. 157-186). New York: Plenum.

Women's Bureau. (1986). Facts on U.S. working women: Caring for elderly family members. Washington, DC: U.S. Department of Labor.

Wright, S. E., & Rosenblatt, P. C. (1988). Isolation and farm loss: Why neighbors may not be supportive. In R. Marotz-Baden, C. B. Hennon, & T. H. Brubaker (Eds.), *Families in rural America: Stress, adaptation and revitalization* (pp. 208-215). St. Paul, MN: National Council on Family Relations.

Young, M., & Willmott, P. (1973). *The symmetrical family*. New York: Penguin.

Youngblade, L. M., & Belsky, J. (1990). Social and emotional consequences of child maltreatment. In R. T. Ammerman & M. Hersen (Eds.), *Children at risk* (pp. 109-148). New York: Plenum.

Zaslow, M. J. (1989). Sex difference in children's response to parental divorce. *American Journal of Orthopsychiatry, 59*(1), 118-141.

Zimmerman, S. (1988). *Understanding family policy: Theoretical approaches*. Newbury Park, CA: Sage.

Zimmerman, S., & Owens, P. (1989). Comparing the family policies of three states: A content analysis. *Family Relations, 38,* 190-195.

Zuravin, S. (1989). The ecology of child abuse and neglect: Review of the literature and presentation of data. *Violence and Victims, 4,* 101-120.

Author Index

Frisch, R., 49
Frude, N., 137
Furstenberg, F., 61, 112, 116, 125
Fusfeld, D., 53

Galinsky, E., 81, 83, 87
Galston, W., 82
Gander, A. M., 122, 124
Ganong, L. H., 6, 7, 119
Garbarino, J., 130, 133
Geffner, R., 140, 141, 143, 144, 145, 146
Gelles, R. J., 12, 130, 132, 133, 134, 135, 136, 143, 227
Genovese, R., 234
Gerber, S. C., 87
Gershuny, J., 56
Giblin, P., 191, 204
Giele, J. A., 56
Gilbert, M. K., 106
Giordiano, J. A., 217, 219
Gjerde, P., 117
Gladstone, J., 125
Glahe, F., 234
Glass, J., 52
Gleberman, L., 145
Glenn, N. D., 5, 7
Glick, P. C., 216
Glover, K. E., 191
Glynn, T., 166
Gnezda, T., 236, 237
Goldin, C., 46
Goldstein, M. Z., 147
Goode, W., 113
Goodnow, J. J., 87
Goody, J., 44
Gordon, L., 138, 146
Gordon, T., 190
Gossett, J. T., 203
Gottfredson, G. D., 215
Gove, W. R., 77, 78, 122
Gray, M., 118
Green, K. C., 224
Green, S., 66
Greenberg, J., 39
Greenberg, M. T., 85
Greenblat, C. S., 62
Greenhalgh, S., 49

Greenwald, E., 138
Greenwood, L., 140
Griffin, S., 118
Groves, D., 103
Guerney, B., 206
Guerney, B., Jr., 191, 206
Gurman, A. S., 215
Gwartney-Gibbs, P. A., 139

Haas, J., 109
Habenstein, R., 162
Hagestad, G. O., 120, 123, 124
Haines, M., 49
Hall, D. T., 101, 103
Hall, F. S., 101, 103
Halpern, R., 89
Hamilton, A., 131
Hampe, G., 125
Hampson, R. B., 23, 25
Handy, E. S., 162
Hanson, C. L., 33
Hanson, D. A., 153, 223
Hardy, K., 219
Harmin, D., 190
Harrison, B., 8
Harry, J., 101
Hart, H., 49
Hartmann, H. I., 99
Haskins, R., 83
Hayes, C. D., 108
Hayghe, H. V., 98
Health and Welfare Canada, 186, 187
Heaton, T., 54
Heckart, K., 250
Heinicke, C. M., 92
Hekimian, E., 131
Henderson, D. A., 139
Henggler, S. W., 33
Hennon, C. B., 122, 123, 124, 199, 203, 206, 207, 208
Henton, J. M., 141, 142, 143, 148, 149, 150, 152
Hershberg, T., 61
Hetherington, E. M., 226
Hey, R., 181
Hickey, T., 147, 148, 149, 150
Hicks, M., 55

Subject Index

291

About the Contributors

Margaret Arcus is a Professor in Family Sciences in the School of Family and Nutritional Sciences at the University of British Columbia, Vancouver. She has published numerous articles on family life education and has been active in the National Council on Family Relations.

Timothy H. Brubaker is Professor in the Department of Family and Consumer Sciences and is Director of the Family and Child Studies Center at Miami University, Oxford, Ohio. His books include *Family Relationships in Later Life* (1990, 1988), *Family Caregivers and Dependent Elderly* (coauthored, 1984), *Later Life Families* (1985), *Aging, Health and Family* (edited, 1987), and *Families in Rural America* (coedited, 1988). His research has been published in a number of scholarly journals, and he has contributed chapters to many books. Currently, he is editor of *Family Relations,* published by the National Council on Family Relations.

Marilyn Coleman is Professor and Chair of the Department of Human Development and Family Studies at the University of Missouri-Columbia. She has coauthored nearly 60 articles and one book, *Bibliotherapy With Stepchildren* (1988). She has conducted remarriage and stepfamily research for more than 10 years and also has investigated the effects of family structure stereotyping, sex-role stereotyping, marital expectations, and divorce. She has made presentations and conducted workshops throughout the United States and in Europe.

Beth C. Emery is Assistant Professor of Human Sciences at Middle Tennessee State University, Murfreesboro. Her research interests are focused on violence in premarital relationships, interpersonal communication skills, conflict, and feminist methodology.

Judith L. Fischer is a Professor in the Department of Human Development and Family Studies at Texas Tech University, Lubbock. Her research has appeared in numerous scholarly journals. She focuses her research on adolescence, transitions in young adulthood, and family development across the life course.

Lawrence H. Ganong is Professor of Human Development and Family Studies/Nursing at the University of Missouri-Columbia. He has coauthored nearly 60 articles and one book, *Bibliotherapy With Stepchildren* (1988). He has conducted remarriage and stepfamily research for more than 10 years and also has investigated the effects of family structure stereotyping, sex-role stereotyping, marital expectations, and divorce. He has made presentations and conducted workshops throughout the United States and Europe.

Charles B. Hennon is a Professor in the Department of Family and Consumer Sciences and Associate Director of the Family and Child Studies Center, Miami University, Oxford, Ohio. His research focuses on divorce, family stress, and international family patterns. His research has been published in numerous scholarly journals and books.

Joan Huber is Senior Vice-President for Academic Affairs and Provost at The Ohio State University, Columbus. Her major research interest is in the macrosociology of gender stratification. She served as president of the American Sociological Association in 1989.

Anthony P. Jurich is a Professor of Human Development and Family Studies at Kansas State University where he works with the accredited Marriage and Family Therapy Program. He is the coauthor of *Marital and Family Therapy: New Perspectives in Theory, Research, and Practice* (1983) and has published more than 100 articles and book chapters.

He has served as Chair of the Family Therapy Section of the National Council on Family Relations and has served on its Board of Directors. He was the 1988 winner of the Osborne Award for Outstanding Teaching. He is presently the secretary of the American Association for Marriage and Family Therapy and is a clinical member and Fellow of that organization.

Judy A. Kimberly is a master's candidate in Family Studies and assistant at the Family and Child Studies Center at Miami University, Oxford, Ohio. Her research interests are focused around sociocultural and ethnic differences between families.

Sally A. Lloyd is Professor and Chair of Family and Consumer Sciences at Miami University, Oxford, Ohio. Her research interests include family violence, interaction in abusive relationships, courtship violence, courtship processes, and conflict. In addition to numerous articles and chapters, she is the coauthor (with R. Cate) of the forthcoming book *Courtship.*

Hamilton I. McCubbin is Dean and Professor, School of Family Resources and Consumer Sciences, University of Wisconsin-Madison. He is currently the Director of the Family Stress, Coping and Health Project. His recent work focuses on family responses to economic stress in both rural and urban communities with special interest in the development of measures of family coping and adaptation. He is particularly interested in ethnic minority families.

Marilyn A. McCubbin is Assistant Professor, School of Nursing, University of Wisconsin-Madison, and codirector of the graduate program in community health nursing. She is currently principal investigator for a five-year NIH-funded study on parent and family adaptation to the initial diagnosis and long-term care of a child with a chronic health condition. She is particularly interested in families and chronic illness.

David H. Olson, Ph.D., is Professor, Family Social Science at the University of Minnesota, St. Paul. He is past President of the National Council on Family Relations (NCFR) and has published more than 100 articles and 20 books in the marriage and family field. He has developed the Circumplex Model of Family Systems, which is used as the theoretical base for more than 600 ongoing studies. He is on the editorial board of eight family journals. He is a Fellow in the American Psychological Association (APA) and the American Association of Marital and Family Therapists (AAMFT).

Douglas R. Powell is Professor and Head, Department of Child Development and Family Studies, Purdue University, West Lafayette, Indiana. He has conducted research on the processes and effects of parent educational support programs, and was founder and director of a parent-child support program in a low-income neighborhood while serving on the faculty at the Merrill-Palmer Institute in Detroit. Professor Powell has published extensively and currently is Editor of the *Early Childhood Research Quarterly.*

Candyce S. Russell is the Vera Mowery McAninch Professor of Human Development and Family Studies at Kansas State University where she is Director of the accredited Marriage and Family Therapy Program. She is coauthor of *Circumplex Model: Systemic Assessment and Treatment of Families* (1989) and has published in the area of marital and family functioning. She is past secretary of the American Association for Marriage and Family Therapy and is a clinical member and Fellow of that organization.

Donna L. Sollie is an Associate Professor in the Department of Family and Child Development at Auburn University, Auburn, Alabama. She has published numerous articles in scholarly journals, focusing on transitions during young adulthood and factors that influence satisfaction in marriages and friendships.

Anne I. Thompson is the Assistant Dean, School of Family Resources and Consumer Sciences, University of Wisconsin-Madison. She is currently the Associate Director of the Family Stress, Coping and Health Project. Her most recent work focuses on family types, functioning, and stabilizing forces in family life. She is particularly interested in women and work.

Patricia Voydanoff is Director of the Center for the Study of Family Development, University of Dayton. She is the author of *Work and Family Life* (1987), coauthor of *Adolescent Sexuality and Pregnancy* (1990), editor of *Work and Family: Changing Roles of Men and Women*

(1984), and coeditor of *Families and Economic Distress: Coping Strategies and Social Policy* (1988) and *The Changing Family: Reflections on Familiaris Consortio* (1984). She is editor of the *Journal of Family Issues.*

Steven K. Wisensale is an Associate Professor of Public Policy in the School of Family Studies at the University of Connecticut. A political scientist by training, he received his Ph.D. in Social Welfare Policy from the Heller School at Brandeis University. His research to date has focused primarily on family policy at the state level and he has published his work in such journals as *Policy Studies Review, The Gerontologist, Public Administration Review, Family Relations,* and *Journal of Management Science and Policy Analysis.* His teaching responsibilities include courses on family policy, family law, aging policy, and planning and managing human service programs.